# Daddy-O

BEST WISHES —

# Daddy-O
## Iguana Heads & Texas Tales

## Bob "Daddy-O" Wade

*with* **Keith** *and* **Kent Zimmerman**

*foreword by* **Linda Ellerbee**

*afterword by* **Kinky Friedman**

BOB
"DADDY-O" WADE
'01

ST. MARTIN'S PRESS ⚏ NEW YORK

Design by Sara Stemen

*Left-hand endpaper art: Waco*, 1972, black-and-white photo emulsion on canvas, 8 feet by 10 feet. (Original photo: Harry Hornby) Note: Subjects were photographed in Uvalde, Texas, in 1969, the day man walked on the moon.

*Right-hand endpaper art: Texas Boys*, 1975, photo oil on photo linen, 4 feet by 7 feet. Production still from 1975 Ken Harrison film, *Jackelope*. (Photo: James R. King. Collection of Michael Graves)

ISBN 0-312-13459-2

Library of Congress Cataloging-in-Publication Data

Wade, Bob, 1943—
    Daddy-O : iguana heads and Texas tales / Bob Wade with Keith and Kent Zimmerman:
foreword by Linda Ellerbee : afterword by Kinky Friedman.
        p.  cm.
    ISBN 0-312-13459-2
    1. Wade, Bob, 1943-       .2. Artists—United States—Biography.
I. Zimmerman, Keith.  II. Zimmerman, Kent. 1953-     .  III. Title.
N6537.W218A2   1995
709'.2—dc20
    [B]                                                          95-82919
                                                                 CIP

First Edition: November 1995

10  9  8  7  6  5  4  3  2  1

This book is dedicated to the Wade girls—
Lisa, Christine, and Rachel—
who put up with Daddy-O, Daddy, and Daddy-Bob.

When I went back East to meet my wife Lisa's grandparents,
her grandmother asked, "What religion is he?"
Lisa said, "Texan."

# Contents

## Iguanacknowledgments

**N** Texas if the truth in a story is not necessarily held in high regard, the way you tell a story is.

My way of telling the stories in this book was similar to working on any of my art projects: Get some hip experts to help.

My Dallas writer friend Mike Shropshire steered me to Dallas fox and literary agent Jan Miller who, along with her eager associate David Hale Smith, steered me to St. Martin's visionary editor and fellow El Pasoan Jim Fitzgerald. Jim and Jan steered me to the longhaired twin San Francisco writer dudes Keith and Kent Zimmerman, who steered me through many hours of egocentric exaggeration on tape (they could make anybody's bullshit read well). St. Martin's Charles Woods designed a great cover, Santa Fe's James

Hart did lots of photo work, and Linda Ellerbee and Kinky Friedman graciously spoke their minds in the front and back.

Sincere thanks and hats off to these experts as well as numerous encouraging advisers: Michael Korda, Michael and Suzanne Wallis, Jane and Michael Stern, Bill Wittliff, Monk White, and my wife, Lisa, a patient and loving companion, an insightful and keen observer who has endured a lot.

Of course there wouldn't be any tales and projects if I hadn't been fortunate enough to have had hundreds of friends and patrons who pitched in one way or another to help Daddy-O over the hump—I am deeply indebted for all of that and to all of you.

While my parents Pattie and Chaffin always encouraged my artistic inclinations, the teachers used to say, "Don't laugh at him, kids, he'll just do it again."

And while Mom and Dad always said I knew right from wrong, there were times I preferred wrong.

Anyway, this is the stuff you like if you like this kind of stuff.

—Bob Wade, Tesuque, New Mexico

Thank you Jim Fitzgerald, Jan Miller, David Smith, Dean Williamson, and Evie Greenbaum. Also John Lydon, Paul Slavit, Adrienne McDonnell, David Dalton and the *Gavin* folks, Beverly Mire, James Lewis, Howard Pearlstein, Kinky Friedman, Linda Ellerbee, Monk White, Mike Shropshire, John Alexander, Lionel Bevan, Rick Hernandez, Henry Hopkins, Johnny Langdon, Joe Longley, Jack Mims, Bull Pettit, James Rutherford, Mac Whitney, Shannon Wynne, Mike Young, the Stoneleigh P, Joe and Doris Zimmerman, the Rybickis,

and especially—

Deborah Zimmerman and Gladys Zimmerman for putting up with all the strangeness and madness we constantly parade through our never-boring lives.

Thank you Bob, Lisa, and Rachel for the loaves of toast and always making us feel warm and welcome.

xxxooo, The Zimmermen

*Keith and Kent Zimmerman appear courtesy of Bio Brothers.*

**B**ACK in the '70s, when I first moved to New York and God and Kinky Friedman were both lads, I was just one more Texan real lonesome for some other Texans. However, as good fortune would have it, there was this place called the Lone Star Café. Real Texans went there. Drank there. Got drunk there. Made music there. Made friends there. Or worse.

Happily, the Lone Star Café was easy to find in New York City. There weren't any other buildings that had a giant sculpture of an iguana on the roof. Lord, I loved that iguana.

"What we have here," I said to anyone who would listen, "is the product of a truly twisted brain. I like twisted. Twisted is good."

Later, I found out the artist was a man named Bob Wade. A weird man named Bob Wade. Met him right there in the Lone Star. Being smart, Bob was not living in New York City at the time. But being *too* smart, he was living in Dallas. (I am from Houston. They do not mix.)

Bob and I got to be friends. Some said it had to do with a shared bad attitude. When the city wanted to take the lizard off the roof (they are foolish that way here in New York City), I wrote stories to try to make them stop it (read this book to find out if that kind of thing actually works).

Later, after I earned two nickels to rub together, I started buying some of Bob Wade's art, although I swear his prices go up faster than my income. Knowing Bob, it may be on purpose.

I have this memory of sitting, some years later, with Bob and his family in their house outside Santa Fe, watching one of those this-can't-be-real-can-it-Jesus? sunsets they get there. Bob seemed happier than he had been, and okay, maybe a little calmer, too. Hey, we all get old or sober or sane or all of the above eventually. But I remember wondering if sanity would ruin his art. Well, by God, it hasn't.

Texan? Yes.

Renegade? Yes.

Artist? Absolutely.

And now a storyteller.

Careful, Bob Wade, you're starting to tread on my turf. If this turns out to be a best-seller, the friendship is over.

Linda Ellerbee
New York
May, 1995

P.S. Dear reader: You're going to like this tale. You're going to like this man. And if you can't figure out why, hell, don't call *me*. I don't understand it either.

# Chapter One

# Braving the Perils of the Trail

KAY, let's go to 'co!"

"Pigpen'll take his car and Gut's got a gas card. Town Bull has some beer. Be in the parking lot in ten minutes!"

Thus the Kappa "Swigs" once again were itching to not call it a night but instead were hell-bent on driving the four and a half hours from Austin to Laredo, Mexico, at one in the morning. This was Austin, Texas, 1963. It was just another crazed road trip with multicultural implications. It, along with hundreds of others, paved the way for many future Daddy-O trips.

"Out of the chute" has always been an exciting visual image for me. Here comes a Brahma bull or bucking bronco out of the chute.

Or in the case of my early hot rod drag racing days, "off the line": two custom shorts revving up the r.p.m.'s, waiting for the guy to jump up, waving the checkered flag. Open the gate. Wave the flag. Get in the car and go to 'co. Watch my dust.

Remembering the whirlwind trips the Daddy-O has taken over the years is like recalling the mythology of Pecos Bill, roping tornadoes, single-handedly taming the wild elements. Stories of Pecos Bill are to Texas what the myths were to the Greeks and Romans; they're the tradition of Texas tall tales told around the campfire or on the porch, stories from the *vaqueros* right on up to Stanley Kubrick's *Dr. Strangelove*, where Slim Pickens rides a bucking bomb, hauling ass, waving his hat in the air.

When Texans ask how far away someplace is, what they really mean is, how many hours does it take to get there? They hop in the big Suburban, crank on the AC, put the kids in the back with the tapes and the dog, and hit the road. Dallas to San Antonio—four and a half hours. Dallas to Santa Fe—twelve hours.

Willie Nelson, Mr. On the Road Again, was once asked where home was. He replied, "Home is where the heart is."

Asked about the particular house where he was being interviewed, he replied further, "This is where I come to get well."

5110 Lemmon, also known as Daddy-O's Patios, became my "place to get well" following projects like the Giant Iguana and the Boots built bigger than Dallas. After these projects were finished, I'd limp back to Dallas and lay it down at old fifty-one-ten.

A good road trip can be wilder than a Christmas goose. Some of my first road trips began with trips to the national drag races, some as far away as Pomona, California, in Gaylord's customized '57 Ford with my car club buddies, the Roadrunners.

And the road continued.

I'd made the run from El Paso to Austin in my '51 Ford to go to college. Later on I drove around Austin in a '55 Ford convertible filled with coeds and college buddies. Then there were the infamous Kappa Sig runs to Laredo, Mexico, or the spring break trips—called Splash Day—down to the beaches of Galveston or Corpus Christi.

I remember reading Jack Kerouac's book, *On The Road*, in 1963. Just like old Sal, my mother used to say, "Get it out of your system." At the time I was as restless as a mule in a tin barn.

The road continued to unfold.

Me and my Oak Cliff Four held wild exhibitions everywhere along the road, including New Orleans. We drove up to Taos, over to Tyler, and took an occasional trip to New York City. There was the road documentary I did through Texas with filmmaker Ken Harrison called *Jackelope*. The story finishes up with me driving through Texas, and ending up in New York City once again. Then there was the great 1978 road trip with Ron Phillips driving my entire show to Los Angeles. I wasn't quite finished with some of the paintings, so I spent most of the time swaying in the back of my van trying to scrub just a little more oil paint onto my big photo canvases, which resulted in an awkward mixture of car sickness and paint fumes. Boyd "El Chingadero" and I burned up my station wagon on the way to Del Rio to check on my Six Shooter, eventually limping into El Paso so I could chase divorcees at my high school reunion (I caught two!).

The Bonnie & Clyde Mobile road trip in 1982 marked the Daddy-O trek down to New Orleans for the art car rolling exhibition which was part of the Mardi Gras parade. Later on we were chased out of Houston by an angry local whose eccentric front yard art we had innocently photographed. Rick Hernandez and I made the long haul to Buffalo for the Art Park gathering and produced the Giant Iguana right next to the roar of beautiful Niagara Falls. Afterward Rick, Jim Napierala, and I made the trip from Buffalo to New York City in the largest U-Haul truck we could rent, with the dismantled giant iguana inside, its head roped to a makeshift platform.

Sometimes the road crossed oceans.

Monk White and I journeyed to Paris twice, first for the Paris Biennale, then on a wild goose chase looking for the lost Texas Mobile Home Museum trailer. We scoured art bars all over Europe with color Xeroxes of the mobile trailer, asking if anyone had seen this thing. Other trips included Jorge, Flex, and me shoulder to shoulder in an El Camino with Funeral Wagon the stuffed horse in the back. Jim Harithas, Mark Lombardi, and I drove off to El Paso and Amarillo.

Most recently there was the Texas road trip with the Zimmerman boys, researching this very Daddy-O book. We ran into all my old cronies—old fraternity guys, scalawags and lots of former girlfriends peppered all over Texas: Dallas-Fort Worth, Carl's Corner, Waco, Austin, San Antonio. We returned to Fort Worth for the all-girl national rodeo finals and swung back over to Dallas again. We quickly ran up a $350 bar tab at the Stoneleigh P when a crowd of friends and past associates came by to swap their favorite Daddy-O stories.

By the time this book comes out, my next work will be in progress. Of course it will involve the road; this time a traveling Iguanamobile, a cross between my giant Iguana and the traveling Texas Mobile Museum.

After all, it was John Wayne who talked about "braving the perils of the trail." So, ride out the perils of these pages and by the way, don't look back, I never do.

# Chapter Two

## El Paso and the Doggies

My family didn't buy a car until we moved to El Paso in 1952. It was a 1947 Chevy, a huge, funny thing. Up until that time my dad had always been in the hotel business and when you grow up in hotels, more often than not, you really don't need a car. You live in the downtown area of whatever city you're in. You live in the manager's suite. The hotel is your life.

My dad, Robert Chaffin Wade, was very artistic. He decorated the big swinging hotel double doors every Christmas and I would help him design large elaborate nativity scenes. My mother, Patricia Schrope Wade, was also very fussy over how things looked around the house. If ever there was a blank patch on the Christmas tree, she would have my dad take one of the limbs he originally cut from the bottom to make the tree fit into the stand, drill a hole in the trunk, then carve down and insert the limb into the trunk. Nobody would ever know it was put there. To this day, I still do that with my own tree.

We never had big money, but if you're in a hotel, you're living the high life. Fine hotels attract celebrities. Somebody famous is always either staying at the place or drinking in the bar. Early on I was required to have good manners. Boy, if I messed up, I was jumped on quick, quicker than God could get the news. If Mom, Dad, and I were in the elevator going down to dinner to the dining room and I didn't say hello politely to Mrs. Jones or whomever, I was in trouble. I soon learned that the way you were treated was directly proportional to how you were perceived.

We moved around a lot, like a military family. As a kid I lived all over Texas. Austin, San Antonio, Waco, Beaumont, Galveston, and Marfa. In Marfa Dennis Hopper and crew had just finished the movie *Giant* and the vibes surrounding that era still affect me greatly. Soon we were off to El Paso for a spell. Hotel brats will tell you: These gigs eventually run out because sometimes new owners will come in and toss everybody out.

As the new kid, I was a stranger to the Mexican culture that pervaded El Paso. I went to Houston Elementary School where I met Danny and Sammy Fuentes, two notorious brothers who were the kings of the schoolyard. They were a year apart from each other.

When I was in the fourth grade, one of the Fuentes brothers was picking on some kid, and I walked up and told him to leave him alone.

He stopped and turned around, almost in slow motion, looked at me, and said, in a thick Latino accent: "You spoke to me." A long silence fueled by disbelief. "You said something to me?"

"Yeah!" I said.

"Ohhhh." Another long, methodical pause. "You must be *crazy.*"

I thought the Fuentes brothers would pound the fuck out of me immediately, but because of my attitude I didn't get beat up. Having moved around all my life, I had the ability to socialize real quick. It was almost like prison life. You had to get with it, get in the scene, or get stepped on.

In class, I was the kid who could draw better than anybody else. I had art in my blood. My fascination with custom cars can be traced back to one of my earliest and favorite childhood toys, a little metal race car that I got when I was four. I painted the outside black and the interior blue, and, using my mother's fingernail polish, added a red flame job to the front. When we built soap box racers that you steered with a rope down a long hill, mine always looked just a little bit cooler than the others.

At fourteen, I talked my parents into letting me buy a motor scooter to get around for my paper route. We went down to buy a Cushman scooter, and since my father was so straight-arrow, and since I didn't have my license yet, he drove the scooter home. Just at the last curve before our house, he turned the gas the wrong way. As my mother and I followed behind in the car, my father drove straight into an embankment. He spent a week in the hospital after nearly breaking his back.

A year later, I got the next level up, an Italian Vespa. It was some pitiful color, and at fifteen, I immediately painted a red flame job on it.

After motor scooters, the next step was getting a car. When I was a junior in high school in 1960, my parents presented me with their 1951 Ford, a two-door, hardtop convertible Crown Victoria—a pretty flashy car for a family. To make it my own, the first thing I did to it was put moon-eye decals on the side.

El Paso was all about cars, a huge automotive phenomenon that was around long before I got there in the '50s. Though we were a hell of a long way from L.A., the custom car craze was happening big. Like Phoenix and Tucson, nobody walks anywhere around El Paso. It's a wide, spread-out city.

I felt socially comfortable with the custom car world. The hip hot rod guys and I would be sitting in the drive-in joints drinking sodas with our dates. You had to sit just the right way in your cool car. Here would come another car, maybe a convertible, and sure it was a nice car, but we would think it was all wrong. Wrong color, wrong style, and way too high off the ground. Then we'd see four or five guys in the cars, all wearing short haircuts.

"Oh, shit! Here comes a carload of doggies."

We used to call the soldiers stationed in El Paso doggies, from the "dog tags" they wore around their necks. Even the locals called them doggies. They were all from outside El Paso.

There was this big circular concrete fenced-in area located right in the middle of the downtown plaza in El Paso. Inside they had four or five gigantic alligators. They were huge, didn't move around much, and just laid around all day long. Doggies would be standing around this concrete fence not knowing what else to do, while all the local punks would be hanging out watching the doggies. During this social interaction of bored people, cigarette butts, pennies, and dimes would get thrown into the alligator pit, lodged between the scaly notches of those elaborate alligator backs. Of course the alligators' skin was so thick the cigarette butts couldn't burn them. There was also a big park over in San Antonio that had live alligators. Sometimes guys would wrestle the alligators, and after the performance, little kids would walk around with a tray among the crowd and serve alligator meat on toothpicks.

Why are these landlocked towns so fascinated with alligators? My theory is the alligators gave them some tropical tie with neighboring coastal Mexican towns like Acapulco or Puerto Vallarta. For instance, seafood is much more popular in Juarez than in El Paso, which is right next door. Juarez, far from any lakes and oceans, relates to Mexico's tropical side.

Later in my life, tropical reptiles and amphibians played a big role in my work. I call it border town sensibility. Juarez is one of the few border towns in the world where one city stops—El Paso—and another just begins—Juarez. When you visit a Mexican border town, you find all this wonderful stuff, quirky critter souvenirs like stuffed swordfish, sailfish, armadillos, frogs, and iguanas. Border town culture has to do with plucking influences from here and there. It has to do with the style and cool that comes from a border town experience. It's always profoundly affected my life and art, and it's how some of my funniest ideas came about.

# Chapter Three

# Horseshit Cigarettes, Taco Wagons, and

# the Streets of Juarez

**AKE** little 'Pard' (short for "partner") over to Juarez for haircuts and shoeshines."

The border between El Paso and Juarez was a very easy walk. I would go over the border with my dad every Saturday, great father-and-son outings.

Getting a shoeshine in Juarez was a real experience, unlike any others, really. The Mexican shoeshiners whistled to the tunes of the mariachis playing in the background. Right behind were legions of drunks from the sports bars. The smells of lime, booze, and puke permeated the air above the streets and sidewalks.

When people would visit from out of town, we'd always take them to the Juarez seafood restaurants. They had walls adorned with velvet paintings of marlins and sailfish outlined in neon, and all had that neat, tacky Mexican grotto sensibility. Some bars were even designed to look like grottoes or caverns. Mexicans and Catholics love the concept of grottoes. It's exotic.

My dad and I would always bring home crazy souvenirs. They were cheap and plentiful in Juarez. My dad would buy a pack of Horseshit Cigarettes, bad-smelling Mexican cigarettes made of low-rent tobacco with a picture of a horse on the pack. You could buy them from most of the outdoor stands. To this day, I still have a pack stashed somewhere. I'd get wooden snakes, Mexican yoyos, or Chinese handcuffs. My father would also come back with a glass or a coaster that had a picture of a beautiful girl in a bathing suit on the front side. When you flipped it over, she was naked on the back side. Leave it to the Mexicans to come up with ingenious risqué stuff. Kids in grade school would have dirty little pen-and-ink comics from Mexico, twisted stuff showing some of the famous American cartoon characters like Snow White getting banged doggie style by a long-dicked Mexican guy wearing shades.

At fifteen, I was finally old enough to go into Juarez at night on my own—without my parents' consent, of course. This was considered pretty fearless for an El Paso teenager. A group of us drove down to the bridge on our motor scooters. If you were old enough to drive a scooter to the border on your own, chances are you already had a sense of what kind of adventure lurked in Juarez. You knew from the older boys that there was action. Plenty of it.

The bridge rose up and over the Rio Grande. We'd hit the main drag right away, a powerful first image of Juarez as you came down what we called the walkover bridge, the equivalent of maybe three city blocks. You'd be right on the main drag! There were floor-show joints, seafood restaurants, liquor stores, barkers outside of the floor shows—it was a lot like New Orleans' Bourbon Street or San Francisco's North Beach, but this was Mexico. Stripper photos in glass cases were out front of the tease joints, and inside the bar there was a photo gallery of bullfighters and Mexican prizefighters.

I learned the shady sides of life sooner than those guys who grew up in Dallas or Houston. We had our own brand of sex education, border town style. For 50 cents you could end up in a room where they showed dirty movies, or you could go to the strip shows—and then there was always the donkey show. . . . The legal drinking age in Mexico was "sorta sixteen," so if you were lucky enough to be of age, you could go to Juarez and drink, or you could buy a whole quart jug of Bacardi rum for around 99 cents.

I went over the border many times with my friends. We'd park our scooters—I can't believe they weren't ever stolen—and go about two blocks in. You always saw the doggies having a great time, getting drunk for next to nothing. Juarez was a wide-open town, with prostitutes roaming the streets.

Prostitution was still legal in Mexico, provided you conformed to a series of laughable health regulations. The law was that there had to be a nurse present in the brothels. She'd check each person before you went back for the real business. These retired nurses were like grandmothers, clad in white uniforms in a white cubicle. Once you paid your money and the deal was fixin' to happen, you had to go into the white room with the nurse. You pulled your weenie out and yanked on it. If some weird stuff started coming out the end or if you jerked back when she yanked it, she knew you had a little problem. She'd look around for any sores, and provided you passed the test, which everyone always did, you paid your 50 cents.

As a fifteen-year-old kid going into one of those joints, the most you could get for a buck was a hand job. You thought you were going to get a suckie-suckie, but what you got was a fake one, which consisted of a naked prostitute leaning across you in such a way that she had you pinned down with a fistful of grease or whatever, and she could manipulate a kid into thinking "Boy, now that was some good blow job."

These were the most bizarre/exciting/strange experiences of my boyhood. Most young men in America might bang the neighborhood girl or meet one on vacation, but to go to a foreign country, pay a couple of bucks, go to the nurse, go inside a tiny room smelling of disinfectant and then have sex with a teenage girl—I must say, it's a rare sexual initiation.

I first heard the term "peter belly" in Juarez. Many of the girls were either pregnant or had been so many times that their bellies retained a pregnant shape. Lots of Mexican prostitutes had permanent peter bellies, wearing prom dresses that hid the fact until you got into the back room, then the real truth jumped out. We'd sit on banco seats at the bar as the girls would come over and sit next to us or on our knees in such a way that the big petticoat and the full party skirt would flare out. Our legs would disappear underneath their flamboyant attire. It was an unwritten rule that you were allowed to play around under there to get a sense of things, enticing you to go to the next stage.

We thought we were the coolest guys of the whole El Paso/Juarez scene, learning at fifteen how not to get thrown in jail. Don't be a wise-ass; don't get drunk in Mexico and do something stupid. We grew up with a laid-back Chicano attitude and behavior. Basically, how to be cool.

To this day, when I encounter a loud, obnoxious drunk, I'm always reminded of my Juarez days, especially when I would visit the hard-core rock 'n' roll bars in Juarez, the most famous being the Lobby Lounge. We watched as the bouncers beat at least five or six guys to a pulp every night, usually doggies, mostly from Midwest states like Michigan or Iowa who didn't know not to cross the line and aggravate the Mexican bouncers.

Doggies and tourists would stagger in drunk. Once they did something stupid, the bouncer would nod to the bartender behind the bar and he would quickly dispense the billy clubs. The bouncers would beat the doggies senseless. The rest of us would run out and watch as the bouncers chased them down the sidewalk, beating them from behind for another half a block. Being underage, even by Mexican drinking laws, we'd let out a relieved sigh, go back inside, and start drinking again.

A guy named Long John played an electric guitar at the Lobby Lounge. An outrageous guitarist, he was so far beyond Hendrix it was unbelievable. He could play guitar with his teeth as he swung out into the audience from a rope tied to a rafter. If some doggie or tourist did do something stupid, Long John would reach out and kick the guy right in the head. Then the bouncers went to work.

There were always ways for me and my dates to get drunk. My parents kept their liquor in the closet, and I used to pour rum into a Coke bottle, replacing the missing rum with water. Sure, I was watering their booze down, but, hell, Mexican booze was watered down anyway. When our hot rod club and their dates ended up at the drive-in movies, I would always bring my Coke bottle filled with rum and try to neck before my date puked.

While I was not in any gangs in El Paso, a lot of friends were. The Gypsy Kings. The Poker Kings. The Hearts. These were the Hispanic gangs that seldom had gringos in them, possibly one. They wore cool jackets and a Pachuco mark, a cross with three little marks. When the Chicanos were first being harassed by the gringos in the '40s, they formed a Pachuco organization to take care of their buddies—a kind of good-guy gang although not averse to beating up rival gangs that lived on the other side of town. At the end of football games, our gangs of Mexicans would go over to fight the other school's gangs of Mexicans. There would be a "Chingaso"—twenty guys with bicycle chains beating each other until the police and the ambulances showed up.

Oftentimes we'd drive to New Mexico, since their drinking age was lower than in Texas. Griggs Restaurant was a fairly nice restaurant/cocktail lounge about thirty minutes from El Paso toward Las Cruces. You either took your dates there for dinner and mixed drinks or you gave them a big thrill and took them to Mexico after a high school function. As a teenager in 1960, besides visiting the red-light districts, another reason to visit Juarez was to take a girlfriend to the infamous Cavern of Music for a highball.

The Cavern of Music was a downstairs fake grotto with Carlsbad Caverns–type decor, leopard-skin upholstered booths, and a piano bar. Musicians would play romantic songs on the piano—typical American songs, Mexican love songs, and requests—as we ordered our cocktails. One Mexican guy in our hot rod club spoke Spanish, so he knew all the Spanish titles to Spanish songs, like "Maria Elena." He'd request a few, which would impress our dates into thinking we were worldly guys.

During my high school days in El Paso, I was part of the whole custom car scene. Our hot rod club, me and twelve other guys, were called the Road Runners. My 1951 customized Ford became more than just spiffy. We drove fast, drag racing almost every Sunday, and the Road Runners won a lot of trophies.

I designed all kinds of elaborate engine modifications on my '51 Ford: traction bars, three-speed conversion kits, meth fuel in the gas tank when I raced. I had to look good at the strip, so I gave the car a detailed custom treatment. In a funny way there seemed to be unwritten parameters of what you could and could not do, and there was always some new *vato* who came up with some new accepted way of chopping, channeling, or bull-nosing his car.

We'd get a lot of the body work done on our cars in Juarez. First you'd nose and deck the car, meaning you removed all the chrome. Welding, torching, body work—it had to be a clean slick design removing all superfluous chrome. Everything off the nose at the front of the hood had to go. Plates that said Ford or Chevy or any of the little chrome Vs had to go too. Since you opened the trunk by pulling a cable inside the car, the chrome lock mechanisms were stripped as well.

I had to figure out a new place to put the license plate. I replaced my '51 Ford grille with that of a '53 Pontiac. With a little modification, it fit perfectly, and the design of the Pontiac grille looked much cooler than the Ford stock.

If you had the bucks, you would delve into the interior. Again, the only place to go was Mexico, which was always a little bit hairy because leaving your car there for a couple of days was risky. Depending on the money you had, they would do the whole headliner, a beautiful Naugahyde treatment with piping everywhere, two colors, rolls and pleats, bucket seat designs. Then you had to figure out what kind of carpet you'd use for the floor and the back window. Mexican car sensibility had more to do with craft and the ability to make and do stuff with your hands.

I could spot a car from Juarez even before checking the license plate. We referred to cars from Juarez as "taco wagons." Many of them were taxi cabs. Like cabs from other countries, they were painted in unusual colors that you wouldn't normally see—funny blues and greens. A taco wagon usually had a lot of fringe dangling by the rearview mirror, maybe some religious stuff on the dashboard or some extra lights bolted on the bumpers and fenders.

Custom gringo cars from El Paso fit more into the concept of the official *Hot Rod* magazine or *Custom Car* magazine look, more devoted to the standards set by Ed "Big Daddy" Roth and Chuck Barris in Los Angeles.

My car was low in the front like L.A. cars. There was a cheap way of lowering the front end by heating the coils near the shock absorbers, causing them to compress. It left you with no shocks, but it looked cool. We called it "raked in the front." White kids dropped their cars in the front while they were "up" in the back, a drag strip practicality. Punching down, you gained traction. Conversely, Chicano customizers raked their cars lower in the back. They were early examples of what low-riders look like now: low or perfectly level, inches off the ground or really low in the back and fairly high in the front. Today they have hydraulic systems installed so that if the car is level, at the hit of a button they can make the car rise up in the front or "jump" and "hop."

In the '60's, drag race aesthetics were important. How to go faster on a quarter mile dictated how your car should look. Very few low-riders were involved in racing. Although they might have cars that could crank up to 120 mph, they weren't nearly as preoccupied with going from here to there in eight seconds as we were. They favored elegant paint jobs with murals, long chrome exhaust pipes, and velvet interiors; a cool surface cruising look.

Customizing hot rods was basically creating art and sculpture. We adhered to the unwritten codes with ease and nonchalance.

"Boy, did he get the right metallic sierra gold on that Ford!"

Or—"That's a little too high."

Artists who didn't go through a custom car phase as teenagers often ended up in art school adopting a more traditional concept of making sculpture, chiseling stone with lots of intense labor. The idea of having some aspect of your artwork farmed out or done by someone else seemed sacrilegious to them. Conversely, I admired and adopted the techniques of "customizing" where a lot of the work was done by skilled technicians and craftsmen.

Custom cars and hot rod clubs and being a teenager, period, soon gave way to higher education. In 1961 my home base days in El Paso ended when I went off to college. My parents reentered the hotel business and moved to Corpus Christi. It was time to put the chairs in the wagon and move along.

My Daddy-O days were now sitting on the horizon.

*Chapter Four*

# Kappa Sigs and Berkeley

**N** college we'd drive hours to Mexico, which never closed. We got drunk, got laid, ate, and puked. Then we'd drive back and miss a bunch of classes. That's how it was. My wild fraternity life consisted of two or three parties every weekend, hanging out in the college bars, and 'co.

Daddy-O's higher education. I got accepted into the University of Texas and the great thing the local guys told me to do was to check out the fraternities.

I left El Paso in 1961 in my '51 custom Ford to go to college at the University of Texas in Austin. I noticed that most frat guys there had shorter haircuts and wore tan slacks and loafers. I arrived in my

'51 Crown Victoria two-door wearing the El Paso correct length blue jeans, a pair of chukka desert boots, and an attitude.

Lots of my friends in my fraternity ended up being fat cats out of Houston, Dallas, Fort Worth, or San Antonio. I was taught when I first joined that they were going to be my friends for the rest of my life. And they were right. Guys I met between 1961 through 1965 at the University of Texas have continued to be great friends and associates. They became my cronies, contacts, and my network. When I went down to UT, there were 19,500 kids. I thought that was big. Now they have over 50,000.

The guys from the fraternities had fairly new cars, and so eventually I traded my '51 for a '55 Ford convertible. I had gotten myself into one of the wildest fraternities on campus, Kappa Sigma. "Machine Gun Kelly" from El Paso had been a Kappa Sig and he recommended me. Everybody had a nickname. One short fat guy was named Pig Pen because, like the cartoon character, he was trashy. There was Melon Head, Doc, Spot, Cowboy, Monk, Skate Key, Blanco, and Mush Head.

The Dallas-Houston types didn't know much about a border town guy like me. I was different. I talked different. My El Paso accent was closer to a choppy, New Mexico Chicano accent—so choppy that in northern New Mexico it's often referred to as "machine gun." I spoke in a "ratta-tat-tat" monotone, a staccato rhythm with few ups or downs.

To most Kappa Sigs, my accent made me sound like I was a Pachuco. I reminded them of a *Blackboard Jungle/West Side Story*–type movie character. One look at my hot rod and long hair combed back was all "Bull" Pettit needed to nickname me "Daddy-O." The name stuck all through college and afterward when I moved on to Dallas. It became my character, my alter ego of sorts.

Fraternity life could be both wild and hell. Superchicken Gallagher blamed it on the GI Bill that put a lot of jaded guys from the Korean War on campus. At two or three o'clock in the morning pledges were ordered to congregate at "pledge rallies" held at the fraternity house. A pledge trainer would put us through a series of exercise drills—normal stuff like push-ups, sit-ups, running in place, on our backs, on our bellies, up and running. After everyone was tired and the whole room was heated up, with the windows all fogged over from the heat, they'd bring out the Bee, an evil contraption, and put it on a sedan chair. All the lights would be out and we could see the glow of this blue arc. The Bee was an old cattle prod gizmo hooked up to a twelve-volt battery. It looked a little like a shaver with two protruding metal arcs. Flick the switch and you'd hear a mad-scientist buzzing sound of electricity. It was very impressive and scary the first time you saw it. The first time they put it on your ass was also very impressive. The second time they put it on your ass, you were trying not let them put it there anymore.

Kappa Sigma reveled in the stereotypical notions that perpetuated the typical Texas attitude: Texas being bigger and better; Austin being the state capital; the University of Texas Longhorns, rah, rah, rah.

The Kappa Sigs were high class *Animal House* types. They could be mean, they could be cruel, but then on the other hand, they could be your best buddies. Everybody wanted to be a Kappa Sig. It was the country club of frats. We were the big red house on the hill. We had staff who would wake us up in the morning with tomato or orange juice. They'd pull on our toe so we'd get up to go to class.

In addition to the Fourth of July, every year Texans celebrate their own Independence Day, marking the day we declared ourselves free from Mexican rule. Every year the university would shoot a cannon in celebration, and that cannon was always pointed toward our fraternity house. Traditionally we dressed up like Santa Anna and the Mexicans with our sombreros, serapes, mustaches, guns, and rifles, and shot blanks back at the university cannon. Our roof was filled with drunk Kappa Sigs dressed up like *Zapatistas*. Afterward we'd go to Mexico and carry on throughout the entire weekend.

Most of my fraternity brothers were pretty cool. Richard Rainwater was also a dragster guy, and others, like Joe Longley, were music freaks. We used to book a band for our parties called the Hot Nuts, a bunch of racy R&B musicians with a filthy sense of humor. Basically we brought them in to gross out our dates, the sorority girls. It was the reverse of the custom in El Paso. Instead of taking them to nice places for cocktails, the idea was to be as horrible as you could. It was easy for me to participate. I would get shit-faced and slip, slide, and take down a couple of coeds onto the beer-soaked floor. It would go on for hours.

The Hot Nuts were up on the stage playing the blues with occasional digressions into racy stuff about nuts and where to get 'em.

There was a guy we used to call Buddha mainly because he was little and round. Buddha was very entertaining. At the end of the fraternity parties every weekend, after the Hot Nuts had packed up their instruments and left, after the last coed had been dragged out, Buddha would manage to get one more foamy spot of beer out of the keg. Because he had a low center of gravity, like a sumo wrestler, he could unscrew the spigot, toss it aside, and lift the big aluminum container up to his mouth to let the last bit of that green beer sludge dribble into his mouth.

If there was no beer left and it was too late to buy any on a Friday night, maybe we'd drive to 'co. Excited, we'd haul out of Austin on our way to Laredo, making one stop at a place just past San Marcos and before San Antonio called the Acapulco, a restaurant/bar/cantina where they sold beer a little later than the places in Austin. If nothing else, you could at least get out of the car and bleed your lizard.

One weekend, Buddha got out of the car at the Acapulco to stretch a little bit. He was feeling a little bit tired, so he lay spread-eagle on the hood of the car, belly-down, facing the windshield. Come time to go, Buddha wouldn't get up.

"Okay, Buddha, let's go," we said, "Gotta go to 'co to get some beer, see the girls and a donkey show. I've gotta buy some Black Mollies and Dexedrine for finals."

All Buddha could offer was a groan.

"Okay, Buddha, tell you what. We're gonna count to ten, and if you're not off that hood we're drivin' outta here. It won't be fun when you roll off onto the highway."

Buddha realized what was fixin' to happen. He also realized he wasn't getting off, so he grabbed the windshield wipers and we drove all the way to Mexico with Buddha on the hood.

For some reason, my parents never questioned me about majoring in art. I enrolled in all the correct art major courses at UT. During college, I was too busy drinking beer and chasing coeds to even think about what I was going to do after graduation. I was never much of a gambler, though there were a lot of guys in college who spent every dime, including their tuition money, playing cards. I'd see card games run for two days straight with nobody getting any sleep. They'd be up five thousand bucks, then next thing you'd know they'd owe five thousand.

One of the Kappa Sig brothers, whose granddad came from Mid-

land and found oil, was once deep in a poker game at the Kappa
Sig house. He called home and said, "Dad, I've lost two thousand
dollars in this damn poker game. What should I do?"

His father said, "Keep anteing. I'll be right there."

He got on an airplane, flew to the university to get in the poker
game to try to win back his $2,000. These were wild Texans.

While I excelled in all studio classes, I'd arrive at my Art History
classes hung over, pass out, and sleep through the entire lecture. I
earned some D's in Art History. Drawing and design came easy for
me. I would walk into three-hour studio courses wearing ragged blue
jeans and work shirts. The other Kappa Sigs were wearing preppy
slacks. They would say, "Hey Daddy-O, you should go get yourself
a new pair of pants."

"Luckily," I'd answer back, "I don't need to wear that corny shit
to my classes. I'll be drawing naked women. In fact, not only do I
sit and draw naked women all day long, but your girlfriend sits at
the next easel drawing naked men."

I'd construct big metal abstract sculptures by welding car bumpers
in the Kappa Sigma basement where we held our gambling mara-
thons. Soon I took over the basement, welding and bolting for a
couple days straight, becoming the crazy artist of the fraternity. I
knew only one other frat guy who was an art major—an S.A.E.

When we'd sit in off-campus bars, occasionally some tight-ass
asked what we each majored in. Pre-Law. Pre-Med. Economics.
When it came around to me, sometimes instead of saying art, I'd
say advertising because advertising made money. In those days, art
sounded like you didn't want to amount to anything. Frat cats had
negative notions about it. Mothers, not dads, painted and decorated.
Majoring in art implied that you were on the feminine side.

Texas college kids—especially UT frat boys—could be cruel fuck-
ers: rich, wise ass, chips on their shoulders, better than you with
families from money, whether it be oil and gas, real estate, insurance,
or law. It seemed tough from time to time, but having moved around
a lot I was able to finagle the best of these characters. They didn't
know about macho painters like Jackson Pollock and Franz Kline,
the New York school of hard-drinkin' tough-paintin' bad boys that
made these Kappa Sigs look like putzes.

I had a friend in Austin who was a Tigua indian, so during my
second or third year of college, I had a mystical, psychedelic expe-

rience before it was fashionable to do any kind of drugs. I got some peyote buttons, cut them up, stuck them inside a double cheese-burger and ate it with an order of hash browns and a big slice of butterscotch pie.

Nothing happened.

After a few beers, me and my buddies went back to the house and I went to my bedroom. According to my friends who were still up late studying, I suddenly broke into their rooms with a machete, my eyes wide open, asking, "Did you see that son of a bitch?"

"What?" my buddy Joe Longley wondered.

"You didn't see that son of a bitch come down this way?"

"What are you talking about?" Joe asked.

"That goddamn cockroach, a giant cockroach in a top hat and tuxedo came into my room."

"Bob," he suggested. "It's the peyote."

"No, this was real. It said something to me."

"What did he say?"

"Come with me, my god is stronger than yours."

My fraternity buddies and I used to go down to Del Rio. Being another border town, it was an alternate 'co location. At the time, the Mexican border town across from Del Rio was called Villa Cuña, which means "the village of Cuña." Now it's called Ciudad Cuña or "the city of Cuña." In the Villa Cuña days, it was a real low-life Mexican border town.

It was a tradition that every year all of the pledges would take a trip together down to Mexico. It goes back as far as 1909, before Pancho Villa. Pledges would rent a bus and then "kidnap" a bunch of the older, "active" guys (the guys who were the biggest partyers) and "make" them go down. No one had to kidnap Daddy-O; I was already waiting on the bus. We drove close to Villa Cuña, Mexico, where the bus driver knew better than to go across the bridge. He stopped and let us all out on the U.S. side.

It was one of those foolish nights that everyone spent every penny he had without holding back enough money to pay for a cab ride back to the border. Still, we boosted a cab ride to within walking distance. When it came time to jump out and pay the driver, every-body bolted, including me. We were totally wiped out, but hightailed it with what little strength we had toward the border.

The cab driver, shaking his fist, yelled out to us in broken English. "Three dollars, three dollars."

Everybody was supposed to meet at three in the morning back at the private bus that the pledges had rented. I was one of the older guys "kidnapped to go down to 'co," the self-proclaimed smart guy from El Paso who could speak Spanish. I was the guy who told everybody how to act and what not to do.

"Don't act like doggies!" I warned, but I guess we sorta acted like doggies when we stiffed the cabby.

All five of us sprayed in different directions from the cab and hid in the shadows and doorways of the old buildings. The cabby was yelling, *"Policía, policía!"*

We hung around in the back alley for about an hour until we were convinced that the incident had blown over. Then, like little cockroaches, we sneaked the last half mile to the border.

The plan was to separate again and, in a low-key fashion, keep walking. We were hoping some old clunker would amble down the road so we could hitch a ride. Sure enough, here came a little 1949 two-door Ford coupe, just like one my buddies from the Road Runners drove in high school. I jumped out and gave the old Ford a thumb and it pulled right over. The driver in the front pulled the seat forward as my partner and I jumped in the back. There were only a few hours until sunup, and we were still kinda foggy as the car drove toward the border.

After half a block, the driver turned his head around very slowly as he put on his policeman's cap.

*"Buenas noches,* boys."

The police knew there were more than two of us, so all he had to do was take his hat off and cruise around. When the other fraternity brothers saw us in the backseat they would wave the car down. We weren't in a position to warn them. Soon all five of us were crammed in the backseat and headed straight to the jailhouse.

Of all the border towns in Mexico, Villa Cuña was supposedly the worst place to end up in jail. [The village brothels there were notorious for having the highest incidents of what our fraternity brothers called "dead head clap." As the legend goes, the end of your dick falls off. Dead head.] But the jails were another story.

After the federales rounded up all five of us, we all met in the jailhouse. I managed to huddle the guys together when we first got out of the car.

"Look," I hissed in an urgent whisper, "I know how this works. They'll want money from our parents because they think we're rich college boys. They'll keep us down here until our parents send lots of money to bail us out. Don't give them your real names."

I was the border-town smart guy, so everybody made up a fake name.

"*¿Nombre?*" asked the desk policeman.

I was Robert Johnson, the last guy down the line.

They put us all in this little cubicle and it smelled like a dungeon. One Mexican prisoner inside couldn't remember how long he had been there. He looked pathetic, with one ear missing. Some of my friends were dry-heaving. This was not good.

There was a whole row of small cells and as you held on to the bars and looked out you'd see an open air common area. In front of every third cell, mounted on these concrete slabs, was a toilet. The jailers might let us out from time to time to do our business on the little toilets.

"Golly. I wouldn't use that toilet if I had to," choked one of my dry-heaving buddies.

As the sun was coming up, we had yet to see anybody come looking for us. But we had given the *policía* bogus names, so who would know we were here?

It was time for the changing of the guard. The new guy came to start his shift, yawning and stretching his arms like he had just woken up. The big fat guard grunted as he took off his hat and walked over to the toilet. He jerked his pants down, turned around, and sat down on the toilet, doing his business right there in front of us as we clung to the bars, watching like animals in the zoo, following his every move.

After the guard finished, he pulled his pants up, flushed, turned back around and stuck his hands down into the water in the topless tank . . .

. . . and washed his face!

Back across the border, the other thirty guys on the bus chose to head back to Austin without us. But before leaving, they took up a collection and left a bunch of money with three volunteers who decided to stay behind and crisscross the back streets of this godforsaken border town to look for us. They had already been to the jailhouse twice. Frustrated, they came back to the police station for a third time. Maybe there had been a mistake, they figured, and they asked if they could go back in the jail to take a look and see if maybe we were there.

Back in the cell, we were beyond dry-heaving. Since the sun had come out, we could clearly see how awful the jail cell looked. It looked as bad as it smelled. We were sinking fast when in walked our search party. At first they pretended not to know who we were as the *policía* walked along with them. Then they said to the cop, "We'll take this one, this one, this one, this one, and this one."

Everyone except the guy without the ear, poor bastard. We felt like mongrels being claimed at the dog pound. Just as we were leaving, in came some doggies from Fort Hood to take our place in the cell. It was seven in the morning and they were just being thrown into jail. As we're leaving, they were yelling to us, "Please! Somebody help us, somebody help us. Could you please call our commanding officer?"

"What were you accused of?" we asked. "Being drunk?"

"No! Starting a revolution."

Evidently, they bought some low-rent fireworks from a guy on the street and were setting them off when the cops arrived. The official charge was starting a revolution. We called Fort Hood on the way out of Del Rio.

Poor doggies.

When I was getting ready to leave UT in 1965, there still weren't many longhairs on campus. The freaks came a little bit later. Partying aside, zip, zip, zip, zip—I was out of UT with a B.F.A. in four years. I had a few scholarships under my belt plus one to the Brooklyn Museum school. I asked my professors to suggest some exciting graduate schools, and since the University of California, Berkeley, came up a number of times, I applied there and got in. Or so I thought. By then I had sold my '55 convertible, and my mom and dad had given me a great, two-door '55 Bel Air Chevy V-8 automatic.

Fraternity and campus antics laid a good foundation for my future Berkeley protests and, later, art antics. In the ambiance of the University of California and the Bay Area, I would meet characters who

were a cool jump back to the Beat poets, reminding me of the characters from *On the Road*.

When I left Austin to take the road trip with my roommate from
Waco, Bob Maddin, we went to Berkley by way of Albuquerque and
Las Vegas. Maddin and I used to go on weekend road trips to the
illegal dog races in little towns outside of Austin, where they used
live rabbits as opposed to the little mechanical ones they use now.
We were about to get a whole new cultural rush.

The San Francisco Bay Area had what we later called in Texas
"hipdogs"—longhaired, seasoned hippies. They were a weird combination of the starry-eyed Haight Ashbury set and the idealistic and
angry Berkeley campus activists. As far as the eye could see down
Berkeley's Telegraph Avenue they swarmed, students and professors
alike looking like Beat poets. There were no Texas-style preppies to
be found in Berkeley. Women wore their hair down past their asses,
with sandals, cut-offs, and no bras. Maddin and I couldn't believe
our eyes. We whipped right over to the first coffee house we could
find to see if it was like being back in UT in some fraternity bar . . .
It wasn't.

I probably looked like a narc with my hair parted on the right
side, madras shorts, buttoned-down shirt, and loafers with no socks.
Maddin tried to start up a conversation with a couple of "hippie
chicks" and came back rubbing his ears. They told us to go away.
At that point, for the first time, it occurred to me that there was a
whole new trip going down out here. Ten minutes later I had finished my beer and we climbed back into the '55 Chevy. Not too far
down the road were the same two hippie chicks who blew us off,
standing on the road hitchhiking. Texas coeds didn't hitchhike
around the campus like that.

When I went to enroll at graduate school, I thought my records
were in order, so I went into the office and gave them my name.

"Gee, Mr. Wade, it says here that you were not accepted into
graduate school. You got a D in art history."

I talked to a professor who advised me to go ahead and take the
full load of classes that summer anyway. If I did well, I'd be a full-
fledged grad student. I enrolled, took the classes, scored all A's and
ended up finishing sooner than the Fall enrollees. An M.A. from
Berkeley was better than an M.F.A. from another school.

I arrived in Berkeley at the beginning of the Free Speech Movement. Students carried signs reading "fuck." I would attend huge gatherings (mainly out of curiosity), whether there were marches down Telegraph Avenue or protests in Sproul Plaza with Mario Savio and Carol Doda. The next year, 1966, I saw Hell's Angels beating up Telegraph Avenue marchers on their way to the Oakland induction center. I took photographs of the crowds and the cops. Signs that year read:

WHY ARE WE BOMBING ENTIRE REGIONS
OF INNOCENT CIVILIANS?

DON'T VOTE FOR WAR.

WE'VE COME FROM SELMA TO OAKLAND.

It wasn't until I went to Berkeley that I met artists both on campus and off campus in the thriving, jumping San Francisco North Beach Beat culture milieu.

Berkeley had the rough, organic, visceral quality I was accustomed to in Texas humor and adolescent fraternity behavior. I ran across an item in the art department student lounge. It was an almost empty coffee cup into which someone had poured urethane foam. It had erupted, creating a big geyser that had risen out of the cup and hardened into a gross-looking blob. For some reason, I took that piece and I've kept it to this day. It was an omen that the art department in Berkeley was right for me.

One well-known sculptor and professor was Peter Volkous, a raucous guy who worked with clay. Volkous helped develop a free-form attitude toward ceramics. Just that attitude influenced my whole artistic activity. Another Berkeley professor of mine was Jim Melchert, who eventually became head of visual arts at the National Endowment for the Arts in Washington, D.C. George Myasaki, another teacher, did a lot of pop art printmaking, and Harold Paris and Elmer Bischoff produced their style of Bay Area work.

All these characters were ultra-cool, ultra-hip and had a great creative attitude—a Bay Area live-and-let-live mind-set that meshed with what was becoming known during that period of the sixties as "funk art." That stylistic term was coined by curator/art historian Peter Seltz, who organized the important funk exhibition at Berkeley. The term "funk" already existed in the music community: It loosely referred to something that was not squeaky clean, not necessarily pure and straight up.

Whether it was figurative or non-representational, funk art was visually organic and humorous. It made reference to machinery and sex, resurrecting the interests the early Dadaists and surrealists had with regard to anti-art and anti-beauty. Funk art ultimately created its own type of beauty. When I left UT for UC, I felt I was moving on so I could get more involved with contemporary art and real life. When I was an undergraduate, the art scene in Austin was fairly young. It didn't have as many "names" as the Bay Area did, but Charles Umlauf, Robert Levers, and others did have national reputations. Lester and Everett Spruce had established regional styles as well. Berkeley was my initiation into the real art scene and pop culture—Berkeley was the Sixties.

I saw an ad for Andy Warhol's *Exploding Plastic Inevitable*, so I went to San Francisco's Fillmore Auditorium to see the Velvet Underground. Work by Warhol and Rauschenberg and their kind of pop stuff was big in the Bay Area—more so than down south in L.A. Billy Al Binkston, Ron Cooper, Larry Bell, and all the others who lived around Venice in Southern California were more into the cool, clean, immaculate, beautifully sprayed look. The Bay Area, with its jazz and Beat poets, fueled a gutsy, grittier art scene. The exception was Ed Kienholz, who created controversy with his exhibition of *Back Seat Dodge* at the Los Angeles County Museum of Art.

I don't remember that much overt political art, surprisingly. I did a little of it, leaning more toward an assemblage technique that combined doll babies smeared with red acrylic paint. They resembled bodies in Vietnam, and were mixed with detritus and weird materials glued down and fiberglassed together with urethane foam poured in. Organic urethane foam (remember the coffee cup?) influenced a lot of my work later on in terms of shapes, building techniques, and eccentric subject matter.

Nobody ever told me or explained to me what I could do with a degree in painting; I just assumed that most good art students went to graduate school to become art professors. The choice seemed automatic. I planned to get a master's degree, then hustle and land a teaching job somewhere, rent a studio, paint, and be in shows. I thought maybe I'd get tenure, marry, travel to Europe, or write a book. Meanwhile, one of my part-time jobs at Berkeley was showing slides for Jan Adlman's art history classes—the same class that I failed at UT that nearly kept me out of graduate school.

I met my first wife while attending Berkeley. I was an assistant manager at an Oakland movie theater and in the process of flirting with the candy girl, I lost my head and got engaged. Susie Immel from L.A. was to become my wife.

Susie was not political: She was a nice girl from Los Angeles who ran up to the Bay Area to go to Merritt College and escape parental control. She later accused me of marrying her to avoid going to Vietnam, but in reality the military exemption for marriage had already passed.

I called my old college buddies in Austin to find out what was happening and if the counterculture was starting there too. Before I left, nothing was happening at all. Now there was an underground club called the Vulcan Gas Company which was featuring all the early Texas psychedelic bands. A lot of the local talented cartoonists ultimately became famous—guys like Gilbert Shelton and his Furry Freak Brothers, and Jim Franklin with his Armadillos. The Austin counterculture had finally taken off. Of course Austin would soon be a complete freak show with the Armadillo World Headquarters' music scene. A lot of the Texas guys that I hung around with had started smoking dope big time, and the pot dealers were making big bucks. Thinking that one day pot was going to be legalized, outlaw Texas dealers began stocking up, figuring they could lay low until legalization. I told my bad boy friends I was engaged and they nearly died laughing. How bizarre, they thought. "Wade! We left you out of our sight for a few months and now . . . you're fuckin' engaged?" True, but looking back, by studying in California I avoided the possibility of being thrown in with all of these pot entrepreneurs who, by the way, occasionally went to jail.

After graduating from UC Berkeley, I drove back to Texas to introduce my fiancée to my family, stopping in Austin to introduce her to some of my cousins. I dropped by UT to check the bulletin boards to see if, by chance, there were any notices for jobs.

I had dutifully sent out my résumés in Berkeley, but hadn't gotten a single taker. I checked a bulletin board that wasn't even in the art department that said:

> New college opening in Waco, Texas.
> Need faculty members.

I wrote down the information and called immediately.

Since we were scheduled to go to Los Angeles to meet my fiancée's relatives and get married, I called up the school in Waco and told them I had to be back in California soon. They told me to drive up to Waco right away and they would interview me immediately. I drove up with my fiancée and the interview went well. They needed someone to start an art department.

Bingo! A week later, I was getting dressed for my rehearsal dinner in L.A. My parents and I were staying in a hotel and the phone rang in my room. Just as I was getting into my suit and tie, the dean of the college in Waco was calling. "Still want that job in Waco?"

"Boy, you better believe it."

"Well it's yours."

I was relieved. Now I was able to tell my fiancée and our families that I had a job waiting. Susie and I spent our honeymoon in Mexico, then drove up to Waco. After doing a little graphics work during the summer, I started a teaching career that was to last almost eleven years. Professor Daddy-O hits Waco. Here I was, trying to be an adult, a professor, and a husband all at the same time, with no previous experience in any of them.

# Chapter Five

# Professor Daddy-O and the

# Photographic Canvas

**N** the late '60s, unless you were "4F" or became a teacher, you went to Vietnam. I became a nice guy college art teacher. I was married, owned a little house, lived the great life. My first year's salary was $6,500. A year later, my first house was purchased for another $6,500.

I started visiting Dallas galleries in 1966 and entered work in the Dallas Museum's annual competition. They handed me a cash award of $1,000. I was so shocked I photographed the check. Encouraged, I did more airbrush "Berkeley-style" paintings of hotdog-looking images. I also used a sewing machine and created stuffed soft sculptures for the floor. Most of these works were called weenies. They were "funky," curvy, colorful, humorous, and sexy, especially for Waco and Dallas. An outdoor sculpture I made in '68, "Funny Farm Family," is still on the McLennan campus.

There was a beautiful Mexican theater in Dallas that showed Spanish movies. On weekends at midnight they would show underground films. Hundreds of stoned hippies would turn up. There was so much pot-smoking in the theater you could barely see the screen.

One of my favorite visual recollections involves the theater's big red velvet curtain. The hipdogs would bring a bag of spaghetti balloons to the movie. We'd blow them up and instead of tying the knot, we'd let them fly toward the screen. The object was to lodge them into the folds of the curtain. The balloons resembled sperm traveling toward a big old ovary. If a balloon went all the way over the top of the curtain, everyone in the audience would go nuts with applause.

My earliest paintings were based on those late-night follies. The designs on canvas were influenced by spaghetti balloons flying through space at the movie theater.

Waco in the late '60s was a strange environment. To this day, you still can't dance on campus at Baylor University. The Vietnam War was raging and many of my friends from Waco were on the lam for one reason or another. Other friends were dropouts or just plain "Waco crazy."

The McNamara brothers of Waco drove around during hunting season with dead deer tied onto their dad's gold Cadillac. They'd pull up to a school playground and as the kids ran over to look, they'd say, "Looks like Santa Claus won't be making it this year."

I was lucky; I was a teacher. My dean wrote a letter each year to the draft board saying they needed me on campus. I was listed in "Outstanding Educators Of America." Also, every year I taught I could reduce my student loan repayment by a certain percentage. I had run up some expensive out-of-state tuition going to UC Berkeley, and could reduce my debt by a whole 50 percent by continuing teaching. Everything was secure and smooth for four full years.

Something had to give.

Northwood Institute, a private school near Dallas, specialized in professional courses and was sponsored by the business community.

Local art patrons including Betty Guiberson and Evelyn Lambert joined museum professionals like Henry Hopkins and Douglas McCagy in developing a professional art program. Their plan was to bring visiting lecturers to the institute, well-known art world figures in all disciplines. I was invited to attend the Summer Arts Festival in 1968 in the rambling hill campus south of Dallas. Artists Peter Forakis and Alfred Leslie were the first guests. The stage was set for an important new art influence in Dallas.

More and more I was driving up from Waco to see painters and sculptors who had been flown in from London and New York. On one of these junkets the director of the art school asked if I would be interested in going on a freebie to New York. They needed an extra chaperone to accompany ten students while they visited galleries, museums, and art studios. I accepted and found myself flying to New York for the first time ever. In New York I bumped into sculptor Luis Jimenez, an old friend from El Paso and UT, who was coming down the stairs of one of the galleries as I was going up. Coincidence? Nah.

Being in New York for the first time was unbelievable. I immediately realized that my living in Waco and being a junior college teacher was over with. I had to get with the program.

The SoHo art scene didn't really exist yet except for a couple of people, like Luis Jimenez, who were living there. On my second trip to New York, I crashed at his studio on West Broadway. There wasn't an extra bed or even a piece of foam rubber to lie on, only half a dozen U-Haul pads that Luis used to wrap sculptures. Although his German shepherd slept on top of them, he told me I was welcome to pile them in the corner. I caroused at the artists' bars and crashed on the U-haul pads for three days. When I got back to Waco, I had the crabs.

There was young Robert the college teacher, back home in Waco, telling his wife that the ointment that he had just purchased down at the pharmacy was to be applied to both of our pubic areas. My wife, Susie, was sweet and asked, "Why?"

I scratched myself and answered, "I think it has to do with Luis Jimenez's dog."

The head of the art department at Northwood, Alberto Collie, suggested I give up my Waco job and become an artist-in-residence at Cedar Hill. He said I could live out near the rolling hills in a modern apartment with a studio attached. I only had to teach about fifteen students, and it would be in a less structured, more experimental curriculum.

It was tough, but I did go back and tell Susie I was giving up my tenured job (that I could have kept for the rest of my life), that we were going to have to sell our house, and that we were about to move into one of the faculty apartments near Northwood. We did it, and we moved. One of my first jobs at Northwood involved the big-name artists who came in to town to lecture. I was the guy who picked them up at the airport and showed them around. When I went to New York, they reciprocated. Italo Scanga, Robert Smithson, Doug Davis, Bill Wegman, and Rafi Ferrer became friends of mine while visiting Northwood. These artists, while under my wing, enjoyed "Big D," cowgirls, and chicken-fried steaks.

The art program at Northwood was partially oriented toward experimental art and technology, abetted by an anti-gravity sculptor named Alberto Collie from South America. Alberto would invite guest engineers from Texas Instruments to come and give lectures. It was kinda like a little M.I.T. sometimes, complete with anti-gravity sculptures with stage magnets manipulating beautiful flying saucer objects.

It was precisely that experimental attitude that got me interested in putting photographic images onto canvas. In 1969 I did some research and found a place that manufactured a special photo emulsion that I could apply to canvas. Even though I didn't have any formal training in photography, I rigged a darkroom with giant trays and developed my first six-foot photo canvas on the floor.

The art department at Cedar Hill then moved near downtown Dallas in order to be closer to the action—the money, really. One of the patrons loaned us a three-story apartment building in a hardcore area of town where winos hung out. It was finally gettin' funky.

When I first showed my stuff around New York in 1970, I knew a curator at the Whitney Museum, Robert M. Doty, who had come down to Texas to find artists to include in the Whitney's annual shows. He really liked my weenie paintings and in 1969 he had put one of them in that year's show. Doty and I stayed in touch during my early trips to New York, and in 1973 he included one of my "Waco Boys" photo emulsions in the annual. Whenever I was in New York he would take me to a lot of galleries. At that time, it was unusual for a museum curator to take you around for an introduction.

I had just started doing photo pieces. They weren't on stretchers, but were loose canvases with little grommets around the edges so you could push-pin them to the wall. I'd roll about four or five pieces—each about five feet long—into a cardboard tube, and take them with me in a cab, the bus, or the subway to these galleries.

It worked out that before a gallery owner or assistant could say, "No, we're not looking at work or slides now," I'd drop to my knees and unroll these canvases like a Persian rug salesman.

Most artists spend half their careers sending out slides and cold-calling, only to be abused by some little art school snit sitting at the front desk making three bucks an hour to be rude to people. I avoided that shit.

I had shown my weenie paintings and, later, my early photo canvases at the Chapman Kelley Gallery in Dallas. "Atelier" Chapman Kelley was among the first contemporary galleries in Dallas to show younger, emerging artists and gave a lot of people their start. Murray Smither worked there. A lot of gay guys showed up at my first Chapman Kelley show in 1969, with all my weenie paintings on display. Word had gotten out that this guy Robert Wade was going to put up an exhibition of penis paintings. Not aware of that at the time, I thought it was curious that so many men showed up.

In 1971 New York artist Mon Levinson saw my photo canvas show at Chapman's and told his New York dealer, Jill Kornblee, about the work. The Kornblee Gallery contacted me and that became my first solo show in New York. Italo Scanga said if you didn't have a solo in NYC before you were thirty, you'd have to wait till you were forty. I was twenty-eight.

I began collecting photos of weird stuff when I drove through Florida in 1970. I was making the rounds of tacky roadside museums when a certain sign enticed me:

SEE OSWALD'S BEDROOM.

I pulled into the parking lot of this strange roadside museum. There was already a great wax exhibit on the same subject: a tableau in Grand Prairie, Texas, of the window on the floor of the school book depository building, with a figure of Oswald leaning out over the window pointing the rifle. There was also another wax exhibit of Jack Ruby engaged in the famous shooting of Oswald. I'd already done some Oswald pieces; I even tried to buy Oswald's original screen door and ultimately did a replica that was featured in an exhibition at the University of Texas in Arlington. I'd also done an earlier piece titled *The Criminal Wall*, which was a wall of morgue shots of outlaws—including Bonnie and Clyde—featuring proud cops standing over the bullet-riddled corpses. Another piece was Pancho Villa lying dead in the bed in Parral, Mexico, where he was ambushed and shot full of holes. Boy, I get carried away sometimes.

So you can now imagine how excited I was to see Oswald's bedroom.

Someone had gone to the boardinghouse where Oswald lived and either bought or reproduced the same dresser drawers and assorted bedroom furniture, measured out the size of his room, put up duplicate wallpaper, and re-created his room. On the wall was a framed photo enlargement of Oswald that somebody had snapped after his brutal autopsy. He looked like a hand-sewn two-dollar football.

At that time, I used to carry my big bulky Nikon loaded with high contrast black-and-white film everywhere I went in case I saw something strange. I "appropriated" the image of Oswald right off the wall and later produced a giant unsettling photo canvas that I wanted to exhibit in New York at that first solo exhibit. The gallery owner refused to let me put it on the wall. I remember saying, "Wait a minute, this is my show," to which she replied, "Yes, but this is my gallery." Case dismissed.

However, there were other exotic images Kornblee did allow. Since Cedar Hill was in the "country," my interest in Texana heightened. While out riding my motorcycle, I snapped a photo of two cows humping. Actually, they call it bulling. It happens in the spring when the heifers get horny and there are no bulls around. They jump up on each other and hunch around. I turned the image into a large photo canvas for the Kornblee show. It was reviewed in *Art Forum* by Robert Pincus-Witten. If you had anything reviewed in *Art Forum*, you were pretty lucky. My work had been in gallery ads, but this was the first time I'd actually gotten a review *with* a reproduction. Sometimes you'd get a review without a photo, but, as

Pincus-Witten used to say, a reproduction in a well-respected art magazine is the equivalent of two solo exhibitions. The name of the cow piece was *Gettin' It Near Cedar Hill*.

Meanwhile, art and Texas were beginning to form a strange alliance. An insecurity syndrome was evolving, which resulted in the upgrading of regional Texas culture in population centers like Dallas and Houston. In an attempt to measure up to the Northeast and Europe, locals felt it was time to improve their symphonies, ballets, and museums.

It became apparent to me and some of my contemporaries that battle lines were being drawn between the cultural elite who were importing culture and a small group of visceral Texans who had their own existing culture, right then, right there. As individualistic Texas artists, we wanted to declare our independence and make our move.

It was time for Daddy-O—and we who were proud of our Texas roots—to fish or cut bait.

*Chapter Six*

# The Horse Crippler and Other

# Taxidermic Tales

**Y**ou hear a lot about National Endowment for the Arts grants these days, but up until 1973, I'd never heard of one, much less applied for one. When you're an academic, a teacher, or an artist, you sometimes need grants to help support yourself or conduct research. There was a notice in one of the art magazines about an experimental NEA Special Projects grant that had been set up to provide limited funding to projects that didn't fall into traditional categories of painting and sculpture.

In my application I requested $3,500 to drive around the state of Texas during the summer of 1973, and go back to a lot of the places

I'd been over the years as a hotel brat, college guy, and starving artist. My idea was to take photographs and buy weird Texas objects. I would be "researching" the Texas phenomena—bigger, taller, more flamboyant, grandiose—an exploration of the Texas myth. My plan was to document roadside attractions like giant teepee souvenir stands, roadside junk stores, taxidermy shops where I could purchase and photograph strange front yard phenomena—quaint, sentimental, ornamental tableaux. Not necessarily folk art, more like people's stuff, really.

Roadside museums had always been favorites. Oswald's room or the Billy the Kid Museum in New Mexico housed things like petrified dinosaur droppings, real roadside curios. You would go in and see "something unusual" in a jar. Further in the back, for another quarter, you could see something more exotic than what you saw up front.

When I got that first NEA grant I was living in my loft in Oak Cliff. I was scheduled to start teaching at North Texas State in Denton at the end of the summer. I was in an interesting life transition stage (whatever that means). I was in the process of moving from Dallas to Denton. I was still married and my first daughter Christine had been born, yet there I was, out on the road alone, looking for deer butts. A strange situation, I know, but when you get these grants, you do what you can. I wasn't about to drag a wife and a six-month-old infant around Texas, particularly in the summertime. I did manage to drag 'em down to Dripping Springs for Willie Nelson's first picnic, though.

I owned a red Ford van, and it was loaded with cameras and film. I slept on the road and did whatever it took to collect my photos and Texas curios. Of course I knew people all over the state, so I'd go from one place to another, starting in Waco where I ran across eccentric front yard stuff. With my thirty-five hundred dollars, I bought things like concrete chickens and stuffed roadkill. I'll always say good things about the NEA because, for me, they've been a life saver. On a number of occasions, I might add. A lot of things that happened on this road trip paid off for me the very next year, including a film crew returning to retrace my steps for a PBS documentary, *Jackelope*.

On the first leg, in Waco, I ran into Byron Jernigan, one of my favorite people on this planet. He's a classic character, slow-talking and heavy-accented, and runs a taxidermy shop called Jernigan's Taxidermy. I was stopping at a lot of taxidermy shops because that's where I'd find odd mounted critters, but never in my life had I seen a stuffed deer ass. Mounted parts are all made the same way, from a fiberglass mold. Every deer head you see is a skin stretched over a large, medium, or small mold, which is why the heads are usually three standard sizes. Usually a taxidermist mounts heads and maybe hooves, but Byron was clever enough to come up with more unique molds.

I can't say enough about Byron Jernigan and his stuffed deer asses. At the time, he was selling hundreds of stuffed armadillos to the Japanese. He had an amazing inventory of strange horns, coyote, wolf, and bobcat skins, lamps made from three deer legs forming a triangular stand, and assorted skulls. Jernigan's was the beginning of my NEA trip. Once I started buying, I began to focus on what I needed for truly incredible exhibits. For the record, a stuffed armadillo is actually stuffed as opposed to stretched over a fiberglass form. When you buy them, especially in Mexico, you can see how they sew up an armadillo's belly almost as poorly as they stitched up Oswald. After putting the critter out of his misery, they slice its belly, remove all the innards, sew him back up, insert a spray can up his asshole and fill him with urethane foam. There's a quick little lesson for you in armadillo taxidermy.

When you begin really studying and buying Texana paraphernalia, you begin to notice an abundance of maps. An interesting thing about Texas cartography is that if you take a map of the United States and think of it like a puzzle in which Texas is a piece that can be lifted out or flipped, the southern tip of Texas—if flipped toward the north—would go all the way into Canada. If you flipped it toward the West Coast, it would touch the Pacific. If you flipped it toward the right, it would go into the Atlantic. Goes to show how big Texas really is.

Sometimes when you go into a good ol' boy truck stop and get a map of Texas on a red paper place mat that the waitress puts your chicken-fried steak on top of, you'll notice that the place mat might have all the highways, and next to each city a symbol of what each area is known for. Sweetwater would have a rattlesnake because every year they have the Rattlesnake Roundup, where hundreds of rattlesnakes are put into a pit and milked. Each area and little town in Texas strives to be known for something special.

Something suddenly clicked in my mind. I could see where my trip around Texas was going to end up—some kind of exhibition resulting from all this road research. I started buying things that would serve as community icons for a large state map. That big Texas map was the beginning of a series of installations, room-sized art layouts that would later swell to gigantic proportions once my career began really to take bizarre turns.

I firmed up a series of exhibitions at universities all around Texas. These were to be installations, meaning you would bring weird stuff into an exhibition space, lay it out, keep it there for a month, go back with your van, pick everything up, and set up the next exhibition. My first venue was to be in my old stompin' grounds of Waco.

I took all the stuff I had gathered up on my summer trip, got my buddy James King, and headed on off to Waco. We re-created a long skinny rambling installation in the foyer of the new library at Baylor University, a very conservative place certainly not known for being avant-garde. There was a seventy-five-foot trail of findings from my road trip, stuffed armadillos, concrete wagon wheels, coyote skins hanging from poles, bark chunks, and logs—all representing Texas. We laid it out in the foyer in such a way that students would have to pass it all in order to go into the library. The title of the piece was *Waco*. Then Earl Staley invited me to do something in Houston. Jack Boynton was there too. We gathered up more stuff, stopped in Waco, picked all of that material up, and drove down to Houston, at the University of St. Thomas. I made a forty-by-forty-foot piece called *Map of Texas*. The exhibition area was perfect for what I needed. Besides being able to walk straight into the installation, there was a balcony above where you could look over it. In order to fully appreciate the piece, you needed to be able to look down into the space like you were flying over Texas. My earthwork friend Robert Smithson's influence was kicking in.

Among the goodies I had accumulated for this *Map of Texas* was a big ol' electric Lone Star Beer sign, which I placed near San Antonio. There was also a Pearl Beer sign with a picture of Judge Roy Bean's saloon. The map was even made up of different kinds of regional Texas soil. Along the Gulf Coast, near Galveston and Corpus

Christi, was sand decorated with mounted fish, nets, and shells. East Texas had black dirt which changed to tan as you got toward Central Texas. In West Texas, where it was rocky and mountainous, I stacked weird rocks and stuffed javelina. In the elevated northern part, near the panhandle, the installation became eye level as the altitude increased. I stacked hay bales to make that work. Dump trucks delivered the sand, dirt, and rocks while a half dozen students helped me wheelbarrow it in. After the terrain was filled in, I placed the corresponding symbols inspired by the paper place mats including chickens, cow skulls, salt licks, fruit in the valley, and a serape, and tortillas near border towns like El Paso and Brownsville. Plastic bluebonnets decorated Interstate 35 from North Texas to Dallas, just like the ones Lady Bird Johnson originally planted. A black cowboy held a mythical jackelope, a rabbit with horns. I placed stuffed armadillos—including a flattened run-over armadillo—near Austin, the armadillo capital of the universe. The whole piece was truly reminiscent of the funk art I learned about in Berkeley some seven years earlier.

Dismantling the Texas map in Houston ("the art schlep") was quite a task, especially moving the cactus. Because it's so hard to transport cactus, I borrowed some exotic stuff from one of the big nurseries. I remember James King brushing his leg on one. He fell down and rolled around on the ground and went nuts. I found out later that the name of that cactus was the Horse Crippler.

One of my student volunteers, Andy Feehan, helped me get the dirt out before heading back to grad school at North Texas. Years later, I would sign his master's degree paperwork for tattooing a pig.

*Chapter Seven*

# Daddy-O and the Oak Cliff Four

**HE** Trinity River runs near downtown Dallas, and because there are levees on each side, there's this funny blank space right down the middle of the city. The Trinity is a non-river—a huge excavation serving as overspill and flood control, and it's usually reduced to a trickle. It's more like a water-stained concrete line of demarcation between the haves and the have-nots. The original plan was to make the Trinity a full-fledged river flowing all the way to Houston.

On one side of the river is a town, separate from Dallas, called Oak Cliff. A lot of artists began living there because it was inexpensive and you could rent old houses and buildings for cheap.

Geographically, Oak Cliff is situated higher than Dallas. There are beautiful cliffs and views and oak trees, hence its name. Dallas is very flat, but what distinguishes it is the skyline. There are probably as many articles about architecture in Dallas newspapers and magazines as there are art columns. In Dallas, art takes a backseat to architecture and certainly to sports.

When the Northwood art program moved into town, I had to decide where I was going to live. I'd been hanging around with two buddies who each had big houses with a lot of space to work, but they weren't giant, cool, open spaces like a New York loft. Most artists in Texas were pretty handy, but for some reason didn't have that thing down about going into an industrial building and turning it into a living space. Creating a bathroom. Creating a kitchen. Starting from scratch.

I found a building for rent on the corner of Jefferson and Beckley in Oak Cliff, about three blocks from the boardinghouse where Lee Harvey Oswald had lived. The theater where Oswald was nabbed while watching John Wayne's *War Is Hell* was a block and a half up Jefferson. Oak Cliff. Texas. The Kennedy shooting. The crazed connection went on.

Jefferson and Beckley was a great corner. The rent was seventy-five bucks. It was a whole floor with a couple of giant rooms, both perfectly sized for large canvases and sculpture, two smaller rooms, and another in the back that had a toilet but no shower. I had seen how New York artists settled into the early SoHo scene; they built their lofts, brought in bathtubs, and rigged up showers. I decided to do just that. Susie was now being dragged through the whole art scene. She had gone from living in a cute home in Waco and a regular income as a professor's wife to hoisting a used bathtub up the stairs in Oak Cliff.

I was one of the first artists in Dallas to work and live in a SoHo-style loft. There's a picture of me inside that loft in *Newsweek* magazine, posing with my three cohorts—James William Roche, George Thurman Green and Jack Alan Mims. We eventually became known as the Oak Cliff Four. Kent Biffle's story read in part:

> Oak Cliff used to be a Baptist bastion, but now it's multiracial, offering low rent and high-ceiling manses that make good studios. One of the favorite haunts here for collectors

and curators as well as artists is the huge loft owned by Robert Wade, an artist who saturates large canvases with photo emulsions, creating large half-real figure studies. Furnished with two old barber chairs, it is a home for crammed chili dinners and bravado conversation. Wade and his friends seem determined to make it, both nationally and internationally, from Dallas. "This may be a perverse attitude," admits one of them, Jack Mims, a painter. "We want to see if we can succeed out here on our own."

The Oak Cliff Four had all participated in Dave Hickey's "South Texas Sweet Funk" show in Austin in 1971 and had some similar sensibilities. Roche and Mims already lived just a few blocks away; sculptor Mac Whitney had his studio nearby; Green came later. We soon created a small art community—an artist neighborhood in Oak Cliff—and it was the first time a group of artists had congregated that closely in a Dallas neighborhood. We hung out at one another's places and discussed everything from aardvarks to zippers.

Oak Cliff was dry; you couldn't buy beer there. You had to drive fifteen minutes across the bridge into Dallas to buy a six-pack. You can buy beer there now but you still can't get hard liquor. Oak Cliff did have private clubs and if you brought a bottle of booze in a brown sack they would provide the setups.

Susie at the time was trying to go along with this new art regime as well as trying to complete her own degree. I was racing back and forth between Northwood Institute and my studio, carousing, drinking, and going off to shows from time to time.

I was the typical fool. Italo Scanga, an artist friend of mine, told me that the very first thing that happens to artists when they get a little bit successful is they get divorced. After a few gallery shows, they get too big for their britches. My time was coming.

I was featured in the Annual at the Whitney Museum in New York in 1973, just before my oldest daughter Christine was born. I took a chance, raced up to New York, then made it back in time for her birth. Mac Whitney suggested her name. I can still remember the look on my mother-in-law's face when she visited our loft. Beulah was horrified at the artist's lifestyle, preferring the good life in Los Angeles and playing golf with celebrities. Maybe she was right.

"Who is this guy?" she probably thought. "He's a college teacher who does funny paintings, does shows in galleries and museums. What is that?" In-laws and outlaws!

During the Oak Cliff Four era between 1969 and 1974, we had a valuable ally in Henry Hopkins, the director of the Fort Worth Art Museum. Hopkins had come from the West Coast, and was one of those directors who was a good friend and advisor to younger artists like us. He would help put together exhibitions.

The Oak Cliff Four weren't necessarily four artists doing group art. Our attitudes, temperaments, and eventual output differed as much as it overlapped. The one thing we had in common was that we all pushed the envelope from the outside. That united us in fighting a regional battle in a city that looked to the outside for direction.

We did have gallery support with Janie C. Lee showing Roche, and Mr. Murray Smither showing the rest of us. Later, Laura Carpenter represented some of us at her Delahunty Gallery.

Being part of the Oak Cliff movement was similar to being in high school. Being in the hot rod club wasn't much different than being an Oak Cliff guy. What both did was give me a sense of security in that I had friends who were like-minded and who, theoretically, would stick up for me. Like any fraternal organization or gang, we were supposed to help our brothers.

The art world can be a very jealous one. In a loose group like the Oak Cliff Four, each person had his own career to tend to. Let's face it, some art has more commercial potential than other works. We tried never to be commercial. We were supposed to create art that probably wouldn't sell. But we would take the money.

Jack Mims was from Dallas: a quiet, intellectual guy, tall—six foot, three inches—and good-looking. His father had a golf course near Oak Cliff. I could relate to Jack because he also taught right out of graduate school. Mims, along with George Green and Jim Roche, went to the University of Dallas, a private Catholic school that had a good graduate art department.

Jack did beautiful, soft, photo-realistic figures that were airbrushed and spray gunned—huge long paintings of eight-foot nudes. They were allegorical and filled with myth. Artists always go to other artists' studios to look around. We all loved going to Jack's house because he always had buck naked photos of good-looking models lying around. He made big paintings from eight-by-ten-inch photographs. We tried to act casual as we walked by, looking at the nude shots, but, like Jesus' experience in the desert, it was hard.

Even though we had never even met, Jim Roche's early works were similar to mine—sculptures that looked like titties. While Roche was really doing titties, I guess I was doing dicks. He created big colorful ceramic sculptures that looked like big pots. Coming out of the pots were maybe ten bizarre-looking breasts. Jim then moved more into mass media stuff. He would extract things from newspapers and magazines, stitch them up into clear vinyl pouches, and push-pin them, creating a thirty-foot wall of stuff. He found massive amounts of printed material, including redneck leaflets, and used them to create a strange social montage. While Jim was a conservative guy in a lot of funny ways, the message of the walls was "Look how fucked up our society is." You'd certainly get his message.

Roche was originally from Tallahassee, Florida. He was the most funky, real guy you could ever imagine. He dressed like a swamp rat car mechanic and had a long ponytail which he usually braided. He wore tight blue jeans and big work boots, had a knife clipped to his belt—he was a grease monkey who drove around on a motorcycle. Roche was a sharp schemer; he planned things well in advance. Jim had no interest in teaching after graduate school. He wanted to go right out into the art world and didn't mind living as broke as a stick horse.

Every one of the Oak Cliff Four was married when we first met. Mims and George Green were teaching at Dallas junior colleges. Mims and I related to each other because we both knew art history. Since we were used to delivering lectures and slide presentations, we could effortlessly rattle off the proper names and dates. George, teaching on the other side of Dallas, was the last of the four to move to Oak Cliff. He would eventually give up his teaching job to be an artist, and struggle around Oak Cliff.

George came from Lubbock. He was the goofiest one of the lot. He looked like one of Buddy Holly's Crickets—the buck-toothed guy with glasses—and had one of those unbearable whiny Lubbock accents, but George was a good artist. He once worked for Hallmark Cards in Kansas City painting immaculate illustrations, but he also did a piece called *Chastity Belt for Reptiles*. He worked a lot in linoleum making urinals for reptiles.

The Oak Cliff Four arranged a group show over at the Tyler Museum which was associated with Tyler Junior College, home of some high-kicking halftime drill team girls called the Apache Belles. The museum was on the campus and the director at the time, Robert Kjorlien, was an unusually cool guy as far as the museum world went.

Kjorlien wanted to put up a major group exhibition showcasing all four guys and put together an unusual catalogue to go with it. Henry Hopkins wrote an introduction and Kjorlien wrote the foreword. Each artist had his own placard with black-and-white photos of his work.

Mims was photographed standing in front of one of his immense photo-realistic murals, almost lost in the massive twenty-foot nude figures parading across the canvas. Roche had his seemingly endless cryptic push-pin wall of plastic-wrapped sociopolitical curiosities, such as anti-drug posters and right-wing leaflets. Green's portion showed a photo of a sprawling linoleum sculpture whose odd three-dimensional objects cast strange silhouettes against another linoleum backdrop, with bizarre life-support-looking hoses plugged into each shadowy figure on the wall. My placard depicted my original ten foot Waco Boys' rattlesnake hunt photo-canvas; the infamous black-and-white *Criminal Wall* featuring huge morgue shots of Bonnie & Clyde, Pancho Villa, and John Wesley Harding, all shot full of holes; plus *Colorblind In Waco*, which was a fourteen-foot-by-fourteen-foot camouflaged hunter named Johnny Stewart holding a scope rifle, standing in front of a pickup truck encrusted with branches and foliage. All my stuff had this horrifying, Texas gun-toting feeling.

The catalogue also consisted of four 45 rpm records on which we had recorded spoken words, music, and sound effects relating to our work. I used military machine gun recordings and Waco deer hunting sounds. Each record was signed and numbered in an edition of five hundred. The catalogue came in a slim box about the same size as the 45s. The cover was our Texas driver's licenses reproduced as non-photogenic, four-color mug shots. The catalogue was acclaimed and the Oak Cliff group and Kjorlien got a big write-up in one of the national museum trade journals.

We wondered whether Kjorlien would catch any kind of flak over the giant painting that Jack Mims had worked on forever and ever to get done in time for the Tyler show. It was an allegorical history of Texas, with European-style nude figures easily twice the size of a normal human. Sure enough, the campus people caused a big flap once the show was installed and before the opening. When the college big shots toured the exhibition, Kjorlien was asked to remove Mims's piece. Because it was especially done for the exhibition, nothing could replace it. No question about it, it was there to stay. In fact, all the work was done and designed for that specific room. We said, "No way," and the painting stood.

We had finally scored this big museum show as a group. We had done gallery shows together, and even though the Tyler exhibition wasn't some famous museum, it was a totally legitimate showing in a beautiful, high-ceilinged space. We got great critical reviews in the Dallas and Fort Worth papers, courtesy of Janet Kutner and Jan Butterfield.

We were known as the Oak Cliff Four, and some people wondered who the hell we thought we were: the Beatles? Still, we wanted to do it up big-time, once and for all, before our partnership started to dissolve.

We placed an ad in this new art magazine called *Avalanche*, run by a guy named Willoughby Sharp. It was filled with beautiful art gallery and museum ads and would help make us known throughout the international art scene.

To take it to the max we also decided to rent a limo to take us from Dallas to Tyler, which was an hour and a half's drive into East Texas. It is an extremely conservative area. Northwood student James King talked the limo owner into letting him be the driver, and he dressed up in a chauffeur's outfit. All the museum officials were excited, but we were still four eccentric artist guys coming into their town, and hence, still a problem. They had already asked that we remove Mims's offensive painting.

When we were all dressed up and ready to go, we lined up in front of the long limo to take a photograph for our ad in *Avalanche* magazine. Someone needed to take the picture, so Italo Scanga, who happened to be in town, took the picture and then rode with us. It turned out to be one of the best group shots of the Oak Cliff guys I've ever seen and it looked great in *Avalanche*.

There was no room in the limo for Jack's and Jim's wives (Susie was home pregnant), so they followed behind the limo in a little foreign car. I lucked out. Pulling up to the Tyler Museum with the women behind the limo made for an awkward moment for the people waiting for us.

Between Mims' nudes and my grotesque hunting canvases, there was a lot of tension at the show. All these well-dressed ladies in fur coats from the conservative East Texas social scene who came to check out these crazy Dallas egomaniac artists simply gasped. We looked like some weird rock group, but the show was a great success with reviews in *Arts* and *Art News* magazines.

The Oak Cliff boys had a hip friend at the Fort Worth Art Museum named Pam. She moved to Taos, but we stayed in touch with her and word reached us that she was working for a gallery owned by actor/artist Dennis Hopper. Pam told Dennis about the Oak Cliff Four, and soon after, Dennis invited us up to Taos for a four-person show. We had met him before in Fort Worth when he had a photo exhibition of his own work. He was familiar with the Oak Cliff Four, and had bought one of Mims's pieces.

Like everything in Taos, the gallery, simply called Dennis Hopper Works of Art, was small and quaint, but we were bent on making it work. The deal was on; we set a date and got our works organized. Jim Roche was scheduled to do a major floor installation that tied in with a motorcycle trip he had taken from Texas to Canada and back. He had audiotapes of Indian chants that served as a protest of the slaughter of caribou in the wilderness. It would fit right in with the Taos sensitivity. Mims and Green had something wild up their sleeves, and I had a few oddball, twisted photographic canvases—one an antique photo of the Taos pueblo, which had something about apartments printed across the bottom.

We loaded up into two different vans. George Green manned one and Mims drove the other. We made it all the way to Santa Fe by dark, and almost got to Taos before Green's van broke down and skidded into a ditch. We finally pulled it out, but the engine needed a part so we left Green behind in the cold with a bunch of U-Haul blankets. It was winter and there was snow on the ground.

We rode into Taos at about eleven o'clock that night. It had been a twelve-hour drive from Dallas to Santa Fe, then another hour and a half up to Taos. When we called from the road, Pam told us to drive straight to the gallery. The lights were still on. Dennis Hopper

"Buckaroo" Bob, age six, with hobby horse made by Dad, Galveston, Texas, 1949.

Pattie Wade, Roy Rogers, Chaffin Wade, and Robert, age seven. Behind the chutes at a rodeo, Beaumont, Texas, 1950.

Gene Autry examines Robert's six-shooter, Galveston, 1949.

El Paso High, 1961.
Robert's artwork and
award ribbons.

Custom '51 Ford,
Road Runners
car-club shirt, and
drag-strip trophy,
El Paso, Texas,
1961.

The Road Runners at Curly's Club, Juarez, Mexico, 1961.
Bob is third from the right.

Susie, Bob's first wife,
Berkeley, 1966.

Back at Curly's Club,
Juarez, 1974. Bob is third
from the right again.

The Oak Cliff Four. *Left to right*: Jack Mims; James King, acting as chauffeur;
Jim Roche; George Green; and Robert Wade. Oak Cliff, Texas, 1973.
(Photo: Italo Scanga)

Daddy-O sits on his *Map of the U.S.A.*, Farmers Branch, Texas, 1976. Notice the tornado brewing in the background. (Photo: Burt Finger)

*Left to right:* The Texas Kid, John "Flex" Fleming, and Daddy-O in the Texas Kid's front yard. Dallas, 1983. (Photo: Andy Reisberg)

Cronies in Dallas, 1993. *Left to right:* Mike Shropshire, Daddy-O, and Monk White. (Photo: Lisa Wade)

Daddy-O as outlaw Texas wheeler-dealer, 1976. (Photo: Burt Finger)

Bob at Northwood Institute with "weenie painting," 1969. Shown at Whitney Museum of American Art Annual, 1969.

*Ridin' It Out,* pontoon performance, Waco, Texas, 1968. (Photo: Waco Tommy)

Daddy-O and "the Kinkster"— Kinky Friedman *(left)*, San Antonio, 1993.

Daddy-O and Stanley Marsh 3 *(right)*, on *The Boots,* Washington, D.C., 1979.

Dennis Hopper *(left)* and Daddy-O at the Menil Collection grand opening, Houston, 1987. (Photo: Ed Daniels)

Bob presents Texas governor Ann Richards with a denim "cowgirl" jacket at governor's office in Austin, 1992. (Photo: Elizabeth Grivas)

Playwright/actor Sam Shepard inspects the Iguana.
Keswick, Virginia, 1991. (Photo: David E. Wynne)

Daddy-O with Rosalea Murphy, proprietor of the Pink
Adobe Restaurant in Santa Fe, and Glenn Frey of the
Eagles, 1992. (Photo: Lisa Wade)

Larry Hagman, Rosalea Murphy, Maj Hagman, and
Daddy-O at "the Pink" in Santa Fe, 1994.
(Photo: Lisa Wade)

Bob, Rachel, and Lisa Wade,
Santa Fe, 1993.
(Photo: James Hart)

Daddy-O-Daddy with daughters
Christine (*left*) and Rachel at his
Elaine Horwitch Gallery opening,
Santa Fe, 1993.
(Photo: Lisa Wade)

sat behind the gallery director's desk with his feet up. He had long straggly hair, wore old boots and a funky Pendleton coat.

That night in Taos, Hopper was feelin' good.

"Yeee-haa! C'mon in boys! Good to see ya. Let's hang this god-damn show up." He had been waiting.

He was scufflin' around the gallery with a bottle of tequila. The combination of our brand of work and Dennis's condition looked like the makings of a good rodeo to me.

With Roche's installation, we really couldn't just "hang" this show. Plus, what the fuck, we had just driven in. With some careful per-suasion, we finagled our way out of having to hang the show then and there.

Hopper disappeared into the night and we crashed at Pam's house. I can still recall the smell of the woodstove stuffed with won-derful pieces of piñon wood. It would be almost ten years before I would smell it again.

Taos in the early '70s was a great hippie hideaway filled with totally unconventional literati and artists, including Fort Worth's Leon Walters and "Owl Head" Thomas. It had a nationwide repu-tation. Dennis was in and out of the area over the years, and was very active on the arts scene. He had a huge, rambling, three-story house with lots of bedrooms, located on the Mabel Dodge Luhan compound. Before she died, Luhan encouraged famous painters, actors, and writers (like D. H. Lawrence) she knew from New York to come out and spend time in New Mexico. She ended up marrying a famous Indian from Taos. Hopper lived at this literary retreat. The following day we moved over to his house.

Hopper had a huge collection of art by Bruce Connor, a San Francisco artist who created macabre assemblage pieces. They were made with parts of broken baby dolls and odd bloody pieces of broken glass with cobwebs. Evidently Hopper walked into one of Connor's shows and bought the whole exhibit. Spread throughout this famous old house, in every bedroom and every nook and cranny, were Bruce Connor pieces. You'd wake up in the morning and these bizarre art objects would be staring at you. I suddenly felt like I was back in Berkeley.

Dennis himself has been part of the art scene since the fifties, and had done the first covers for *Art Forum* magazine when it was

launched by his friend Charlie Cowles. That L.A. scene included
Walter Hopps, Ed Kienholz, Larry Bell, and more.

It soon was time to hang the damned show. Roche's contribution
was elaborate and involved, while Green, Mims, and I merely had
to hang our stuff on the wall. Dennis was pretty excited about the
show, which got him and us partying again, so it seemed like a perfect time to show him and Pam this strange limited edition I had
surreptitiously brought with me to Taos. It was a shallow wooden
box about fourteen inches square, and inside were some small canvas
photo pieces.

I had initially picked up these photos from a man in Clearwater,
Florida, who had been selling me strange five-by-seven circus photos—the fat lady, the tall man, midgets, guys with no arms. When I
had showed up in person at this guy's house in Florida, I found him
in his front yard with these large galvanized washtubs filled with
water that he stirred with a big stick. Floating inside were dozens
of five-by-sevens, and as he was rinsing off his latest batch of circus
photos, we were chatting. Finally he told me that he had photographs that might interest me, ones that he had no use for. Since
they were so gross, he felt they were almost illegal to send through
the mail. I bought the entire photo collection plus the negatives.
They ranged from World War II atrocities to sexual aberrations and
deformities.

I put ten of the most grotesque of these shots on small photographic canvases and put them in a box. Flipping through these
canvases one at a time, you'd see guys with pierced penises, a lineup
of Africans with elephantiasis of the balls—they were almost as big
as basketballs—and other shockers. Late at night I used to show
them to mixed company just to hear people's remarks.

"Dennis," I asked sportingly, "are you ready for the Dirty Box?"

Of course he said yes.

Each canvas was more shocking than the one before. As I showed
them to Pam and Dennis, I explained that the Dirty Box was filled
with prototype canvases that I planned to sell as a limited edition.
If someone wanted one, I'd go back and make them a set. As I
flipped through the miniature canvases and showed them to Dennis,
he waved his arms.

"Oh, no! You don't understand," exclaimed Hopper. "These can't be hidden away in a box! They've got to go up on that wall right over there."

He pointed to a small leftover wall space about four feet wide. We left a clean space as you first came into the gallery to give the exhibit a little valuable breathing room.

"Dennis," I pleaded, "you can't put these on a wall! They're gross enough just hiding in the Dirty Box."

"No, Daddy-O," he insisted, "these have to go on that wall right there!"

Dennis took another swill of tequila and demanded, "Now!"

"Put 'em on the goddamn wall."

I looked around nervously. Somebody said, in a hushed tone, "Put 'em on the fuckin' wall."

They're gonna have our heads, I thought.

After hanging them, we left the gallery to eat. The opening was slated for that very evening. Jim Roche's spread featured the tapes of the chanting Indians. Then there were Green's weird works, Mims's large realist canvases, and my photo pieces on another wall. The Dirty Box was right on the front wall. The Oak Cliff boys do Taos.

People streamed in for the opening preview. About halfway through the show it became obvious that some who approached the Dirty Box canvases were not happy. It was beginning to turn ugly. It looked like I had defiantly shoved these pieces into people's faces.

We were scheduled to leave town the next afternoon, so we went back by the gallery at ten o'clock that morning for one last look and a few quick photos of the exhibit. Sure enough, the Dirty Box canvases were literally and figuratively off the wall. People had called, created a minor stir, causing the canvases to be scuttled into their little home, back into the Dirty Box where they live to this day.

Another time some of the group drove down to New Orleans for our show at Gallery Simone Stern. Walter Hopps, a highly respected curator, was in town for the museum biennial. We were sitting in a bar when Hopps walked in and had a drink with us. Realizing we were just starting out, he offered, "Let me give you guys just one piece of advice."

We were curious. "What's that?"

"Whatever you do, don't hold back."

We all looked at each other as Hopps finished his drink and left. I'm not sure if anybody else thought about it much at the time, but I did. We were all young guys, pretty sharp, cool, and hip, and that was probably the best piece of advice anybody could have given us.

We didn't hold back. Each of us was going as fast and as furious as he could.

By fall 1973 I left Northwood for North Texas State in Denton. Denton was another place where old hip dogs hung out. It was funky and had one of the best music departments in the country. Doc Severinsen came from there and supported the jazz bands.

Between the musicians, the art faculty, and the older students, there was a scene going on. I had a good reputation as an up-and-coming Texas artist and I was anxious to work with grad students. It was a fast and furious four years. The students were great, and worked with me on a number of projects like the *Map of the U.S.A.*

I taught for a total of ten and a half years, from 1966 in Waco until I resigned much later in 1977 from North Texas State to pursue full-time projects and occasional residencies. I was married for the same period of time. I quit teaching and got a divorce in almost the same month. Italo had been right. All four Oak Cliff boys had gotten divorced.

The importance of the Oak Cliff Four was that we bucked the '70s/New York aesthetics that were being shoved down everybody's throats in Texas. New York supposedly dictated the way things ought to be done everywhere. But we didn't belong in the New York/ European continuum. We were educated guys who knew enough about what was happening in Europe, New York, and L.A. to know there was such a thing as an alternative. We had all been represented in shows everywhere. I had been to Europe a number of times. I had won NEA grants. We weren't rednecks with M.F.A.'s; we just felt there was an aesthetic that needed to be explored that had its roots in Texas, or (as in Jim Roche's case) a more Southern feel. The Oak Cliff Four got with it, hit it, and did it. Times changed and we scattered into different directions. As for my career and my life, it was time to call in the dogs and piss on the fire. I was hitting the road.

# Chapter Eight

# Enchilada Entropy: Daddy-O on the Road

**T'S** hard to believe, but I still had some NEA money stashed aside from my *Map of Texas* project. I was invited by the University of Texas in El Paso to do a new installation, and was introduced to a student who went on to become one of my best friends. Rick Hernandez is now number two in command at the Texas Commission on the Arts. I had an idea for a new piece called *El Paso*, which I planned as a forty-foot floor piece incorporating two aspects of Southwestern life indigenous to locales like El Paso, Phoenix, and Albuquerque.

In lieu of normal things like grass and trees, folks in the Southwest decorate their front yards with rocks, crushed gravel, and, because water is scarce, cactus. The other aspect of the piece had to do with food. I planned to portray a yard in the spirit of a really great-looking combination plate of Mexican food: a burrito, enchilada, flauta, a plop of beans, rice, and chili peppers, all nicely designed on an oval plate/space. I combined those two traditions with things I found in the El Paso area, including velvet paintings and paper flowers from Juarez. All I had to do to prepare was cruise around with Rick and load up my car. Rick spoke fluent Spanish and I knew pretty good border Spanish, so it was like shooting fish in a barrel. In Juarez we became big shots, big buyers.

"How much for thirty velvet paintings?" I'd ask. "How much for one hundred multicolored place mats? Two hundred round coasters? Tortilla chips, chili peppers, corn husks, broken glass, rocks, bricks, cacti . . . the list went on, the car got fuller.

*El Paso* was a very pretty piece. I hung religious items that lit up on the end walls. Sections inside the oval included a Pachuco gang symbol made of crushed taco shells, surrounded by green chili peppers. I lit the piece very dramatically; the whole thing glowed.

Another section consisted of velvet paintings of bull fighters, nudes, sunsets, and a scarred Pancho Villa bad guy. Another was a skull that was smoking a cigarette through a cigarette holder, surrounded by vials of drugs, hypodermic syringes, and a marijuana cigarette—all of the evils that I remember seeing when I was a kid.

I've since done photographic night scenes of Juarez with cars driving past the bright, flashing neon lights. These pieces were exhibited in the El Paso Museum as part of a show called *Shot in El Paso*, an exhibition of photographs taken by people who have either lived there or who were passing through. David Byrne and other well-known artists contributed photos of strange and odd sights in and around Juarez and El Paso.

When Jim Harithas arrived in Houston in 1974 to direct the Twelve Contemporary Art Museum, the first show he put together was *Texas*, an exhibition of twelve artists who he felt deserved recognition, including James Surls, John Alexander, Mel Casas, Dorothy Hood, Rafael Martini, and me. Harithas wanted to meet with each artist to get a feel for his or her work.

At the time I was in El Paso putting the finishing touches on my installation. Luckily, Harithas was driving through Texas at the same time, meeting artists and lining up exhibits. I had just flown into El Paso to finish up, and Harithas and his curator, Mark Lombardi, drove in from Houston. After showing them *El Paso,* I'm pretty sure we went to Juarez and had a good time. That night, I realized they could keep up with Daddy-O. I agreed to drive with Harithas and Lombardi from El Paso, through New Mexico to visit Luis Jimenez, and on to Amarillo.

After we visited Luis, it was my turn to drive because everyone else was half shot. I think I really impressed Harithas during a tire blowout by swigging tequila out of a jug. As our car careened from one side of the road to the other, it was up to me to land it safely on the shoulder. The car swerved to a stop amid clouds of dust and a soundtrack of pinging rocks and gravel. I brought the car to a halt and changed the tire, all without putting down the bottle. Back on the highway, we cut across to Amarillo to see the infamous Stanley Marsh 3 (pronounced "the third") who had just financed the Ant Farm's *Cadillac Ranch.* We were all about to meet our eccentric match.

I had never met Stanley Marsh 3, but like everyone else in the art community, I'd heard of him. When we reached the high-rise in Amarillo where his huge, open office was, we were led into a conference space, where one of the employees announced, "Stanley Marsh 3 will be with you shortly."

Since we had been out on the road for days we were a bit jittery. In walked big, tall, funky Stanley. He had funny hair, big glasses, and a droopy mustache. He was a large guy and one of the most eccentric Texans in the world. His family was oil and gas, plus he owned a radio station. He gave us each a limp handshake and asked, "And who are you?"

"I'm Bob Wade."

"Nice to meet you," he said, and moved to the next person. "And who are you?"

All three of us went through this funny routine. Next thing we knew we were in the car with Stanley for a tour of his *Cadillac Ranch,* which had just been completed by the Ant Farm guys. It was truly spectacular. The famous piece is a row of Cadillacs half buried on Stanley's property, which runs parallel to the highway. Occasionally they changed the colors of the cars. For one Valentine's Day, Stanley painted the cars red as a present to his wife. One year they were covered in graffiti. Originally they were different colors, progressing from the early '50s Cadillac to the late-sixties model featuring the big fins. He rented a billboard on the property next door and put up a sign that read, "Coming Soon—Snake Farm!" That kept the area clear for a while.

Some of Stanley's own art was also spectacular. One piece was a giant soft pool table located in the middle of a field of green grass. From a cliff, you could look down and see a green field forming a huge natural pool table with eight-foot pool balls and a rack. Stanley was also fond of highway signs and actually fabricated his own sick humor versions.

When I attended the Ranch's ten-year anniversary in 1984, I wanted to see whether it was true that Stanley had mounted and stuffed my friend Andy Feehan's pet pig. Andy had been my student who received his master's degree by tattooing a set of Harley Davidson wings on his pet pig, Minnesota Fats.

When the pig became impossible for Andy to keep in Denton, I arranged for Stanley to inherit him as a house pet. Andy claimed that the pig died because Stanley fed him M&M's and champagne. If indeed Minnesota Fats died living the high life, I figured it wasn't so bad to have been immortally stuffed. What bothered Andy was the rumor that Stanley had stuffed the pig in the platter position and that he was being used as a footstool. Well, Minnesota Fats hadn't been reincarnated into a footstool, but he had been mounted and stuffed. Before the Andy-Stanley connection turned sour, Stanley underwrote the tattooing of bat wings on the sides of a Chinese golden crested "hairless" dog. After they split, the collaborators shared "Hot Dog" like divorced parents. I always like Stanley's flamboyant, tongue in cheek attitude toward art and the art establishment. Just another Texas millionaire who has fun doing what he wants.

Lombardi, Harithas, and I finally made our way back to Denton, where Daddy-O was poured out of the car and back into his humble professor's world. It took me days to get over that trip, but soon enough I was back out on the road, faster than a sneeze through a screen door.

I'm going across the state to pick up some things for a couple of shows to take to New York City. What do you think they'd like to see up there?
　　　　—Bob Wade to Waco taxidermist Byron Jernigan, *Jackelope*, 1975

I don't know. What don't they have up there?
　　　　—Jernigan's reply as to what stuffed objects the fine people of
　　　　New York might enjoy

In 1975, a number of artists were approached by Ken Harrison, an independent filmmaker, who was setting out to capture different kinds of Texas art sensibilities on film, for the Dallas PBS affiliate. Whereas a lot of documentary directors shot only videotape, Ken worked in film because he could work in half and quarter frames: smaller frames of action edited into one final piece. Ken was a heck of a film guy, not only as a director but as one of the frontline cameramen.

Ken's idea was to produce a documentary that covered half a dozen Texas artists. The same names kept popping up—me, James Surls, and George Green, with cameo appearances by John Alexander, Letitia Eldredge, and others. Ken contacted each artist individually. There we were, careers just starting, trying to get somewhere, and along came PBS to document how we worked. Ain't that being in the right place at the right time.

When Ken came to me to discuss how he was going to incorporate my work with the other artists', I explained that I had a project coming up in New York at 112 Greene Street, a highly respected alternative exhibition space located in the heart of SoHo. It was mostly for artists or group shows that couldn't be shown in conventional galleries. My project was to be part of a group show called *Group Indiscriminate.*

I had been up to New York, seen the space, and this is what I had planned to do: Across the far end of this long gallery, which was meant to be rough, scruffy, and relatively unpainted, were five windows, bricked in from the outside. My idea was to use the windows as niches. I wanted to bring in my weird road stuff, including stuffed snakes, a picture of *The Waco Boys*, and *The Last Legal Hanging in Texas*, and put 'em in these niches.

Harrison wondered how I'd assemble all this stuff for the documentary. As I did when I put together the *Map of Texas*, I planned to go to Jernigan's Taxidermy in Waco and buy some more of the same weird stuff. While I was there I'd go see my buddies who love to blow up cars. Harrison's eyes got bigger when I told him my plans. He immediately saw my art as film action, which for him meant getting in the car, buying the stuff, and following me from Texas to New York. My other role was to narrate my travels and visit other artists like Mel Casas and interview them. As a result I became a cowboy on the road, and was followed by two station wagons: one filled with equipment, the other carrying two camera and sound men, including Phil Lamb, Mark Birnbaum, and Felix Alcala, who's now a respected television director.

In order to perpetuate the Texas myth, I borrowed my parents' gold Cadillac with its leather top. Just like the old B Westerns, I took along a sidekick, James King, the beloved victim of the horse crippler cactus and chauffeur of the Oak Cliff limo. With our film crew intact, we headed on down the road again.

**The line between satire, irony and humor in the Texas mind is very fine. A guy . . . like Byron Jernigan with that really straight face . . . you don't know whether the guy is really serious, really kind of obsessed about those fucked up armadillos laying in that freezer, or is the guy really laughing on the inside about it? Selling deer heads and armadillos to the Japanese, now that's the funniest fucking thing I've ever heard, and I *know* that he knows it's funny.**

**—Bob Wade, *Jackelope*, 1975**

The trip's highlights included visiting Aubrey, Parnell, Mike, and a couple of other guys I called the Waco Boys. They are the guys I liked so much while I was teaching at McLennan Community College. They had a shooting range outside of town where they liked to piddle around with dynamite and blow things up. On film, as one of the guys is shooting a beer can with a gun, one guy warns him, "Be careful, don't kill a neighbor." It was actually easier to find dynamite than firecrackers around there. The Waco Boys had a pretty wild gun collection including semiautomatics, shotguns, silencers, and machine guns, all of which made me think of Bonnie & Clyde. As for me, I nearly fell down when I pulled the trigger on the machine gun. For the film, my friends prerigged a shot-up car with nitroglycerin coils. When they detonated it, the whole thing went up in smoke.

My segment for Harrison's documentary ended up being a travelogue featuring traditional and unnaturally bizarre cultural oddities like Manny Gamage, the famous hat maker who made all the cowboy hats for LBJ, Jerry Jeff Walker, and John Connolly. Then there was the guy with the fried rattlesnake meat that he claimed cured cancer. Even though the Texas landscape was beautiful, I was taking pictures of weird trailer trash and dude ranch signs. I was extremely proud of the job Harrison had done documenting my Texas road trip.

Driving from Dallas, Texas, to 112 Greene Street in New York meant finding someone who had a car that could make it clear to New York. Since we didn't know how long we'd be there, I resorted to my foolproof system that worked if you were broke. The "Drive Someone Else's Car" transport company (not to be confused with carjacking) had proven handy before, so I didn't have a problem qualifying. I was expected to pay for gas while the company figured out a decent timetable, which in our case was three or four days from Dallas to New York. We were to deliver a car to a destination thirty minutes north of New York, and the main rule was that no one else was to drive the car other than me, the bonded, authorized driver. Also, you couldn't tow any kind of trailer or boat.

Of course I had already lined up Flex, Felicitas, and Gene Binder to help me drive what turned out to be a not-so-big car hitched to a twelve-foot U-Haul full of Texas stuff. While snoozing through Nashville, I felt this jerking around. There we were in the middle of this curvy freeway, negotiating S-curves in a downpour. The driver didn't know about braking, she was just hauling ass. I slowed the whole operation down and we kept going until we made it to New York. When we got there, two of the people went their own way, leaving me and Flexible John Fleming to find our way to 112 Greene Street. I decided not to return the car for a couple of days since I had no money for cabs, and we needed to take care of a few loose ends such as filling in the five gallery window niches with cheap plywood so I could nail the skulls and push-pin the photos. I also needed two-by-fours and black plastic to build a museum back space.

After we bought the wood, black plastic, and nails for the exhibition at a lumber yard on Canal Street, we rigged and roped it all to the roof of the car. The problem was, once everything was tied on good and tight through the car doors we had to crawl through the windows to get into the car. There we were in SoHo with someone else's vehicle, all roped up, roof laden with cheap plywood.

Around the first corner the wood started shifting, so I ran a stop sign in front of a cop who eventually stopped us. The cop walked up and asked,

"Would you please get out of the car?"

"Actually, officer, we can't."

Slowly climbing through the window without alarming the policeman, I produced enough paperwork and mustered enough pity so that the cop miraculously let us go without writing us up.

After unloading the wood at 112 Greene, I finally decided to return the car. I got lost driving through Harlem on the way to the expressway. I know I looked peculiar—a Texan driving around Harlem asking how to get to Something-dale in Westchester county. Not much help there.

I finally found the folks and their house, which was in a decent neighborhood somewhere in the suburbs. They were a very nice, well-to-do Asian family with a trim lawn. Before delivering the car, we stopped off at a car wash. The family was happy to see their car, and happier when they saw us leaving.

On the way back to 112 Greene we started wondering where we were going to stay. We knew we had a full day's work of building ahead of us, not to mention installing close to a hundred pieces of Texana for the exhibit, so we asked Jeffrey Lew at the gallery if it was okay to sleep in the back corner with all our goodies. Because of a complicated situation regarding the existence of only one key, they agreed to our staying with one hitch: We were forced to spend the night locked inside the gallery with only our deer heads and two-headed calf (with two legs and two assholes) to keep us company.

In *Jackelope*, just as the detonated car in Waco lands in a cloud of dust and mess, Harrison cuts to the competing smoke and noise of 112 Greene Street. As part of our exhibit, we installed all the stuff we got from Byron Jernigan, plus the photos of the Waco Boys blowing up cars, pictures of Lee Harvey Oswald and Pancho Villa, cowboy hats, beer signs, the Lone Star Brewery's hideous two-headed/two-assholed calf, a homemade cattle prod, and a bulldick cane (made by stretching the foreskin of a bull's dick over a wooden cane). Written on the gallery wall (in my handwriting) was a recipe for homemade armadillo stew with gravy. All this was incorporated into my 112-Greene-Street-Daddy-O-Believe-It-or-Not-backroom-sideshow-roadside-museum-pay-an-extra-quarter-see-something-extra-weird installation. Mona DaVinci wrote a long piece in the *Soho Weekly News* about it, titled "The Texas Ball and Chain Cult." The head of Germany's *Documenta* exhibition saw the show and wanted me to send stuff to Germany. Somebody stole the bull dick cane.

A stuffed horse suddenly came into my life, courtesy of the late Helmut Naumer. Helmut served as the director of the Fort Worth Science History Museum, which was located right next door to the Fort Worth Art Museum. The horse was a fine taxidermic specimen with a steel framework inside. The outside was horsehide, perfectly stretched over a fiberglass mold. Coming out of the back feet were threaded rods sturdy enough to allow the horse to be bolted down to a platform. The horse instantly became art when it was moved from the science museum to the art museum for my *Cowtown* installation in 1975.

I needed the services of the stuffed horse again for a group show at Cal State, Los Angeles, called *TEX/LAX*. I got my friends "Jorge" and "Flexible" to drive with me to L.A. The horse rode upside down with its feet up in the air, in the back of Jorge's El Camino. We were also towing a U-Haul trailer filled with the work of Boyd "El Chingadero" Elder and the other artists.

In order to drive the long stretch, we stopped in El Paso where we partied with Rick Hernandez and I acquired some Mexican No-Dōz and tequila. Instead of buying good tequila, I bought low-rent mescal. Inside the bottle, of course, was a real worm.

As we were driving, we hit a rainstorm in Arizona that made the horse look all sweaty. When we stopped to get gas, a couple of grizzled old filling station guys slowly came out and saw this stuffed horse in the back of Jorge's El Camino. They tried to act casual, but they wouldn't look directly at the horse while we were filling up the tank. Finally, they said "What happened to it?"

We told them an elaborate story of how we were following a horse trailer being pulled down the road in the rain, when the door swung open and this horse just fell out onto the highway. We said we barely missed him and he tumbled around. We went back to get him, but the trailer never even stopped. They didn't even know he'd fallen out, we said, so we were still trying to catch up with the trailer.

Three men in the front seat of an El Camino truck is kinda tight for some guys. We were truckin' down the highway and all of a sudden we all started to itch. Everybody was scratching himself. Maybe the tequila wasn't processed right, or maybe it was distilled during the wrong season, but we came to find out that when you buy low-end cheap tequila you risk getting a severe rash. With a stuffed horse in the back and pulling a U-Haul trailer, we scratched all the way to L.A.

We made it and set up the exhibit. I'd never tried this before, but since the stuffed horse had the long threaded steel rods coming out of its feet, the plan was to drill holes through one of the portable panels, stick the rods through the holes with big washers and bolts out the other side, and hope the horse cantilevered on the wall. It would hang there by its back legs seemingly defying gravity, but actually reinforced with the fiberglass and steel work inside. It worked.

On the road, Jorge had nicknamed the stuffed horse "Funeral Wagon" because we figured that whoever rode that tough old horse was going to end up on a funeral wagon. For the exhibit, we made up a story to go along with it. Thirty different guys who rode Funeral Wagon out of the rodeo chute around Texas had died, we said. We would explain that the horse finally came out of the chute so strong that the rider fell off and Funeral Wagon landed backwards, breaking its back and dying on the spot. In the spirit of preservation, Funeral Wagon was mounted and stuffed like any famous bronco should be. On the gallery wall next to Funeral Wagon, I wrote out this story in pencil. To round out the exhibition, I brought along the two-headed calf, the big photo canvas of the Waco Boys with their guns, a cattle prod (courtesy of Laura Carpenter), a velvet landscape painting, some hay bales and two salt licks—one new and one licked. A crowd of Asian students stared at the horse, studiously reading the story on the wall, the tall Texas tale of Funeral Wagon fueled by itchy tequila and El Paso bennies.

While life on the art road had been fun and as busy as a funeral home fan in July, little did I know that I was fixin' to jump out of the skillet and right into the fire.

# Chapter Nine

# Bob Wade's Jumbo U.S. Map

**M**y *Bicentennial Map of the United States* got a lot of press and editorial space, including a double-page spread in *People*: "Eat your heart out, Rand McNally. Bob Wade is building a map bigger than a football field.... In this bicentennial year, or any other, there's no escaping death or Texas."

The national media began gearing up for the bicentennial in 1974. The government urged every county or municipality, big or small, to do something to honor our nation's two hundredth birthday. I had been teaching at North Texas State for about a year, and at the same time had kept my ties with the Northwood Institute. I was excited about the bicentennial and felt that there should be some way for me to participate. I looked into the possibility of a museum show or an outdoor project. If I could nail down a grant or something, I thought, I could do some kind of gigantic outdoor spectacle that could involve the public. Since it was coming from Texas, I figured it had to be bigger than anybody else's stuff.

There was a group called the Northwood Contemporary Arts Council of Dallas and Fort Worth that included movers and shakers in the Texas scene—museum people, collectors, critics, and the like. Someone in the group suggested I apply for a matching grant through Northwood to work on a large project, perhaps a gigantic, topographical map of the United States in honor of the bicentennial.

Up until then, the biggest art objects I had done were forty feet. I was thinking in terms of three hundred feet, a dimension people could picture in their minds when it came to recruiting funds. It would be a map the size of a football field, a walk-through experience that would represent all the states, incorporating a few state symbols like potatoes for Idaho, an oil well for Texas, and corn for Iowa. This complete Americana spread could be illuminated at night and could feature scaled-down highways, mountain ranges, and rivers that would be visible from the air.

I got the grant. As the project director I was to receive a seed money check for $7,500 with the stipulation that I raise a matching amount in contributions or materials. It was an NEA Works of Art in Public Places Program. This map, as I explained, was about every aspect of America; the various cultures, products, landmarks, and more. A bigger Texas map times fifty.

The whole process became much more complicated than any of my other projects in terms of administration. It went way beyond hustling cowboy hats and urethane-foamed armadillos. I needed to take a major lesson from the real world—the high stakes, wheeler-dealing circles of Dallas real estate and big bidness.

First, I drove around Dallas looking for prospective sites, searching for a large open space on which to erect my most ambitious roadside attraction. It had to be a public place that had easy access and high visibility, and I felt it should be alongside a freeway. I staked out a beautiful piece of land alongside Stemmons Freeway, right across the street from a high-rise office complex. The land was owned by the Stemmons family so I contacted John Stemmons, Jr., and explained my idea.

"I'll tell you what," he said. "I'll take you up to see my father and see if he'll let you use the property."

I went up to the executive offices, and I was nervous as hell. This was the big time: It was a long way from asking for salt licks and cowboy boots. I explained the grant and my need for a viable site the size of a football field. Mr. Stemmons looked out of the window at his property and asked me a few questions.

"What are you going to do about parking? Will you be able to pave one-third of that property so you won't have mud problems when it rains? What about security? How about rest room facilities? Is this going to be a bonded situation? Will there be money set aside for the removal of the project so that piece of property can be returned to its immaculate, original condition?"

I realized I didn't have any clue about what I was about to get into. Hanging my head, I thanked him for his time.

Stemmons was dead right. I needed answers, so I formed an advisory board with—who else?—my friend Monk White, who helped me plan it out properly. Bill and Sheila Jenkins designed a professional prospectus, press releases, and letters of support aimed at a number of people from whom we might get matching funds, products, and services. Money out of my $7,500 was budgeted to hire a development person to organize the financial and press campaign. Volunteer fund-raisers, photographers (Shaw and Finger), and advertising agencies donated their services.

The committee looked at the corporate funding opportunities as well as the possibilities of corporate advertising on-site. "Additional financial support is to come from corporate advertising," read the brochure. "Advertising is part of the American landscape and Wade's *Map of the United States* will include scaled-down billboards and road signs sold to firms and corporations across the country. The money from advertisers will supplement the National Endowment for the Arts grant and add a bit of authentic capitalism."

Since I was already criticized by some for being commercial, I asked myself, What is one of the most prevalent sights across the USA? Billboards! It was an ingenious way to represent one aspect of American culture. I liked the idea of including billboards as a form of art.

I still had appointments with property owners to set up, including one with one of the most famous in the world, Trammel Crow and his company, Heritage Square. Crow had countless square feet of apartment buildings, shopping centers, convention centers, warehouses, and more. Besides, Crow was a genuine patron of the arts, a private man who had purchased and donated a lot of sculpture to various parts of Dallas. Here I was, a thirty-two-year-old artist meeting with one of the seniormost successful real estate heavyweights in the world.

Trammel Crow's headquarters was wall-to-wall desks. There were maps on the walls and a roar of business activity. I met with him personally and this time I had more answers than I had at my meeting with Stemmons.

Crow told me he had a number of different properties that might interest me, lots he could loan for one year during the bicentennial. I walked down the corridor with him into an office conference room. He slid down a hideaway floor-to-ceiling, photo-aerial map of the Dallas area, and seemed responsive to my idea. He grabbed a pointer and pointed out about six locations along a freeway.

"Think about these locations," said Crow, "and call me when you make a decision."

I picked out a site on the north edge of Dallas and along Interstate 635—the LBJ Freeway—one of the major loops. The corner, in a little suburb called Farmers Branch, was where the toll road ended and the regular streets started out again. It had a traffic count of 100,000 cars daily. It was a nice part of town, which meant advertisers would be more likely to spend money. Free and accessible parking was only a few steps away.

The official title of the project was to be *Bicentennial Map of the United States*. I was optimistic and scheduled completion of the map for February of 1976, with a grand opening set for late May. It was a nationally certified bicentennial project, endorsed and supported by community leaders. The mayor of Farmers Branch gave us a citation. An article by art critic Janet Kutner appeared in the *Dallas Morning News*. DBG&H, a Dallas advertising agency, donated press releases, printing matter, and publicity efforts. It was to be a free admission art experience from 9:00 A.M. to 10:00 P.M. and we anticipated that we'd draw a million visitors. The attraction was to be listed in tourist publications across the county, state, and nation as a point of interest.

The first thing I did was put up a big sign on the land explaining the site to the general public. I made arrangements for electricity, telephone, and portable amenities, and started recruiting North Texas State students to help me:

Willard Watson, alias the Texas Kid, was a great character who worked on the map with me and became a lifelong friend. My friend Clare—or as the Texas Kid used to call her, Miss Clara—spotted the Kid in downtown Dallas. He was known for cruising around town, tipping his hat, and being extra friendly. He was an unbelievable Southern gentleman.

"How are you, ma'am. Good to see you, ma'am."

The Kid was born in Shreveport, but was considered a Texan as far back as 1927, when he was seven years old. His cousin gave him the nickname "Texas Kid" because he always looked real young. Anytime he'd go anywhere, people would call him the "kid from Texas." When he used his CB radio in his truck, he went by the handle "Texas Kid."

Clare struck up a relationship with this unique gentleman, and the next thing we knew, here he came in an incredible Cadillac that was jazzed up like Nudie of Hollywood, with horns on the hood and a fancy interior with tooled leather. He arrived at the map and introduced himself to everybody. He did many things for a living, including upholstering and auto repair, and was an all-around guy who could rig anything. He was part Indian, mostly black, and the minute he showed up at the map with his magnificent attitude, I knew he was a wonderful addition to our team.

The Texas Kid became my runnin' buddy for a long time. From time to time I'd use his house as my mailing address or as a place to get phone messages if I was laying low, avoiding people, bein' a gypsy, or out doing art projects. The Texas Kid's wife, Miss Elnora, screened my calls in her gruff voice. She eventually passed away, the sweet thing, my mom away from home.

"Art is something you see in your imagination," the Kid used to say.

Kid also had a truck that was elaborately "Texanized," complete with steer horns, extra chrome, lights, and photos of his friends and family glued all over the sides. It was sort of a soul brother taco wagon.

We used to drive around looking for stuff. According to the Kid, if you pick up the right stick or found object, you could make at least $75 or $100. In fact, he used to brag, "I don't care how much my wife paid for a T-bone steak. I was gonna make thirty-five dollars offa that bone."

One day I was down at the Texas Kid's, hanging out. I was down in the dumps, fairly broke, and said, "Kid! I've been working this artist gig for a long time now, I've taught for years, and I've done all these projects. I've sold some work and done big sculptures every-where. But you know? I feel so bad that I don't really have a whole lot to show for it."

Kid leaned in and smiled. "Oh, Mr. Bob. You is a rich man."

"A rich man? How is that, Kid?"

"Well, you know, it's those cars you rides in and the houses you stays at and the parties you goes to that makes you a rich man in my book."

God bless the Texas Kid, truly a rich man in my book as well.

Kid and I developed a reciprocal relationship. He'd lend me his pickup truck and be the wise old man. I'd help him with his folk art career, photographing his projects and taking him to gallery open-ings. Soon he became famous.

Kid loaned a number of things to the map, including the very Cadillac he first drove up in. He parked it in "Detroit," not far from the pay phone we set up in "Chicago." Nobody burglarized or van-dalized it, which was amazing. Since the Texas Kid was a genuine untrained folk artist, he built other things for us, including a light-house made from found objects like oil barrels. We planted that on the East Coast, in Maine.

Folk artists like the Texas Kid have a natural knack for finding things and putting them out in their front yard. It starts with the urge to improve and decorate beyond having a clean, nicely-mowed lawn. Yard art is the desire to please the public, and some people go so far that their house becomes a roadside attraction. Art like that is slightly eccentric and as wonderful as can be. In fact, we had to testify on behalf of the Texas Kid because the city tried to stop him from decorating his yard. They called it junk and an eyesore.

While we were constructing the map, the Kid had great ideas about building roads, or creating pieces kids would like. He hung around the project, greeted people, shook hands, acting the perfect host. As peo-ple would approach, he'd politely tip his hat. "Howdy ma'am. I'm the Texas Kid. Very nice to see you." He'd answer questions or refer in-quiries to me, Mr. Bob the Artist, the head man, or Mr. Monk.

We constructed a tower from which you could look down on the map. One of the local scaffolding companies agreed to come out and put one up. We outlined the USA in lime powder and hustled up some crushed gravel for the outer edges; ultimately every state was edged in white gravel. We outlined the perimeter with white plastic flags, the kind that flap in the breeze at used car lots. The map fit proportionately to the lay of the land, with a side street on the far side by California and a service road on the other end by New York and Florida. Texas ended up being seventy feet long, whereas Rhode Island was the size of a sheet of plywood.

The tower view was fine, but the real view was from the air. A helicopter company donated six different excursions over the map, that were used by a journalist, me, or a member of the construction staff. Shelly Katz, a photographer from *People* magazine, went up and snapped some fine aerial shots.

Armed with our brochure, aerial photographs, and letters of support, volunteers set out to comb the Metroplex for plumbing, many more square yards of gravel, plants—the list was endless. Most of all, we needed more dough. We put together a rate card. A display featuring your company's logo would cost $3,500. A four-foot-by-eight-foot rectangular billboard with coverage on both sides cost $1,500. For $750, a patron could sponsor a special display such as a water fountain, landscape props, or resting benches for the anticipated throng of visitors. Modest contributions were earmarked for other beautification purposes, and everything was tax deductible, of course.

Companies like Steak and Ale, Century 21, and Bonanza responded. Bob's Big Boy restaurant chain, with its boyish mascot in the checkered overalls, said okay, they were good for an eight-foot Bob. We set the fiberglass Big Boy in cement so he wouldn't disappear into the night—of course, some college kids swiped it and stashed it in Highland Park for a while. A health club donated a couple of plaster gold Venus de Milos.

Kids would come out and run amok. We dug six feet into the ground to create the Great Lakes—concreted like a swimming pool complete with water. The dirt from the Great Lakes and the Mississippi River was hauled over to create the Rockies. The city of Farmers Branch agreed to hydro-mulch the entire map by spritzing it with a mixture of grass seed and fertilizer. An electric company agreed to put in underground wiring, and some guy showed up and offered to install underground PVC pipe for a sprinkler system that watered the plant life. It all seemed to be coming together, except for a shortage of one thing: time.

Looking back, I should have had a three-year lead time to put the map together and a paid staff of twenty. I was still teaching at North Texas State, and I entered into this project influenced by the giant projects of Christo—he of *Running Fence* fame—and the noted Robert Smithson, who did the great spiral jetty out in Utah. Another eccentric folk hero of mine, Clarence Schmidt, rambled around Woodstock and ended up with acres and acres of all this assembled stuff from junk tires, toys, and tar. A lot of New York artists plucked ideas from Clarence while summering at Woodstock.

Artists like Christo finance their endeavors with the sale of drawings, collages, and preliminary paste-ups of each project. I was in no position to do that then. I was shooting for freebies and billboard advertising. Each week was hand to mouth, and I took on the persona of artist turned Texas-style land developer wheeler-dealer.

We mailed a letter to every state chamber of commerce asking them to send anything we could associate with each state. Louisiana and a bunch of others sent flags, which waved in the breeze. One business agreed to build us an outhouse and asked us where to put it. Since we had nothing from Arkansas, we put the outhouse there. Soon after, we received an irate letter from the Arkansas chamber of commerce. I told them to send us a check for $1,500 and we'd move the outhouse to Oklahoma. There was a great spot where the highway hit the Texas gulf coast. A famous racing duo lent us an actual funny car racer. We installed tunnels and bridges in key spots. We had two giant boats, one brand new and the other a junker, which we installed by digging a hole approximately the same size as the hull. We shoved the dirt up very neatly right along the edge and filled in the gravel.

Some days were up, some days were down. At one point we sent out a desperate newsletter: "*The Bicentennial Map of the United States* is a public work of art owned by the residents of Dallas-Farmers Branch Metroplex. It's your map! Ideas and materials are welcome. Without donations all work stops. Water and electricity stop. All services and donations are tax deductible."

Some of the media began expressing their doubts about the map's completion as early as February. They printed rumors that we were broke and that contributions were coming in too slowly. As the newspapers were saying this, someone donated enough one-by-fours to build a fence around the entire map. Neighborhood groups began showing up: Ten couples and their kids would come out on a Saturday and put in fifty posts that held these one-by-four boards and created the fence. Afterward someone donated some white paint, and a boy scout troop and a school group came out and painted the fence from top to bottom on both sides. We were given more bushes, shrubs, and trees. All of the mountains had white-lime snowcaps.

When visiting the map, visitors started at the main gate by the San Francisco Bay area, walked along a four foot wide paved highway (complete with the dotted lines down the center and no pass on curves) and proceeded north, which took them across Oregon and up to Washington state. They could meander eastward to Illinois, across New York state and back down the East Coast, cut across the top of Florida, go down through Louisiana and into East Texas, down to the Gulf, then straight up diagonally through West Texas into northern New Mexico, Arizona, Nevada, and back out of California near Los Angeles. As on most maps we put Alaska and the Hawaiian Islands inside a rectangle below Arizona. The highways were dotted with miniature road signs; for every three steps you crossed one hundred miles.

More and more school kids began to arrive on buses to get the educational experience of walking along miniature highways that gave them a sense of where the various states and mountain ranges were. For braver visitors, there was the large scaffolded vertical tower with elaborate steps that went to a platform forty feet high. It was the second platform we built, because the first one was taken out by a tornado that whirled its way through the map. The new tower was rebuilt taller, stronger, and higher. From the ground, the map seemed more like a miniature golf course.

Every afternoon at four o'clock, "the bar opened," as Monk would say. I had two mobile homes out there that were teeming with sex and rock 'n' roll. They said I had every big-titted girl in Dallas out painting, digging, or something. Despite the distractions, in the back of my eye I saw it all, and sure enough, the map took shape.

Over the period of a year and a half, a number of great characters came into play. One was [Bud]*, an itinerant handyman. He worked pretty good when he wasn't guzzling beer after beer forever.

One morning I arrived at the Map early with a couple of my assistants and the first thing we saw was a squad car with its lights

*Pseudonyms, bracketed the first time they appear, are designed to protect the innocent and the guilty.

flashing. A police officer was talking to an elderly lady with a couple of grandkids in tow.

Every day it was something new.

"What's the trouble, Officer?"

A body had been discovered on the top of the observation tower, but it turned out to be alive. One of the kids had climbed to the top of the stairs and there was Bud. The night before, he was grooving on the aerial view and then decided he was too drunk to climb down, and since it was a hot evening close to the Fourth of July, he went to sleep au naturale. When the kids got to the top, they found Bud out cold, not moving, seemingly not breathing, and buck naked.

We held a big fundraising party for Bob Wade's Jumbo U.S. Map in June. There was free beer and live music on flatbed trucks. We raised a little money but had more fun than anything. Bills were rolling in and here I was, Mr. College Professor Homeowner teaching a full load of classes with a wife and a little daughter, and broke. If we were short on money for gasoline for a dump truck or hardware materials, I'd use my own credit card. My cards were all maxed out and my wife, rightfully, freaked out. My teaching job in Denton was forty-five minutes away and I was racing back and forth every day.

I'll admit it. The map project pretty much did me in. But how the hell was I supposed to back out? I started it. I was the artist, the guy. I couldn't let people like Monk and the volunteers down. I was the entrepreneur behind the *Map of the United States.* I was the guy who put this great big earthwork project together. But I didn't have money for the daily upkeep. There were no funds even to hire someone to pull weeds. I had the land until December, 1976, but it became impossible to maintain what I had started. Every time I'd get one of these bizarre bills for the map, I'd stick it in an old suitcase my father gave me. The case was jammed and there was nothing I could do.

We had our big-bang July Fourth celebration just like we promised. Thousands of people showed up, the press came out, and people were eating barbecue and singing and drinking and yelling. *Art in America* magazine gave it a half-page reproduction and lots of newspapers across the country ran stories and photos. Journalist Roberta Smith referred to me as more of an entrepreneur than an artist.

Despite the celebration, I was heading toward a nervous breakdown, and the college people in Denton thought I was nuts. Like a true road warrior, I bolted to New York City to cool out a couple of days after the party. *People* magazine printed their article on the map on July 26, 1976, and as I walked down Fifth Avenue, I picked up the issue at a newsstand.

There was a double page spread with an insert photo of me.

> The creator of this cartographic curiosity is a 33-year-old avant-garde artist named Bob Wade, who wrangled $7,500 from the National Endowment for the Arts. Wade admits this map is like a circus, but he claims it's a miracle. . . . Wade figures he has spent more than $100,000 in donated materials and labor so far, but insists the project is meant to glorify America, not himself.
>
> "The map is like a movie set," Wade said. "There's no one ego that dominates."

While I was in New York, I would occasionally check back in on the map. Now there were citations from the city of Farmers Branch, the same city that was so proud to have us there in the first place, stuck to the trailer office door. The weeds were getting taller, the phone bills were piling up, and nobody was out there watering. Yet people were still visiting the site and climbing the tower.

Toward the end of '76, there were a lot of technical problems with the map, including the aftereffects of tornadoes, and other natural disasters like rainstorms and hail. It had become the perfect microcosm of America.

Dismantling the map meant giving it all away. A Kentucky log cabin from the map was donated to an orphanage that reassembled it on their grounds. The huge tires and large concrete cylinders used for highway construction were given to schools and playgrounds around the Metroplex. The tower and the trailer offices were returned. The leftover building materials went to people in need. The fake Venus de Milos went to the Texas Kid's controversial front yard. People picked up their boats and the Texas Kid got his Cadillac back. Eventually, at our request, the city of Farmers Branch bulldozed us down and plowed us under. Within six months, a Hilton Hotel was nearly completed on top of the map site, leaving Daddy-O as dazed and confused as a goat on Astroturf.

# Chapter Ten

# Par Lay Voo Texana? The Texas Mobile
# Home Museum

T this point after the map, I felt I'd been ridden hard and put up wet. I was at a personal crossroads. There was no getting around it. I had to make a decision between being a full-time teacher or a full-time artist. One year after I started the map, both my teaching career and my marriage were about to appear in my rearview mirror.

So I made a difficult Daddy-O stand.

I resigned from my teaching assignment and got divorced. One, two. I went back to living in the center of Dallas in a high-rise across the street from the Stoneleigh Hotel, and started work on yet another impossible, implausible project, The Texas Mobile Home Museum. Three, four. With a new life in front of me, I was also scheduled to go to Paris to teach the Europeans a thing or two about Texana bravado.

The Texas Mobile Home Museum was a project put together specifically for a September 1977 exhibition at the Musee d'Art Moderne: the tenth Paris *Biennale des Jeunes Artistes*, which means "biennial of younger artists." Over one hundred international artists were represented. You had to be under thirty-five to participate. An international panel from each country decided the nominees and all of a sudden you got something in the mail saying you'd been nominated to submit materials for possible inclusion in the Paris Biennale. At thirty-four, I got in just under the line. I was one of only ten American artists invited. It was a great honor.

I was asked to submit an advance packet in order to be officially chosen, so I put together a proposal inside a wooden box (not the Dirty Box) housed in a hand-tooled leather cover that slipped over it. Inside the box with the proposal were country-western cassettes, chrome-plated barbed wire strips, plastic bluebonnets, baby cowboy boots, color Xeroxes of my past work, and other Texana weirdness. Most people sent slides and resume bullshit, I sent something different. The exhibit people loved it. Later my dealer Laura Carpenter hand-carried the box with a more extensive selection of color Xeroxes to the Basel, Switzerland, Art Fair.

Now, what was I going to do for the show? Not a clue. I was coming up drier than a desert full of rocks.

The funny thing was, they never even asked me. I had a budget that wasn't huge, but it wasn't bad. I stated that I wanted something that would roll down the road, looking cool on wheels. In the past I'd taken a U-Haul trailer and filled it with a lot of Texana stuff. I'd show up at the museum, unload it, and maybe arrange things in the shape of a star and create an installation, but I'd always wanted to create a show that could be towed from place to place, like a traveling gypsy museum or something. I'd always liked trailers, and not just Airstreams. I'd been taking pictures for years of classic trailers and funny-looking white-trash things parked by the side of the road, and I decided that a funky aluminum job would be the perfect way to box up a whole bunch of Texas, shoot it off to Paris, and travel on to Spain and maybe *Documenta* in Germany. I set out on a trailer

search around Dallas, hitting the used trailer lots and parks. I found
the perfect 1947 Spartan Trailer Coach in one of those lots on the
edge of Dallas heading toward Fort Worth.

Spartans predated Airstreams, and were manufactured in Tulsa.
J. Paul Getty had a World War II airplane factory, and hundreds
of women worked there riveting huge sheets of aircraft aluminum,
a special alloy. When the war ended there was no need for any
more bombers. Everybody at the airplane factory was bummed,
but at least we won the war. The aircraft factory was then turned
into the Spartan Trailer Factory. Same aluminum. Same rivets.
Same little old ladies. As a result of the aircraft-style design—high
tech for its time—the Spartan Trailer Coach looked much like an
airplane. The front end had an aerodynamic curve, and the back
end had a curve like an old fastback Chevy. What struck me the
most was its resemblance to the tour buses used by people like
Bob Wills & His Texas Playboys. They were the coolest buses in
the world with their funny, rounded backs. That's why I associated
the trailer design with Texana. The curved look didn't seem Arkansas, California, or New York. It was Texas: rounded like a
horse's ass or the handle of a six-shooter.

I knew the old Spartan I saw would be perfect, so I pulled right
in and bought it. Well, actually Monk bought it because (a) he had
money, and (b) he's at least as crazy as me.

Although the Spartan was in rough shape, I knew it would shine
up since it was aluminum. In fact, I experimented on one side of it
before we bought it—a little spit and polish—and saw that it was
going to shine up like a mirror and chrome. I went over to the Love
Field airport, around the back where all the repair joints sell all kinds
of aircraft supplies, and bought some aluminum polishing compound. Not just aluminum, mind you, but aircraft aluminum.

First I towed the Spartan over to the Texas Kid's driveway. He
helped me gut the trailer's original insides. By gutting it, I had an
open clean space where I could create my museum. This was my
chance, once and for all, to export Texana weirdness to a big European event.

I'd been stockpiling lots of weird stuff over the years, including a
lot of sideshow freak photos. (Some had been in the Dirty Box.) I've
always been interested in sideshow freaks, and especially a character
named Knotty Knots. The state fair in Dallas always had the best

sideshow freaks. Monkey ladies, Flipper Man, the Little Lobster Boy, and a particularly queer character named Knotty Knots. We'd see him every year. Knotty had golf-ball-sized tumors all over his body. One year when he wasn't there, the head guy said only that modern science was curing freaks and ruining the sideshow business.

Another famous sideshow freak was Lentini. He had a third leg that came out next to his genitals. Next to that third leg was a second complete set of genitalia. Not only did the guy have three legs, he had two dicks and four balls!

During my Oak Cliff period, Jim Roche and I had been talking, when Jim's wife at the time happened to walk by and overhear our conversation about Lentini.

"Lentini?" she asked incredulously. "Why, that's my uncle!"

She confirmed Lentini's physical plight. It seems that when he went outside to go shopping, he'd tuck his extra leg into his pants and wear a big coat so he looked like he was severely overweight.

It dawned on me that since I had my own collection of freak photos, a Texana sideshow in Europe could be fabulous. Maybe Paris was ready for a freaky traveling Texas roadside museum. It was time for another Daddy-O art adventure. It all started with the gathering process.

Years before, I had visited the Lone Star Brewery museum, which had acquired the holdings of a famous downtown San Antonio joint called the Buckhorn Saloon. The Buckhorn's former owner was also into collecting odd mounted heads that ranged from things like dik-diks, which are miniature antelopes, to Siamese twin calves, stuffed and set upright so it looked as if they were dancing. There were hundreds of heads of strange animals that people had shot and stuffed, aberrations of nature such as steers whose horns had taken a cruel U-turn and grown into the poor animal's eyeballs. There were also several two-headed calves, the kind you'd see in funny roadside sideshows. When the Lone Star Brewery moved to new headquarters out on the edge of San Antonio, they used this stuff to embellish their tasting room and named it the Buckhorn Hall of Horns. Visiting it is still one of my favorite things in life.

I managed to meet the curator, not only a wonderful old guy, but also a member of the Topperwien Wild West sharpshooter family. I got to talking to him about my show in Paris and hinted that I needed a two-headed calf. While he wasn't able to loan me any from the museum display, he did have one in the back room he was willing to part with. It was so disgusting that when it was on display, the museum got a number of complaints from old ladies and pregnant women who demanded they remove this two-headed freak of nature. It also had an extra leg growing straight up out of its back.

One look told it all. This was not fake. Plus it had two tails and two assholes.

My traveling twenty-five-foot trailer museum was gaining steam. Now I had a two-headed calf, Funeral Wagon the bucking bronco, stuffed armadillos, and plenty of plastic bluebonnets. Anytime you see an amateur art show in Texas, you see lots of paintings of Texas bluebonnets. It's a corny symbol of Texas that I've used a whole bunch of times.

Next I added a few rattlesnakes that I got from Byron Jernigan, who takes a rattlesnake, guts the sonofabitch, takes urethane foam, and fills the snake right up, giving you a nice, long, hard rattlesnake.

Meanwhile, in addition to gutting the trailer, the Texas Kid had been designing a custom saddle. His payoff was that he got to keep all the stuff that came out of the trailer, including the toilet and the sink. He scored big. Once the trailer was gutted, we set out to create a convincing, high-class art gallery. So it would be like most art galleries, we installed a glossy natural wood floor of knotty pine. Going back to my hot rod aesthetics, I decided we would upholster the interior with white Naugahyde.

In order to get donations together and get this thing over to Paris, I set the trailer up as a nonprofit museum. My Texas Mobile Home Museum was listed as a nonprofit entity, with the board of directors being Monk, Judy Buie, and others. Buffalo George Toomer also advised us.

Shannon Wynne hit the streets looking for upholsterers and found two guys who were the coolest upholsterers known to mankind. They glued thin sheets of foam rubber to the walls and used a spray adhesive to glue on the Naugahyde. To make it curve properly over the rounded, aerodynamic walls, they used hairdryer-like devices.

With the upholstery and fancy wood floor down, we then installed a series of skylights down the middle of the roof. Using the aircraft aluminum polish, we shined the fuck out the trailer with a rented flexible device that was a buffer of sorts. On the end of it was a big spinning disc. While polishing I developed vertigo and had to go to the doctor. If you're up on a ladder for a week, watching this spinning disc, it affects you psychologically to the point where you can't stand up straight. I walked diagonally, my body at a sideways slant, that whole week.

At the time, I was living in an apartment building in Dallas where a lot of designers, writers, and ad agency and television people lived. It was a very hip joint called the Maple Terrace and right across the street was a bar called the Stoneleigh P where my crowd hung out. Tom "Mr. Tom" Garrison had been the patient proprietor there for many years watching endless days and nights of bad behavior. Columnist Nancy Smith usually covered the hijinx if a celeb was involved. Maple Terrace was located on sprawling, elaborate grounds with swimming pools. It also had a very cool parking lot in the very back area and it occurred to me that if we pulled the trailer way back in the far corner of the parking lot, it wouldn't be all that noticeable. I thought maybe I could work on the trailer if I parked it next to a halogen light pole. I talked the maintenance guy into hooking up the electricity so I could work my buffers, saws, and power tools. He finagled the wiring so that I was able to plug things in. For a long time the apartment manager had no idea that we were creating the Texas Mobile Home Museum right in the parking lot of one of the most posh apartment buildings in Dallas.

The back yard scene would occasionally spill over to the Stoneleigh P, which one night was hosting a Czechoslovakian Polka Party. Everyone was in full costume. By the time we got there, we were so fucked up we just thought they were another part of the Daddy-O entourage. Mike Shropshire danced with them and knocked them over. He didn't realize until the next day what had taken place and I remember him saying, "Damn, it takes a hell of lot to fuck up a Czech Polka Party and not even know it."

The parking lot became a real scene. People stopped by all day long. The Woodalls. Monk. The Texas Kid. Shrop, Clare, Toomer, and Shannon, not to mention the workers—carpenters, electricians, upholsterers, and movers. Henry Geldzhaler, the curator from New York, stopped by and left a note: "Nice work!"

I'd stopped teaching at North Texas State so I didn't have a fucking dime. I was broker than the ten commandments. I had a few friends and students who would come to the rescue. That type of assistance has always figured big in my projects. Former students have always hung around, continuing as a part of my life. One was very good with fiberglass and woodworking, so I told him I needed a big pair of longhorns for the inside of the trailer. After all, we were out to blow the French out of the water, so he laminated slabs of wood into the shape of a fourteen-foot pair of horns. Afterward he fiberglassed the horns, which gave them a beautiful, slick finish, and another buddy showed up with an airbrush and did a beautiful horn paint job. He also airbrushed "Texas" on the sides to look like cowhide. Funeral Wagon barely fit through the trailer door. Once we got it through the door, upside down again, we parked it near the inside front. That's where it stayed. It looked great. Inside the trailer we also had snakes, barbed wire, a tape deck—all sorts of crazy things. The final touches included 150 hand-tooled leather belts and chrome-plated barbed wire fender skirts. It looked bizarre and fabulous—and finished.

We started making arrangements to put the trailer on a boat sailing out of Houston. Before towing it to Houston, though, we were determined to throw a big going-away party. By then we'd been notified by the Maple Terrace management that our white-trash horror show in their parking lot had to go. And they asked me to go with it.

We put out a mailer inviting the entire seven stories of apartments to our bash. "You are invited to the going-away party for the Texas Mobile Home Museum. Please do not park in the parking lot tomorrow." We cranked it out that night. We had a band, food, a chimpanzee, and plenty of fools. It was a huge blowout.

A few weeks before we left, we were contacted by a blue jeans manufacturing company whose hook was that their pants had a design down the leg of the pants that was stitched by the same machines that boot companies used. They were looking for publicity, so they made a giant cover that looked like a denim coat and was form-fitted for the trailer. We even got silly about it. Since the trailer curved like an armadillo, we designed a long tail. On the back of the cover, there was a giant pocket so that, if you needed to, you could curl up the tail and stick it in the giant back pocket. We finished up last minute details at our new temporary location "Delahunty Gallery" courtesy Ms. Carpenter.

Finally, we hooked up a pickup truck to the trailer and towed the whole thing to Houston, its sleek blue jeans cover and fifteen-foot-tail dragging at about sixty miles per hour, which was slow enough to keep the cops at bay.

When we got to Houston we experienced a complicated semi-fuck-up: We weren't sure where the boat was. Once we found the right place, we put the trailer on a boat that would get it as far as New Jersey, and then it was on to France where it would land in Le Havre, a city along the English Channel, just northwest of Paris.

Meanwhile, I had been asked by *Art Press* magazine in Paris to write a short piece about my Biennale entry. I ended up saying something about Stanley Marcus bringing French culture to Texas via the "Marie Antoinette" beehive, and that I was reciprocating by exporting a calf with two assholes.

When the Daddy-O crew (including Monk) and the trailer arrived at the Biennale in Paris, everyone else's stuff was already hanging in the museum. There we were with all the other Americans, put up in an artists' residence, waiting for the trailer's arrival. While we were attending a very strange press conference introducing all the artists to the European press, the trailer finally arrived in Paris. It was less than twelve hours before the grand opening of the exhibition.

There were two museums housed in two separate buildings, connected by an open air space. The officials had decided the trailer would look best in the open air space where everybody had to walk by. Trouble was, they had to rig dozens of railroad ties just to push it up the wide stairs. Once they got it upstairs, our Texas Mobile Home Museum stood there—beautiful, immaculate, and ready to go. The Eiffel Tower stood in the background. We had rigged cassette players and funny lighting inside so that once we plugged the whole works in, all the neon popped on, and boom, out kicked Willie, Waylon, and the boys.

There were really only a couple of actual outdoor sculpture pieces that were part of the tenth Paris Biennale. The trailer was shiny and beautiful and had that exotic Texas-in-Paris look. The big skulls up front, the shiny silver metal finish, the inlaid wood, and the stainless steel star made it look like it dropped in from nowhere.

People didn't know what to make of the trailer. It was an imported time warp; it came from the turn of the century when rodeos and Buffalo Bill's Wild West show would travel to Europe. When the exhibit actually opened up, we had things going full tilt. You could hear the music outside, and you could see the shine of the old Spartan trailer coach with the longhorns. The tape deck inside was playing Waylon Jennings's "Luckenbach Texas." It immediately drew a crowd; from that moment on, a throng of French art fans always surrounded the trailer. There was a feeling of action on the site. People filed in and out like a sideshow; it was a museum within a museum.

The fabricated longhorns were an exaggerated fourteen feet across. One Frenchman wanted to know where the horns came from. He must have believed that they originally came from some critter. I shrugged my shoulders and said, "I'm not sure, but I think Mexico."

In terms of gasp reaction, the trailer and its art had what art critic Jan Butterfield would refer to as "the willing suspension of disbelief." Viewers wondered just what it was. It was constructed so invitingly that when people approached it and walked around to the side where the door was open, the music and the polished wood floor would pull them right into the display. The very first thing viewers would see at their right-hand side was Funeral Wagon, my famous stuffed horse, upside down, shoved against the front end. Their reaction was similar to the reactions I had when I traveled through the South in the '70s, visiting all those freakshow roadside attractions like Bonnie & Clyde's car or Oswald's bedroom.

During the exhibition, I had to attend an artists' meeting so Monk agreed to lock up the trailer. Our daily routine consisted of taking in the three longhorn skulls which hung on little hooks on the outside. We were afraid of thieves, so we'd put them inside the trailer each night. There was also an old funny saddle that the Texas Kid had jazzed up with a special paint job, and a Mexican blanket that had to go inside.

On that particular evening, Monk came over to lock things up for the night and we made arrangements to meet for dinner later. When we finally met up, Monk shook his head, saying that he screwed up. He accidentally locked the door before putting the skulls and saddle inside. Everybody was gone and he didn't know what to do, so he found an old plastic garbage bag, put the skulls inside, and brought them with him. Monk—in his blue jeans, ostrich-skin boots, and a western-style shirt—got on the Paris subway with his sack full of longhorn skulls and a saddle thrown over his shoulder. Looking back I picture Monk, with his long hair flying, roaming the streets of Paris looking like Joe Buck in *Midnight Cowboy*.

Two artists were singled out by the Biennale committee to receive a special acknowledgment and a cash award that was the equivalent of $1,000. After all that work and barely getting there on time, I received one. When the committee presented it, they told me that in the tradition of the Paris Biennale, the artist who receives the cash has to treat the committee to a typical Parisian lunch.

I wasn't sure how many people were supposed to be part of this lunch. I thought maybe a half-dozen people at the most, counting assistants and cohorts. I ended up taking thirty people to lunch. Wine flowed for hours. When the bill came, it translated to almost exactly $1,000.

Texana exportation mission accomplished, the trailer was a big success, and far too soon it was time to return to the States. Our free room had expired; the deal was up, the money was gone. My big plan was to go back to the States, take care of business, regroup, get more money, go back to Europe, and tow the trailer from country to country. We had museums lined up in Spain, Germany, and Italy, whatever it took to make the rounds.

When I got home, it was back to the impoverished life of an artist. I broke up with my girlfriend. My life was now a total mess. What else was new? My beautiful gold 1971 Cadillac, which had a collection of photos of buck-naked coeds and various companions stashed in the trunk, was gone. A friend of mine was supposed to move it from one place to another to avoid it being towed. I'm sure I owed a fortune on past-due tickets. But he forgot about it, so eventually it was towed away. By the time I returned from France, enough weeks had passed that the impound amount and the tickets were far more money than the damned thing was worth. When I finally got the money together, my car had been auctioned off. Somewhere, someplace, there's a gold Cadillac with dozens of compromising photos of me and all kinds of women in the trunk.

One of the American artists involved with the Biennale exhibit stayed in Paris and promised he would take care of the trailer. A few months had passed when I received a letter asking me to loan the trailer to an Italian film director. Great, I thought, the trailer will be in a movie and someone is going to take care of it for free. I was finally hitting two birds with one stone. But somewhere along the line, the movie director pawned the trailer off onto someone else and, from what we heard, eventually it fell into the hands of a band of Gypsies.

Monk and I decided to go back to Europe and look for the trailer. We were both single at the time, and after a few Lone Star beers we decided we could do a whole lot worse than driving around Europe chasing women and looking for a damned trailer. We brought a color Xerox of the Mobile Home Museum and hit all the bars from Paris to Athens and back, asking if anyone had seen our long-lost trailer. We went everywhere in Europe. We never found the trailer, but we drank lots of beer.

Three years later, a letter arrived from the Biennale exhibit office saying, in effect, that my "caravan" had been purchased by an unsuspecting man who was having trouble with the paperwork, so he wanted to sell it back to me for $900. Figuring a lawsuit in Paris would be nuts, and still obsessed with the trailer, I bought it back and arranged for it to be towed to the outskirts of Paris for storage.

It was years later—1985—when my wife, Lisa, and I went on our honeymoon, and went to see the trailer. We found the corner where the mechanic had it stored. He was away, but there it was, my long-lost Texas Mobile Home Museum! We could see through the back window that everything was gone. No bucking bronco, no two-headed calf, no snakes. In the middle of the trailer, however, on the knotty pine floor, one stuffed armadillo was sitting there like a little dog waiting for his mama to give him supper.

The window wasn't locked so I climbed inside, snapped a few photos, and grabbed the stuffed armadillo before noticing the saddle designed by the Texas Kid. I loaded the saddle and the armadillo into our French rent-a-car. Back at the hotel, we dragged the stuff through the lobby, looking somewhat like Monk had years earlier. I put the armadillo in the bathtub and cleaned up the saddle. Meanwhile, a friend of mine from Dallas had just opened up a Tex-Mex barbecue ribs joint in Paris, and since we were supposed to go see his restaurant that night, I decided to give him the armadillo and the saddle. I sure as hell wasn't going to check this stuff on a plane and fly it all back to Dallas.

As for the trailer, I'm still working it out. The Texas Mobile Home Museum still lives outside of Paris. As for the guy who's storing it, he sends me a bill every so often. At last count, the tab was somewhere over $10,000. Actually, I'd be happy just to get the stuffed horse and two-headed calf back, and I wouldn't mind seeing those photos from the trunk of the Cadillac either.

*Chapter Eleven*

# Years of the Iguana, Part I:

# The Invasion of Art Park

**THIS** is the story of the Iguana—one of the most complete, fulfilling, bizarre, and media-charged projects I've ever been involved with, and ever want to be involved with.

My projects are like children. You can raise them, but you don't know how or where they're going to end up, what's going to happen to them, or how they're going to manifest themselves. The Iguana is a perfect example of what happens to me when I immerse myself in a project: how I come up with an idea, how it is built, how my work site is set up, how it evolves, the interaction of the people who work on the project, finishing it, and seeing the public's reaction to it.

The Iguana is the epitome of that process and more.

Long, long ago there was once a program called Art Park. It was located near Niagara Falls, and was built for summer tourists who came through every year. It was sponsored by the New York State Office of Parks and Recreation, the National Endowment for the Arts, and other agencies. Art Park is devoted not just to outdoor sculpture, but also performance arts like music, dance, and symphonies. Situated on the rolling acres along the Niagara River, you could hear the roar of the falls at all times. It was a wonderful place to be during the summer. Nice and cool.

People from nearby Buffalo reminded me of Texans. There were rough and tough good ol' boys—survivors. Some of my Texas art buddies, James Surls, Joe Hobbs, and Andy Strout, had all been up there before me. I knew what the program was going to be, and since I had a few large-scale projects under my belt, I actually lusted to try something at Art Park. After finishing the *Map of the United States* and the Texas Mobile Home Museum, I felt like I could accomplish just about anything, anywhere.

There was snow on the ground in Dallas in early '78, when Ray Tyson, director of the visual arts part of Art Park, was scheduled to give a lecture at the University of Texas at Arlington.

Gallery owner Laura Carpenter had suggested me to Art Park, so I went to the lecture, picked Ray Tyson up in my funky white van after the lecture, and took him to Dallas. On the way, Tyson looked through my leather book—*Bob Wade's Texas*—that detailed my past projects. He got a good sense of what I'd done over the years and as a result, I was in the running to be invited up to Art Park.

The idea of the program was that an artist would come to Art Park for a month and build a huge outdoor piece. People who came through could stop and watch you work. It's what I call "monkey-in-the-zoo performance art." Some artists, whether they're introverts or not, don't like interacting with the public, don't want to be watched. You have to be able to handle the wisecracks.

To some extent I operate like Tom Sawyer and Huckleberry Finn. If somebody stops by, I immediately put them to work. "Could you please bring that hammer over here? Do you know where I can get some yellow paint for free?"

Art Park staggered their projects; artists would arrive a couple of weeks apart, resulting in different levels of progress between the various ongoing works. I was invited for the upcoming summer so I sat down and got serious about the scale of the piece. I had seen photos of the park, and having seen Tyson's slide lecture, I had a pretty good idea of the outdoor possibilities.

I decided that I should build some kind of armadillo or other huge critter. The biggest piece I had ever done (not counting the map!) averaged about forty feet across. I was thinking along the lines of something about the size of a small suburban home.

In the beginning I decided that it would be interesting to create something inflatable like what you see at the Macy's Thanksgiving Day Parade. The Texas connection would be that most of the helium these objects were filled with came from Amarillo.

I called a bunch of places that manufactured and fabricated parade inflatables and gave them the dimensions and a basic description. A place in New Jersey got back to me with a figure of over $25,000. My plans could be sent in and all I would have to do was fill it with helium and watch it float around. I scrapped the idea of an inflatable critter.

Friends of mine like Monk and his wife, Pam, were still making trips to Mexico—Puerto Vallarta and Acapulco. They knew I was a fan of Mexican border town kitsch, and although Monk grew up in Fort Worth, his taste was similar to mine. Usually he would bring back funny little stuffed frogs. My big score came when he brought me back a stuffed iguana from Puerto Vallarta. It was the biggest one I had ever seen—stuffed or unstuffed. Generally iguanas are about eighteen inches long, but this one was two feet long from the tip of the nose to where the tail curves up over its back. They're strange-looking creatures, kind of dinosaur-like.

When Monk brought me this new stuffed critter from Mexico, I thought, This is it! The armadillo (a Texas hero) was almost a cliché by then. In tropical Mexico, people have iguanas running around their houses. I found out months later that there were a lot of pet iguanas in New York City, more so than in many other large cities. The iguana is at least as weird as the armadillo. Sculpturally speaking it has a more dynamic look. An armadillo, while funky and interesting, is passive—it's like a football with a tail, four legs, and a funny little head—but the iguana has a certain automotive quality. It's lower in the back, like a low-rider. Its tail comes up over its back with a swooping, flamboyant quality. Standing with its head high in the air gives it a cocky, self-confident posture—a macho Texas attitude. So I decided: an iguana.

Ron Phillips helped photograph an iguana for my photo show that spring in Venice, California, at Jan Turner's Janus Gallery. The four-foot-by-six-foot blow up looked great. So maybe bigger would be better.

I met up with one of my design friends, Gary Ferguson, at the Stoneleigh P in the spring of '78. He was an architect bad boy drinking pal who had been helpful over the years. After three or four beers, ideas began to roll as we discussed the iguana project. I had brought my new iguana to the bar and sat it on the booth. We started getting really bizarre ideas. Soon the iguana transformed into a small version of the Concorde, which had just landed in Dallas.

Over the years I've always had good luck with the number 40. I had done a lot of installations that were forty feet wide or forty feet long. Indoor museum and gallery spaces lent themselves well to a forty-foot-wide structure. Maybe it has to do with human scale and its grasp. Once you go beyond fifty- or sixty-foot projects, it goes past what you can see, perceive, and control.

I flashed back to when I built model airplanes as a kid. I assembled little thin wood pieces and struts, covered them with paper, and painted the plane. Paint caused the paper to shrink up tight. Later on I made bigger planes with gasoline motors and a thirty-foot wire with a U-control handle that would make the plane do loop-de-loops. I used to win trophies at hobby shop contests. I was also a yo-yo champ . . . but I'm getting off track here.

Looking at the iguana's body as a fuselage, I wondered, Who do we know that fiddles around with airplanes? Maybe we can build this sculpture according to airplane technology, keeping it lightweight and sturdy.

Gary and I thought of a mutual friend who lived and worked in a little town near Dallas called Ponder, which was close to Denton. We used to drive out to the Ponder Steakhouse, which had the best T-bones and desserts in the state. A character named Richard worked across the street from that steak house, in a broken-down brick building. Inside it were parts of airplanes, wings and fuselages.

Richard was an aircraft expert. When Texas businessmen flew around in their little Piper Cubs, occasionally they would flip them over or bang them up, and Richard would repair them. Fergie and I figured Richard could give us some ideas on this iguana.

Richard told us to make a lightweight steel tubular framework, using electrical conduit. Having fixed up my loft in Oak Cliff, I was familiar with building materials. He told us to construct struts like a model airplane, cover the whole sculpture with wire mesh, and then spray it over with urethane foam.

What a funny coincidence. That old coffee cup from Berkeley had been mixed up with urethane foam, and Jernigan and the Mexicans used the same material to fill up the stuffed frogs and iguanas they sold as souvenirs. They sometimes used sawdust, but more often than not they resorted to urethane foam. You could spray it either out of a can or, more industrially, out of pressurized drums in trucks. Urethane foam was also used to coat leaky roofs, insulate walls, and build flotation docks. After seeing Richard, we left feeling very secure about how to build our iguana.

I had a photographer take side, front, above, below, and back views of my stuffed iguana. Then I transferred these images onto grid paper, drawn exactly to scale. These drawings became the first working blueprint plans for the critter.

I knew that by the time I got to upstate New York, I'd have a loose idea of where the internal structure would go and where the support system would be. I calculated how best to wrap the wire mesh, but I hadn't worked with urethane foam on such a large scale. Hopefully, I could find somebody else to do it.

I'd always been a nuts and bolts kind of guy, partly because my dad was handy. Art Park promised to provide me with interns, and I was also hoping I'd meet some students who wanted to help me build this thing.

I talked my friend Rick Hernandez into coming to Dallas and helping me get my white GMC van loaded up with whatever tools, beer coolers, current art magazines, and materials I thought we might need, and driving with me to upstate New York. One thing I always did before hitting the road, especially on my way to New

York, was buy every current art magazine and read it cover to cover. My theory was that when you get to New York, you gotta be smart.

I was living like a Gypsy: I had a five-year-old daughter and ex-wife living in California, and a couple of ex-girlfriends in Dallas, and a long drive to Buffalo and Niagara Falls ahead of me. When we got to Lewiston, New York, we found our way to Art Park's offices, which was a typical work trailer like the one I had at the U.S. map. We arrived wearing cutoffs, flip-flops, T-shirts, and cowboy hats—with cold ones in our hands.

The first people we met were a couple of interns and coeds who were camped out in the woods. It got me pretty excited, damn excited in fact. Then we met Ray and the people who ran the deal, who offered to rent us one of the shanties—a little ten-foot-by-ten-foot work shed—where we could keep our tools and materials. They would run electricity out to it so that we could run our power tools.

After agreeing on a location for our project, we moved the shanty into place in the middle of a big open space. It was like one of those sites you see in dinosaur movies. The terrain along the Niagara River had a prehistoric look, very bizarre and barren. The little paved road that started at the main gateway down toward the beginning of Art Park wound its way up through two or three other artists' projects, then past us and on to the main buildings near Niagara Falls, where all the dances and gatherings were held. We were among the first of the artist attractions the visitors would drive past to get to Niagara Falls and the river.

I thought of my childhood in Texas, growing up around roadside stuff like giant teepees, and remembered the importance of high profile and easy in and easy out. Whether the tourists stopped or not, the Iguana was bound to give them the big thrill of a Texas roadside attraction.

The first thing I did after setting up the shanty and purchasing some materials was instruct my new staff to assist Rick and me in assembling the internal structure. At first the Iguana looked like a stick figure. As it turned out, one of our interns' father was a local welder, so we talked her into convincing him to come down and help us. Again, that's my modus operandi for this kind of project. If an hour has gone by and you haven't hustled something from somebody or made a contact, you're already behind schedule.

Next to the shanty, we built a shade lean-to we called Little Mexico. Having furnished it with the passenger seat from the van, I could listen to the radio and drink beer while making drawings and overseeing the project. Tom the Welder finished the stick-figure's internal structure according to my plans, and the basic framework was right on the money. Using some wood pieces, we created circular parts to round off the body, the belly, the neck area, the tail, and the legs.

The program at Art Park lasted only for a month or two. You had a specific amount of time in which to build your project and then remove it, or else it would either get thrown out or become the property of Art Park. Since I couldn't move a giant forty-foot structure with its huge leg span totally intact, I had to design the creature so that the legs, the head, and parts of the tail would come apart.

I had a month to complete the Iguana, and was moving along pretty good, but one of the problems that slowed us down was that it kept raining. Sometimes these heavy downpours would last an entire day, and half of Lewiston's weird terrain would turn to mush. You couldn't even walk on it much less work in it. During the first week we decided that Rick and I could operate out of the shanty shed we had already turned into a bachelor pad. We had installed a bed and rigged up a little television set I brought along. The curators were appalled when we requested that some of our budget be used for an air-conditioning unit. Hey, we were from Texas. We turned the shanty into the most comfortable place of any artists' working areas. People would come down, hang out, drink beer, and bullshit. Chasing women and carrying on was a principal part of being at Art Park. You couldn't be there without getting laid.

Since the rain definitely presented problems, Rick and I requested a bigger shanty in addition to the one we already had. Renting a twenty-foot shanty for three weeks was going to eat further into our budget, but in the new one we could construct legs, feet, and other components. It also became the "Iguana Museum" for orienting visitors with photos and plans.

When the Iguana frame was finished, we covered the whole thing with wire mesh and window-screen wire. The metal fins were installed down the back and up the long tail. A urethane foam outfit out of Niagara Falls agreed to come out to Art Park and spray the Iguana's exterior for free. The workers were used to spraying roofs, boats, and walls, so they were excited. The texture was perfect. We used kitchen knives to carve out details like eyes, toenails, and the teeth. Every time oversprayed foam hit a blade of grass, it created textured masses we called Iguana toes, which we would hand out as souvenirs to the tourists.

"Have a souvenir! Have an Iguana toe," I offered while I painted and jazzed them up a bit.

It was time to double up and catch up. The schedule allowed me only a few days to paint and finish up. My month was almost over. One of the other artists, Alan Kline, a glass blower, fashioned a pair of beautiful glass spheres with stripes and colors. These "gigantic eyeballs" were rigged into the Iguana's eye sockets. They were bluish with silver-tipped corneas that picked up light reflection.

After perfecting the body shape, we performed a dry run by bolting and unbolting the head. An accident occurred when somebody forgot to put the washers and nuts back on. I was up on the neck and about to move forward. I was shirtless and wearing cutoffs and a big cowboy hat. That's when Andy took the photo of me riding the Giant Iguana (the very cover of this book!). Seconds later, the head fell to the ground, taking me with it; rodeo jargon would be "takin' a header."

I still needed a way to get in and out of the Iguana so we could tighten the bolts from the inside. How could I create an access that would not distract from the design? Simple. I figured I'd cut a hole the size of a manhole cover, right where the asshole would be. Of course it was christened the asshole from El Paso.

Rick Hernandez flew to El Paso to take care of some business, and came back with some homemade tamales just in time for the final Mexican paint and body shop routine. I had already carved out the toes, jowls, mouth, and that great hanging thing under the chin—the dewlap. Next I fabricated little white teeth, and Jim Napierala made a big red tongue. Rick got creative, and the Iguana's body received its first primer coat. Since iguanas have a metallic look anyway, real metallic paint was added as the last coat. The final touches included zigzag stripes around the belly, and details around the eyes and the corner of the mouth.

I had finished on time and that big lizard looked cool, just like something out of a '60s Japanese monster movie. The tourists loved it. I rigged up spotlights so it could be lit up at night. It looked hotter than a Mexican whore in June.

So now, what do you do with a forty-foot iguana? Now that I'd finished, I didn't have a clue as to where the Iguana was going to end up. Since it turned out to be such a great-looking sculpture, I figured it should tour the New York state area and end up in New York City. The roof of the Guggenheim Museum was my immediate thought, but my gut feeling was that it probably wasn't gonna happen.

Rick remembers that putting the Iguana on the roof of the Lone Star Café was actually artist Alice Adams's idea. She was a sculptor from New York and was also at Art Park. We were sitting around in a little circle of about ten people and Alice was talking about the Iguana.

"You know," she said, "that thing ought to be on the roof of the Lone Star Café in New York City. You should call them."

I had visited the Lone Star Café once or twice before to see my friend Kinky Friedman perform. The club also featured a western fashion show coordinated by another Texas friend, Judy Buie. She was one of the first people in New York to help spread the concept of Texas Chic in the '70s. Judy had opened up a fancy cowboy boot shop. During the Travolta *Urban Cowboy* craze, the all-Texas Lone Star Café parties ended up segregated by cities. Transplanted folks from Dallas were on one side, Houston on the other, San Antonio usually closest to the bar. El Paso was usually the tiniest minority, stuck off in the corner, just like it was geographically.

I knew the Lone Star's basic look, its Manhattan location, and its crazy, wild Texas honky-tonk ambiance; but better, I knew that the roof was flat and there was a taller building just behind it which could make an effective backdrop. Since restaurant and bar people are more apt to take something on immediately than museum people, I started thinking the Lone Star was a possibility.

A bunch of us were sitting around another good-bye party, drinking red wine, when I got the urge and ran up to the Art Park trailer and cold-called the Lone Star Café to find out who the owner was and if anybody there knew the dimensions of the roof. Some guy answered the phone and I rambled on about my big lizard, how I knew Kinky Friedman and Judy Buie, and how I sure needed to talk to somebody about putting a big sculpture on their roof.

A perplexed voice on the other end announced, "This is Mort Cooperman, one of the owners. And who is this?"

That might have been one of the last times Mort Cooperman ever answered the phone at the Lone Star Café. As he confessed later, he figures that if he ever answers it again another guy like Daddy-O might try to sell him a lizard or something.

I ran the deal down to him. Of the two partners who owned the joint, Mort was the creative guy. He previously worked at an ad agency so he was always game for publicity, and when I called him about putting a lizard on the roof, he was at least willing to listen. He actually had somebody measure the roof, and called me back.

The Iguana measured forty feet long from front to back, twelve feet across the front feet, and about sixteen feet across its back feet. Two hours later, Mort called back.

"I don't know how long that lizard is, but the roof space you have to work with is about forty-two feet long and twenty feet across."

I couldn't believe it: I had two whole extra feet to fiddle with. If I sat down and drew an ideal rectangle rooftop for this thing to sit on, I couldn't have come much closer than the rooftop of the Lone Star Café.

As my buddy the Texas Kid would say, "Mr. Bob, if it's fer ya, it's fer ya. If it ain't fer ya, it ain't fer ya."

The Iguana on the rooftop of New York City's Lone Star Café musta been "fer me."

*Chapter Twelve*

## Years of the Iguana, Part II:

## The Critter versus the City of New York

 told Mort Cooperman I
needed to get the Iguana out
of Art Park and pronto, even
though I still didn't know if
he was interested in buying or leasing the damn thing.

"Why don't you get on a plane," he suggested, "and fly down here
and do some more measurements? Bring photos of this thing and
I'll get my other partner, Bill Dick, and we'll talk about it."

Bill Dick was a nuts-and-bolts, engineering kind of guy. He had
access to tools, equipment, and sub-contractors. He and Cooperman
were the guys who could handle the job.

Once I got to New York, we sat around all afternoon and

schemed. They loved the look of the Iguana, but it was time to talk money. We settled that they would buy the Iguana for $10,000, which in 1978 wasn't bad. Plus, I figure I had built this thing pretty much for free at Art Park. I hustled a lot of stuff for nothing, had a lot of free labor, and received my stipend and living expenses while I was there.

The money seemed like a pretty good deal, but the conditions were a bit wacky. The Lone Star promised me half in cash and the other half in the form of an open tab at the Lone Star. I could charge pork chops, enchiladas, and giant chicken-fried steaks until the tequila and my five grand ran out.

Man! I thought. Not only am I going to have five thousand bucks in my pocket, I'm gonna have five thousand bucks worth of tab at this joint—some of the best food in New York City, and the kind I prefer to eat anyway! The Lone Star was one of the jumpin'est places in all of New York then. On the corner of Fifth Avenue and 13th Street, not far from Greenwich Village and near Washington Square and NYU, it already had become somewhat of a landmark. Locals and celebrities loved to crowd in to hear the country, blues, and rock 'n' roll.

Rick and I put the disassembled Iguana in a big warehouse in Niagara Falls and drove back to Texas. A few weeks later we flew back to Niagara Falls and rented a U-Haul for the trip to New York. The challenge then became how to fit the Iguana's components into the biggest U-Haul truck we could rent. After hours of shoving stuff around and manhandling lizard parts, the body barely stuck out of a twenty-four-foot truck, but there still wasn't enough room for the head.

I thought back to my youth. "What would they do in Juarez if they were trying to haul something to El Paso and didn't want to spend a bunch of money?"

There was some lumber left over, so we roped some two-by-fours on the front bumper of the U-Haul truck, nailed a sheet of plywood onto the two-by-fours and rested the other end on top of the cab. It was exactly enough of a platform so the head could lay flat sideways, facing forward, mouth open.

In early October 1978, Rick Hernandez, Jim Napierala (one of the volunteers from Buffalo), and I got into the U-Haul and drove down the Thruway from Buffalo to New York City, courtesy of Lionel Bevan, a cowboy philanthropist Fort Worth. We only stopped to pee and gas up. The guys from the gas stations could not believe their eyes, and the tollbooth ladies actually screamed. We couldn't close the back tailgate, so you could see all the weirdness inside, as well as the big head added to the platform. At 50 mph, it was a slow nine-hour drive.

An artist at Art Park named Sally Fisher once said to me, "I have a huge loft on the lower West Side of Manhattan and you guys are welcome to flop there if you dare bring the Iguana down to New York." I took her up on it.

Upon arrival, we made arrangements to park alongside Sally's loft on Hudson Street and sleep in her loft for a couple of days until we got things under control. We rolled in at about two o'clock in the morning, and thank goodness there was a parking space right by her door. For a small price, the parking lot attendant across the street agreed to keep an eye on the truck.

At around four o'clock in the morning we got a phone call from the parking lot attendant. He was yelling and screaming.

"There's a guy stealing the big head. They're taking it off the roof right now! Quick! Quick!"

Rick, Jim, and I pulled on our jeans and ran downstairs onto the street. A big station wagon had pulled up alongside the truck and three would-be thieves had already unroped the head and moved it onto the roof of their station wagon. They were gigantic guys from Brooklyn built like professional wrestlers and drunk out of their minds too.

"Wait, wait, wait, wait!" we shouted. "What' the fuck is goin' on?"

"We thought it'd be funny to drive around the city with this head on the roof of our station wagon."

"Wait a minute," I said. "We've got to put it on the roof of the Lone Star Café tomorrow!"

"Yeah sure, tell you what. We'll drive around with it for a while then bring it back."

"Yeah, sure."

Turns out they thought it was Jaws. They wanted to be the guys who became famous for stealing Jaws.

We talked them out of it. How, I don't know. We told them we had television stations coming tomorrow morning and suggested they meet up with us at the Lone Star tomorrow. We said we'd put it on the roof of their station wagon, and they could come driving up when the TV cameras were there and pretend like they had it all night long. We could point at them, and say, "Look! Here comes the head now. These guys had it last night, but now they're bringing it back.

Damned if they didn't buy our story and drive off. We were afraid they might drive around the block and come back later, so we just managed to fit the Iguana head through the big double doors of the main entrance to the loft. The main floor was a laundry with Sally's loft up the stairs and off to the right. Imagine the workers' surprise when they came in the next morning, opened the door, and found a fucking lizard's head staring back at them.

The Iguana was scheduled to be delivered at 9:00 A.M. The Lone Star guys made arrangements for a publicity event; a crane was going to arrive at noon. The head, the feet, and the tail were scattered along the sidewalk when the crane arrived. The body itself was longer than a Yellow Cab. You could barely walk past. People were taking pictures and filming us. In actuality, the Iguana was so light, we could have hoisted it up, but Mort wanted to make a big deal out of it and Bill wanted professionals.

A couple weeks before, sculptor-welder David Stoltz had bolted steel rigging devices to the parapet walls that would ultimately hold the Iguana in just the right position. On installation day, welders were waiting on the roof with their torches, ready to assemble the sculpture. Platforms had been mounted on the gravel roof, which was a pretty big drop down from the parapet. The crane lifted the Iguana piece by piece to the roof, where it was later assembled. I spent a couple of extra weeks after that putting a new, elaborate paint job and more scales on the critter. I added a lot more detail work and rigged the lighting so a spotlight could shine on the eyes and tongue. Like we did up at Art Park, we added spotlights from below to give it that dramatic look. The back wall had been painted a flat white, so we had a museum-like installation, a perfect sculpture stand, a wonderful backdrop. The crane and welder came back and this time we put it in place for good. We thought.

Just about every hip Texas musician at that time played the Lone Star Café. On occasion I'd run into a friend while he or she was doing soundchecks. The Iguana was on the rooftop, next to a room housing the air conditioning and electrical equipment. There wasn't any room downstairs for a musicians' hangout, so the musicians usually hung out between sets in a flop room which led onto the roof. It was also my staging area, where I'd store tools and materials to work on the sculpture. I was sort of the Lone Star honky-tonk artist-in-residence.

Musicians who were on East Coast tours through Boston or D.C. would finagle their way to New York City by getting a gig at the Lone Star Café. Even though the stage was tiny, it was a much sought-after venue. A small nightclub like the Lone Star was often more happening than bigger joints. I ran into Billy Joe Shaver, Freddy Fender, and Jerry Jeff Walker, who climbed up on top of the Iguana. Song writer Doc Pomus was around in his wheelchair and Delbert McClinton was wailing away on stage.

And then there was Kinky.

Kinky—a fellow University of Texas sicko who made fun of stuff by performing as Kinky Friedman and the Texas Jewboys. He'd been around for years working Texas and both coasts singing songs with verses like "They ain't makin' Jews like Jesus anymore" or "Put your biscuits in the oven and your buns in the bed." He was another Texas eccentric (good thing Stanley Marsh 3 can't sing) and I felt more secure in my work just measuring myself with the Kinkster. He got paid, though.

During the '70s, the Lone Star had kind of a singles bar atmosphere. The clientele was varied—native New Yorkers, transplanted Texans, Texas political types visiting Manhattan, cowboys, and celebrities: Larry King, Ann Richards, Tommy Tune, Dan Rather, John Connolly, Chet Flippo, and Linda Ellerbee, to name a few.

One time a Latino musician was desperately looking for me. He was sent to me because I had keys to this upper level room where I kept my new and very delicate dragonfly sculpture. El Latino wanted to have some quick fun with this groupie he had just met downstairs at the bar.

I told him I was worried about customers breaking into that room, so we made a deal: Since the door only locked from the outside, I would let him and the girl inside and lock them in. Thinking with his dick, he reluctantly agreed but insisted I come back and let him out in thirty minutes. Well, I very seldom wore a watch and I lost track of the fuckin' time. I was back where the action was—at the multi-level bar with the girls, the music, and the characters, plus I didn't like the guy either.

The bartender asked me where El Latino was. Oh God! I raced

back upstairs a half-hour late, and he was pounding on the door, all upset. Apparently the fling was over and he was ready to get the hell out of there. If only that dragonfly could talk.

The Lone Star was housed in an old building complete with an elevator. It had been at one time a Schrafft's ice cream parlor. The banner that hung from the front of the building was emblazoned with the words of a Billy Joe Shaver song: "Too Much Ain't Enough." That's what the Lone Star was all about. I knew there were a lotta complaints about the high-decibel music and drunks swinging out of the notorious revolving front door, but putting an Iguana on the roof was almost too much for the merchants and people living in the high-rise apartments up and down high-class Fifth Avenue. This was at 13th—almost 14th—Street, which was full of hardware stores, riff-raff shops, sidewalk vendors, card tables selling socks and underwear, and three-card monte fly-by-night guys. I loved all of that stuff, but when the Fifth Avenue folks said we were ruining the makeup of Fifth Avenue, I was confused.

Right across the street in a building overlooking the Lone Star was the famous Parsons School of Design. The students who drew and painted used our site as subject matter. At the end of the block, further down Fifth Avenue and across the street, was the world headquarters of *Forbes* magazine. Even farther down was NYU and Washington Square. It hadn't been but a few days before somebody started stirring the fire with a sword. "The merchants are pissed off," said the *Village Voice* on October 23rd.

After all the television and newspaper publicity, the Lone Star had hit the big time, just like Mort hoped. It would cost 'em. They had to hire attorneys to fight mounting problems with the city inspectors. They were pressured by neighboring merchants, but they went ahead with the official unveiling as planned: Halloween night, with a giant, fake, lit-up pumpkin placed between the Iguana's front legs.

The Iguana controversy was in the papers constantly, and Mort kept dragging celebs up to the roof daily. The lizard and I both were gettin' lots of attention, so I had to hunker down in the city for a while. Who wouldn't have?

My painter friend Julian Schnabel had a live-in loft about ten blocks from the Lone Star. Julian and I go back to Texas days (he watched me milk some P.R. in Dallas during the filming of *Jacke-*

*lope*) and I usually visited him on my New York trips. He actually saved my life once when I almost walked into an open elevator shaft.

Schnabel was just beginning his famous "Broken Plate" series then, but was basically broke, so I fed him pork chops on my Lone Star Iguana tab. When Julian told me he was going off to Europe for a month to help Les Levine install art, I jumped at the chance to use his place. One problem: He needed rent money—four hundred bucks. Since I was still doing touch-up work and P.R. for Mort's empire, I worked a deal whereby the Lone Star would pay Julian's rent for me, but reserved the right to house an occasional musician there in a bind. The bind did come once in the person of "Mr. Mendocino," Doug Sahm. Doug stayed about three nights and about wore me out, constantly rambling on, combing his hair, and entertaining fans.

Before Julian left, we made a couple of trades. He wanted my white cowboy boots to impress a European gallery, so he gave me his Gestapo-looking leather coat. He also said I could have one of his "Twig-like" drawings. I never got it.

I also agreed to take care of a couple of things for Julian in his absence: (a) Feed his dog, who shits in the studio; (b) Cooperate with his now famous gallery owner/rep Mary Boone, should collectors come by; and (c) Keep an eye on the bills and alert Mary Boone about them.

One morning Boone called up and said she was bringing an important collector by and could I tidy up the dog turds and help her move Julian's broken plate paintings for "Dr. Panza" to view.

I cleaned up, checked the mail, and found a couple of emergency-cut-off notices.

Here's the high profile Daddy-O cleaning up dog shit and being Mary's lackey so that Julian can make a sale to perhaps the most well known art collector in the world.

When the two left Julian's, I slipped Mary the cut-off bills. She called back a little later to thank me and said that Julian "wasn't very good at business." In case you don't know, Julian is now a famous trillionaire and fixin' to be a movie director.

I was loving the Lone Star scene, especially the part about showing the waitresses some finer points inside the Iguana. I'd remove the butt plug and the interior of the sculpture would become an insulated cozy hideaway. The butt plug finally got stolen. I'd sure like to find the "asshole" that did it.

*Dallas Morning News* society column writer Alan Peppard was at the Lone Star one weekend with his Dallas squeeze, and it was decided that the sweet thing should take a closer look at the internal structure of the sculpture. We still laugh at the snapshot of her standing on a ladder with her head up inside the Iguana's asshole. Alan has always been kind enough and "kinky" enough to mention my exploits in his column, usually associating "Super Broker Monk" with those exploits.

Years later when my wife, Lisa, and I were at the Lone Star, Mort said, "Wade, I want you to take this guy Tom up to the roof and show him the Iguana real close up."

We had a ladder up there so visitors could climb up and have photos made. Kinky posed for an article in *High Times* and TV shows were recorded there. I asked Lisa, "Who is this 'Tom' guy, part of the warm-up band?"

"No, idiot, it's the actor Tom Cruise."

Tom and I got up on an industrial stainless-steel kitchen table—high enough so that the background was the Iguana head with the dewlap under its chin. Cruise's managers and agents were hovering all around him, scared that something was going to happen. I was posing on the table while people were taking photos when I looked around and Cruise was gone. He had slipped off the steel table onto his back and was rolling around on the gravel in pain. His people rushed to his side and leaned over him. Everyone looked back around at me like it was my fault. It wasn't and Cruise took it like a man.

The city of New York finally declared the Iguana to be a sign, and as a sign, it broke various codes to which signs are subject—not attached properly, incorrect permits, and flammability. This went on even though I appeared in court as "the artist" as opposed to "the signmaker."

Numerous "art" experts appeared in court, including a former member of Art Park's advisory staff and a curator from the Brooklyn Museum of Art. My foxy friend Joanne Cassullo who was on the board of the Whitney Museum also made an impassioned plea. On November 4, 1979, the judge found in favor of the Lone Star Café, declaring the Iguana not a sign but a bona fide work of art. In his statement, the judge expressed fears that the city might try to declare the Statue of Liberty a sign. Case dismissed.

To celebrate, we threw a big party at the Lone Star, but while the club celebrated, the city was still getting pressure from the merchants. Meanwhile, the Lone Star had thousands of dollars invested not only in the costs of installing the Iguana, but also in legal fees. The publicity they got made it a New York City landmark. People would tell cab drivers, "Take me to the bar with the giant lizard."

It was in calendars, day books, tour bus routes, and on T-shirts. It was becoming an institution.

Under pressure from the city, the New York City Fire Department conducted continual raids and inspections. Firefighters would frequently come by in the middle of a concert wearing full fire gear and carrying axes. They'd rush in and disrupt the whole evening, counting heads to see if the joint was overpacked. If it was, the club was fined. At that point I should have told New York what Davy Crockett said: "You go to hell, I'm going to Texas."

Back in Texas, I got a call from Mort and Bill.

"Wade. We gotta get this Iguana out of sight because it's costing us a lot of grief and money."

The Iguana had been up for three years when the partners decided to take it down. I flew to New York with a brilliant plan. With some semi-complicated manipulations and by removing the tail, we were able to move the Iguana in between the two roof drop-offs, making it invisible from the street below.

After we moved it, you couldn't see the sculpture unless you walked out into the roof or were floors above in one of the nearby buildings, like the Parsons School of Design, sketching away. After that, the inspectors took an "out of sight, out of mind" attitude. The Lone Star Café decided to lay low for a while, which is what a real iguana might do—go take a little nap.

In this case the nap lasted three years. The *Soho News* would occasionally have photos of the lizard in different locations around the city—the subway, the movies, with Nixon or Kissinger.

Occasionally I'd take a trip to New York and drop by the Lone Star to check up on the "hidden" Iguana. One night, a reggae band was playing, and between sets you could barely walk through the musician room upstairs because the ganja smoke was so thick. The steel door obviously hadn't been opened in a while.

The Rastas were looking at me as I pounded and pried at the door. They wondered what I was doing up there.

"Hey, you guys," I asked. "You want to see a big lizard?"

"What you talkin' 'bout, mon?"

"Right outside this door is a giant iguana lizard. You gotta see it."

I finally got the door loose and open, and there it was—the face and the dewlap shoved up almost against the door, mouth open.

Rasta man refused to go on roof.

During the end of the Iguana's third year, there was a party at the Lone Star. Mayor Ed Koch attended and got to talking with the Lone Star partners.

"Hey! Whatever happened to that big friggin' lizard that was up on the roof here?" he asked.

"Well you ought to know," they answered back. "Your office made us take it down."

"It wasn't my office." replied Koch. "Let me look into it. I thought the Iguana was great. In fact, give me a call on Monday and I'll help you get it back up."

Soon enough I got the call. The Iguana was poised for its first city-sanctioned comeback. Mort called, "Wade. Get your affairs in order. It looks like you might be coming back to New York City. We're waiting for the final paperwork to come through from the mayor's office."

"Dynamite."

"What we want to do is coordinate the Iguana's return with the governor of Texas's visit."

Then-governor Mark White was coming to New York for a fund-raiser because there's always been a huge contingent of Texans there. They had an organization called TINY—Texans in New York—and their own newsletter, and when Texas artists would play the Lone Star there were always dozens of Texans there, drunk as rodeo goats. A lot of Texans stopped by just to taste the barbecue.

I was in Chicago at the time, working on a hundred-foot-long snake at "Sculpture-Chicago." Besides Mark White, Mayor Koch also agreed to appear. On the year of the Texas Sesquicentennial—150-year-birthday—New York was going to stage the reinstallation and the unveiling of the new appearance of the Iguana. They didn't need me there to supervise the cranes when they reassembled the sculpture, so on October 1, 1985, Lisa and I flew in from Chicago and took a cab directly to the festivities.

"Take me to the bar with the . . ."

A giant white cover with ropes was hanging over the Iguana. White and Koch were outside chatting. Mort and Bill were there with all the television stations and the newspaper reporters congregated outside the Lone Star revolving doors. The mayor of New York and the governor of Texas each said a few words, then they pulled the rope and the big cover came off the Iguana. Everybody was yelling and clapping. I had tears in my eyes. The Iguana was back. *My* iguana was back.

The reporters started their questions, and then Mayor Koch asked me, "What sex is the Iguana?"

"Ohhhh," I paused. "It's both!"

We went up to the roof and the governor presented me with an elaborate gold watch to celebrate Texas's 150th anniversary. Reporter Linda Ellerbee, a friend of mine who is from Houston, was on hand.

The Iguana stayed perched on the roof for another four years until things started looking bad for the Lone Star. The partners were worried because the rent kept going up. Business was great but an era was about to end. They decided not to get a new lease on 13th Street, but rather opened up another location on 52nd Street.

Before the move, the owners held a gigantic, flamboyant auction to close the downtown Lone Star. The auction was publicized in the newspapers and on April 26, 1989, celebrity limos pulled up outside and the media covered the big event. I was invited to attend. Even though I didn't own the Iguana, I did own a companion piece: the sixteen-foot-wingspan dragonfly which hung from a chandelier inside the club. I originally made it at the Kansas City Art Institute, and exhibited it in Washington, D.C., as the world's biggest dragonfly. It had been hanging inside the Lone Star wearing cowboy boots on all six legs, and a cowboy hat atop its furry little head and funny compound eyes. They auctioned off the dragonfly and it ended up moving to a bar near Woodstock.

A couple of my buddies were interested in buying the Iguana for their Texas truck stop, Carl's Corner. I was authorized to bid up to $7,000, but when it went beyond the $7,000 mark I began taking pictures of the bidders, the auctioneer, and the action itself. At one point I raised the camera up to take a picture of the group. The auctioneer pointed his gavel my way.

"$10,000!" he yelled.

Luckily the bidding went up and finally ended at $17,500. The winning couple was from Long Island; they had a horse farm in Virginia, not far from where Sam Shepard had just moved from Santa Fe. They wanted the Iguana trucked down two days later. Sam, who used to have a little fellowship with us in Santa Fe, sure was surprised to find out that Wade's critter had followed him to the Virginia countryside. Naturally, I oversaw its dismantling and placement on the truck. I waved goodbye to my Iguana and took some final photos of it as it headed to Virginia, where it has lived ever since. Lisa had bought the "Too Much Ain't Enough" banner and I bought back my Iguana photo piece.

Throughout its lifetime, the Iguana has been in at least two TV movies, one full-length motion picture, and dozens of magazines, newspapers, and television stories. It is still one of my favorite creations. Countless celebrities sat on its head, posed next to it, on it, in front of it, and lots of people have seen it on TV or read about it. It's staggering how famous one funny sculpture became. As for its sex, I sort of lied to Mayor Koch.

For some reason, Mort and I always thought of it as being female.

At one point I tried to borrow the Iguana. I wanted to put it on the back of an eighteen-wheeler and truck it to a big sculpture conference in Washington, D.C., an hour and a half drive from the farm. The move proved too complicated and expensive for such a quick appearance. But at least my Dallas buddies Preston Carter and David "Joe Boy McCoy" Wynne got to see it one more time when they went to visit Sam Shepard. Sam even agreed to one more photo op by climbing up a ladder and putting his head in the refurbished reptile. All of which tempts me to one day construct Son (or Daughter?) of Iguana. Wouldn't it be nice to meet a smaller version, rigged on a trailer as part of a traveling Daddy-O exhibition? Coming to a town near you—the Iguanamobile!

As for the old 13th Street Lone Star location, it went through several name changes and food offerings and is currently a Korean Deli. Did the Koreans ever make any '60s dinosaur movies?

# Chapter Thirteen

# Daddy-O Goes to Washington, or 35,000

# Gallons of Beer to the Boot

**NE** day the phone rang, interrupting me from a nap.

"Bob Wade? My name is Al Nodal from Washington, D.C. While I was in New York having lunch, I saw the giant Iguana you installed on top of the Lone Star Café. Would you be interested in doing a big outdoor piece for our nonprofit group, the WPA, the Washington Project for the Arts? We have a corner lot that has been loaned to us by the city of D.C. and we want to erect a site-specific outdoor sculpture on that corner. You'd be perfect for that kind of situation."

The WPA presented performances, solo shows, group shows, theater and art projects around the city, and had a little book shop at their headquarters. They specialized in alternative spaces (rather than museums or commercial art galleries) supported by the NEA and city funding for artists whose works don't fit into more mainstream categories. One new program was called the Washington Art Site, and I was chosen to be the first artist to put up a project on the corner of 12th and G.

I drove down to D.C. to look the site over. 12th and G was a great corner three blocks from the White House. Lots of traffic rolled by and the city had just opened a subway stop across the street, which guaranteed all kinds of downtown foot traffic.

I was excited about the high visibility, and the close proximity to the White House. I met with the WPA and they talked about a nice budget, a place to stay, and all the materials. Fine, I said, count me in. I went back to New York to finish all my obligations with the Iguana.

Ultimately the Washington Arts Project's promises turned out to be wishful thinking. Nodal and I had to do lots of schmoozing and presentation-making just to get the project off the ground. Being the diplomat he was, and knowing D.C.'s Beltway mentality of embassies, government procedure, and politicians, Nodal knew a plan had to be devised to raise money.

It was the summer of 1979. I quit teaching in '77 and had been on the gypsy trail for a couple of years. Since I owned neither a straight-arrow suit nor a tie, Al Nodal took me down to a men's clothing store and with his credit card bought me an off-white three-piece suit so that we could make the rounds at big nonpartisan breakfasts, cocktail parties, and other social functions. We wanted to push this project through properly, so the WPA didn't want me looking like some stereotyped artist or Texas hayseed. While Nodal was already familiar with some of my photographic pieces, I showed him slides of an exhibition I did in Venice, California. It was the one with the Iguana in it, and two other works having to do with cowboy boots. I described the piece I hoped to do for the WPA: a pair of giant cowboy boots. Nodal suggested I make a preliminary paste-up or maquette that we could use as a model to display at our sales pitch presentations.

Washington, D.C., has a legendary roster of Texas politicians, like LBJ, John Connolly, and Cactus Jack Garner, all of whom wore cowboy boots. They accentuated their Lone Star image. The good ol' boy legislators who left the big house in Austin to go to Washington, D.C., to serve in Congress or the Senate formed a definite Texan power base inside the nation's capital. They frequently held giant barbecues honoring the Texas constituency, and many of the transplanted Texas lawmakers traded in their tweeds for one night of western attire.

I decided they were the group I needed to get into my court.

Projects such as the WPA are called site-specific because the work is made specifically for one location. The lot at 12th and G was a long rectangle, so my sculpture needed to look good not only as a long horizontal, but also as a vertical.

Basically it was a matter of if the boot fits, then make it. Boots seemed to fit the site, the western wear "Texas chic" obsession at the time, the social milieu, and most importantly, the politics—these were all the pluses. Nikon in hand, I analyzed the scale of the neighboring buildings, took photos of the vacant corner and the adjoining areas, scratched out a few quickie drawings, and pasted in a cutout of some cowboy boots clipped from a magazine.

When I arrived in D.C. in July of 1979, one assistant was assigned to work with me; a guy named Michael McCall, nicknamed Captain Squid. He had an art space in an office building nearby. Since D.C. artists didn't have much of a loft scene, they often used rundown, inner city office spaces. I needed a welder. McCall didn't know how to weld, but he sure as hell was fixin' to learn. Mary Pettus became my development director.

I kept my luggage and tools in my car while the WPA worked on my accommodations. That's when I began to realize that again, I was going to have to finagle my way through another project. Washingtonian bureaucrats were about to get a lesson in the Texas hustle. "Shameless exploitation for the community good," as Paul Newman says. Looking back, I could have walked away from the project when it became obvious there wasn't a whole bunch of money on hand, but I was determined to let the wheeling and dealing begin. At the very least I could end up owning what I made, and, theoretically, if I could find a home somewhere for those giant cowboy boots, then maybe I'd make money. If it wasn't for that vague monetary reassurance, I'da been gone like a scalded dog. I originally thought I'd be in D.C. for a month. It ended up being closer to three.

The WPA eventually found me a free hotel room in the Washington Hotel, which was located close to the White House. All they needed was for someone to contact the parent company in San Antonio to confirm an arrangement. The Washington Hotel (my father had been a desk clerk there in the early '40s) was owned by a company called Gal-Tex, which also owned the famous Menger Hotel in San Antonio where Teddy Roosevelt and the Rough Riders used to stay. It was across the street from the Alamo. I phoned up the head guy and explained my situation. It turned out he knew my father, Chaffin, who once managed hotels in San Antonio. I explained that I was in Washington, D.C., doing this huge project and was having a problem finding accommodations. All I asked for was a small, undesirable broom closet next to the freight elevator or the ice machine. He called back to set me up with a room for as long as I needed, and it proved to be one of my biggest freebies of all time. I had scored a hotel room for three months overlooking the Washington Monument! I watched the Fourth of July fireworks celebration that year from the window of my room.

Daddy-O Goes to Washington! On a typical day I would meet with two hundred people at a Texas breakfast club and then lobby for my giant cowboy boots project. At a meeting designed for Texas newcomers, I stood up with my maquette, flyers, and presentation as Nodal introduced me.

"I'd like to introduce Mr. Bob Wade, who's associated with the Washington Project for the Arts. He'd like to give you a quick rundown on why he's in town and what he wants to do."

Clad in my new three-piece eggshell suit, I stood up and machine-gunned my pitch.

"*The Biggest Cowboy Boots in the World,* another monumental work of art by Bob Wade, native Texan, June through October, three blocks from the White House on a empty corner lot, 12th and G at the metro center, forty feet high, thirty feet long, heel to toe, simulated ostrich skin, high tops with collars, pointed toes, fashion heels with caps, elaborate stitching, formed by spraying urethane foam over tubular steel and wire armatures, dismantled for easy transport, curated by the Washington Project for the Arts and its new outdoor program, Washington Art Site, and funded in part by the National Endowment for the Arts, matching contributions are tax deductible."

My pitch was successful and I soon received some funding. It was time for Daddy-O to get to work.

12th and G was such a busy intersection that the first thing I needed to do was build a chain-link fence around the empty lot so our supplies wouldn't walk away at night, or people wouldn't swarm us during the day. A plywood fence (like those found on most urban construction sites, where they drilled peepholes and sponsored children's groups to paint murals on the outside) just wouldn't do. As with all of my outdoor art projects, we wanted people to be able to watch the process while walking or driving by.

The first thing I learned was that the minute you walk into a chain-link fenced area with a bucket of junk, wood, and pieces of steel, within minutes of dumping the stuff on the ground, you have twenty people hanging on the fence watching. Not only are they watching, they're yelling things like "Hey, mister! What's this going to be?"

It was kinda like Art Park.

We had to construct the tops of the Boots horizontally rather than up in the air on ladders, because that was impractical and dangerous. Soon the boot tops looked like four long miniature Quonset huts covered with wire mesh. They ran the length of the lot. We told the crowds they were dog cages.

There's usually a nice big professional-looking sign at a project site telling you what's coming—a shopping center, a high-rise, whatever—so I made a four-foot-square painting of what the cowboy boots were going to look like when they were finished. Underneath I added the slogan THE BIGGEST COWBOY BOOTS IN THE WORLD, my name, and Washington Project for the Arts. Even though the sign was only a few feet away, all we heard all day long was "Hey, mister! What's it gonna be?"

One helpful character I met was Uncle Sam—yes, the real deal Uncle Sam. John Rusk was a tall gentleman authorized by the government to march in D.C. parades. He also dispensed flags with certificates saying they had flown over the U.S. Capitol. Some had been hastily run up and down the flagpole, but still had "flown" over the nation's capitol. While I was at work on the Boots, Uncle Sam walked up and down the chain-link fence, greeting people, answering questions, and shaking hands with the kids. He was the perfect glad-handing host and foil. Sometimes he'd wear his Uncle Sam outfit and top hat, sometimes he had on a cowboy outfit with his

pants tucked into his boots because—of all things—this Uncle Sam was from Texas. He was a fine American, as Kinky Friedman would say.

When our Uncle Sam volunteer dropped by, the crowd would be shoulder to shoulder, watching and waiting. Daddy-O's in the cage. Throw him some peanuts. As with the Iguana, we began to construct the Boots with steel framework, wire mesh, and urethane foam. I still had to figure out how to unbolt, dismantle, and transport the Boots after the exhibition. Once they were disassembled, would they fit on two flatbed semi trucks? Wind drag was an issue for a structure the size of a four-story building. At the time this was the tallest sculpture I had ever built.

One of the WPA board members, an engineer, signed on to double-check my figures, design, and three dimensional sketches. When we began asking donations of conduit and materials from suppliers, D.C. was going through some renovation and a lot of the older downtown buildings were being razed. Within some of the rubble we found giant steel beams and rods. We would make our pitch at the demolition sites and load up. As a result, a lot of the Boots' internal materials came from buildings that had been there a hundred years.

Much like building a house, we started from scratch by pouring concrete slabs with bolts sticking out of the foundation. We developed the project in clearly defined stages. As at Art Park, first we created our "backstage" area, a place to get away from the crowds, a quiet place where we could refer to drawings and plans, rest, and have lunch. "Backstage" became a covered wooden deck with car seats and chairs so we could get out of the sun and rain.

At one point, newspapers and television started picking up on us. Joan Mondale (whose husband, Walter, was the vice president at the time) came by several times to discuss public art for her latest book. She had a degree in ceramics and was very interested. A speechwriter for Jimmy Carter came by to talk about the effect government support agencies had on public art getting a higher profile. Most public art in the past was controlled by the architects who placed more importance on the buildings than on the sculptures in front of them. We used to call it "plop art." You make it somewhere and you plop it down. Sometimes it related to the building, but usually it didn't.

When the first boot's skeleton, outlined in steel-galvanized pipe, was bolted into place, you could climb the criss-crosses to the top. At that stage it was time to have a Texas barbecue blowout. We booked a country band to play and invited Texas lawmakers, sponsors, and friends as well as the media to the celebration. Everybody could wander around, visualize the project, and get enthusiastic. Keeping up a steady stream of P.R. and lobbying to fuel the project worked. *Art News* said, "Most people smile as they walk, a rare sight these days in Washington, D.C."

Paul Richards, the D.C. art critic, wrote, "Bob Wade's boots could stomp a bus. Wade's boots are so pretty they could strike Ralph Lauren blind."

Somebody volunteered to make special T-shirts for the crew. A nearby community college sponsored a work program so a couple of art students could come out and help in return for college credit. The city had a teen summer program, so we enlisted a couple of hardworking kids. They were paid through the city; we continued to gather donations for materials with over thirty companies helping out; donations of urethane foam and high tech paint rolled in. My power tools were stolen from the lot only to be recovered by the Washington D.C. police later the same day.

I had gotten so many parking tickets from running errands that by the end of the project, when I went out to my car, I found a "Denver boot" clamped to one of the front wheels. Since it didn't make sense for me to pay hundreds of dollars in tickets while we were collecting donations and local grants for the project, we had the fines expunged with our motto: "Better to make a boot than to get one."

The boots were looking good after only a month. Greyhound buses were pulling up to the curb every day. You could see flash-bulbs popping from inside the buses through the tinted windows. I was building another monument in the city of monuments.

The giant Boots were designed to have a simulated full quill ostrich-skin surface. Ostrich-skin boots have distinct bumps. People who supply the ostrich skin to the boot companies make sure those bumps are as flamboyant as possible. Before the ostrich is "terminated," they jerk the huge feathers out so the hole where the quill comes out of bleeds and scabs over. Then they nix the ostrich.

My timing was perfect. "Boot Fever" was raging coast to coast and everybody wanted a cool pair of boots. They still do.

After bolting the lower front structures into place and spraying urethane foam over the wire mesh, we came back and squirted little blobs spaced evenly all over the toes, stimulating a full quill ostrich. I'd direct the spraying of the blobs:

Put one here.

Plop!
     Over here.
       Plop!
          Now here.
             Plop!

The tops got a white rubberized coating and red lines where stitching creates the intricate upper designs. Then we craned the uppers onto the bottoms and heels, bolted them in place, and finished the paint job using an industrial epoxy paint used for airplanes and fire engines.

After three months we had completed the sculpture. Walter Hopps stopped by; so did Stanley Marsh 3, who rode on one of the toes. Joan Mondale agreed to be present at the unveiling. Much like we did with the Iguana toes we gave out at Art Park, we presented "Joan of Art" with a painted, urethane ostrich bump. Later that night, we were in some bar down the street, all worn out, watching the television, and sure enough, Joan and the Boots were on the eleven o'clock news.

I headed straight to Kansas City to do an artist in residence gig at the Kansas City Art Institute, courtesy of Dale Eldred. While I was there building my Dragonfly, I was desperately making calls trying to track down any possible potential buyer for the Boots. I had to get the Boots out of there because the next artist was scheduled to come in, so the site needed to be cleared out. At the time, I couldn't afford to move them. How unusual.

As with the Iguana, I got lucky as hell. A call was forwarded to me from the Rouse Company of Columbia, Maryland. The Rouse Company purchased art for the shopping centers and corporate headquarters they developed, and had received numerous awards from the national art community for their work. One of the curators,

Becky, had seen the Boots, and was seriously considering purchasing them to send down to one of their shopping centers in Texas.

I called *my* financial advisor—yes, Monk White—and we talked money and figures. The Rouse Company and I made our deal, and we agreed to have the Boots sent to San Antonio where the Rouse Company was renovating the North Star Mall. We made arrangements for a Dallas trucking company to stop on their way back from New York and load up the Boots. As part of the deal, we agreed to split the cost on two trucks—one boot per truck. I was to fly back to D.C. from Kansas City to number every bolt so they could be easily reassembled in San Antonio.

I arrived back at the site and went inside one of the Boots and climbed to the top in the drizzling rain to number the bolts. I was wearing my tennis shoes and slipped on a wet pipe and fell twenty-five feet down through the internal structure, bouncing off one bar after another, banging my head on the way down. I was lying there semiconscious when somebody from the WPA, prompted by a phone call, came looking for me.

"Oh Bob? Are you in there?"

I had a slight concussion and severe back pains and managed to find some painkillers. I had made arrangements to go to an important event later that night at the Corcoran Gallery of Art, featuring a seated dinner and slide lecture by Christo.

Dazed on painkillers, I went by myself. I sat next to Christo's wife, Jeanne-Claude, and across from a State Department staff member who oversaw international exhibitions. At one point I started to feel dizzy and a little queasy. I said to myself, Daddy-O, it's time to get up and walk out the front door quickly. I got up and left without saying good-bye. As I walked down the front stairs of the Corcoran, I noticed a park with a bench across the street. Goofy on cocktails and medication, I maneuvered myself across the street and, like a sleepy child, climbed onto the bench in the fetal position with my three-piece suit on. I dozed off to sleep, which wasn't a smart thing to do at night in downtown . . . or anywhere.

About thirty minutes later I began to hear voices coming from the museum. The gig was letting out and they were spilling out of the Corcoran. I sat up like a hungover wino. One of the people who knew me pointed to the park bench.

"Look! There's Bob Wade!"

It wasn't one of the finest performance pieces in my career.

The cranes and the trucks showed up in the drizzling rain the next morning. The Texas truckers jumped out of their cabs, wearing cowboy boots. First they stared up at the monument, and then back down at their favorite footwear. Meanwhile, a third eighteen-wheel low-boy pulls up. I walked up to the driver in charge. Why was there a third truck? It turned out that he caravaned with them just in case they needed a backup. I cringed. I couldn't afford another thousand bucks for a third trucker.

Three hours later, the stuff was finally rigged up—onto all three trucks. Two of the vehicles had a technically illegal load. Too high, too wide, and too long—the story of my life, come to think of it. I would later write a country-western tune with that title.

The plan called for the three truckers to stay in touch by CB radio and avoid the main road checkpoints all the way back to Texas. The only problem they had was just before they left D.C. The boot peak coming up from the toe was pretty high up, and the truckers miscalculated its height by a few inches. The piece stuck under a bridge, so much so that they had to stop and pry it downward with a crowbar. I was approached by a passerby as I watched the caravan head out of D.C. and back to Texas.

"Hey, mister! What happened to those big boots?"

"Why, they're truckin' to Texas!"

A few days later, I met the drivers at the San Antonio end. The components were going to be stored inside an empty building that housed an old department store while they were being touched up. When they came rolling into that parking lot, I swear it felt just like Christmas. Since I lived in San Antonio as a kid and had so many memories, I felt a surge of homecoming. Grown men and their toys.

Slabs were poured in the same configuration as in they were in D.C. The new concrete footings weighed 84,000 pounds each. The parts were pulled out of storage, the crane arrived, and the Boots finally fell into place. Lots of friends including Monk, Lionel Bevan, and Peter Gill helped with the unveiling. They hired mariachis, brought in margaritas, and kicked off a Texas-style reinstallation party.

San Antonio still remains a happy home for *The World's Biggest*

*Cowboy Boots.* Located near the airport and right alongside the freeway in front of North Star, they're definitely roadside art.

Every year when the rodeo comes to San Antonio, a radio station erects a crow's nest and broadcasts live from the top of one of the Boots. Below, rodeo fans hang out and drink beer. During one of the rowdier celebrations, somebody kicked a three-foot hole in one of the heels. As I made arrangements to fly down and repair it, I received another frantic call from one of the secretaries at the shopping center office.

"Mr. Wade, Mr. Wade," said the voice on the phone. "We need to get you down here fast. The Boots are on fire! We need to see if there's any damage inside."

"How could they burn?" I wondered aloud. "The urethane is fireproof, and the rest is concrete and steel."

White smoke had billowed from the top of one of the Boots. The fire department was called. Sirens wailed as folks surrounded the burning boot. A coughing, disheveled figure of a man emerged from the sculpture. Security had discovered a homeless person living in the left boot. When you consider that it's thirty feet from toe to heel—although it's pointed at the tip—you realize it's fairly spacious inside. It's insulated so it's cool in the summer, warm in the winter. It's not a bad place to crash. The dude had set up peepholes and an exhaust port; he cooked with a sterno can and smoked cigarettes with the high school kids. On that particular day his lunch and his cigs got out of hand and smoke poured out of the top of the boot.

In 1993 while I was in San Antonio, I asked to climb to the top of the Boots one more time. I went there with a television station that thought it would be a classic photo opportunity, but the shopping center security told us no because they were afraid that the Boots wouldn't be structurally sound. I noticed that the trapdoor lock was missing and instructed the film crew to set up fast as security drove away. As I climbed the inner structure, my memories of D.C. flooded back. As I got closer to the top, I passed stray beer bottles and spray-can graffiti messages. I made it up to the old crow's nest, waved to the cameras down below, then climbed back down. I made the six o'clock news that night.

Even now, over 100,000 people see the Boots every week, and 300,000 people see them during a holiday. On any given day there are at least ten tourists sitting on the toes having their photographs taken. If an actual person were in scale with the Boots' foot size, that person would need to be two hundred feet tall to model them. More importantly, how much beer would the Boots hold? According to my calculations, 35,000 gallons each.

Hey mister—do da Boots leak?

# Chapter Fourteen

# The Bronze Age

ONE of the defining trade-
marks of Daddy-O has be-
come critters. In 1982 I was
contacted to compete for a
commission to do a project for a shopping center outside Houston
in Pasadena, Texas. The required subject matter, of all things, was
armadillos. They wanted something bronze and approximately twelve
feet long. The center asked a number of artists to submit their ar-
madyllic ideas. After sending my drawings, I got the commission.
When I met with the head guy, he stressed that he would need a
three-dimensional study—to show what this thing would look like.
Instead of creating an elaborate tiny sculpture, it occurred to me

that I could easily go see Byron Jernigan in Waco and order a fresh armadillo "stuffed" in the position that the sculpture required. My idea was to create a cowboy riding a bucking armadillo. I figured I could go to the dime store and find a plastic cowboy that I could mount onto the armadillo. I then would spray the whole maquette with statuary bronze metallic paint.

I headed down to Waco with my drawings. Byron already had gutted and sewn the "fresh" armadillo. We positioned and mounted it with his front feet nailed to a piece of wood. Next we put the urethane foam can right up to the asshole and filled that bugger right up. As he filled, we bent the poor critter into the bucking position, back legs bent at the knees, pointing upward, head slightly turned, the body twisted just like bulls when they're trying to buck persistent cowboys. We held it in that position until the foam hardened. Once it set, we had ourselves a bucking armadillo. I took it back to Dallas, scrubbed it down, rigged the cowboy on and spray-painted the shit out of the maquette.

Ladies and gentlemen, *Dasypus novemcinctus*!

*Novemcinctus* is rooted in the Latin word for nine—*novem* (as in November)—which is the number of bands on the back of a typical Texas armadillo. The center guys went nuts and the deal was done. Off they went, back to corporate headquarters. Check's in the mail. Let's get started.

I constructed the internal structure at my studio on 5110 Lemmon Avenue (nicknamed Daddy-O's Patios by Monk White) and loaded it into the back of an El Camino—the same vehicle we used to haul Funeral Wagon the stuffed bucking bronco to L.A. With the Bucking Armadillo skeleton—a steel framework covered with wire mesh—in the back of the El Camino, we drove to Weatherford, a little town outside of Fort Worth, where Larry "J.R." Hagman comes from. Larry has always been one of my favorite professional Texans.

It was a correct and realistic piece because one of my buddies, a real cowboy named Lionel Bevan, came out to Weatherford and posed. Because it was a haul to Dallas, I stayed in Fort Worth at my friend Johnny Langdon's guest house for a few weeks. I'd get up in the morning, gather all my goodies, then drive to the foundry. It was the summertime—of all times to be working in a Castleberry foundry pouring bronze. It was so hot, it was unbelievable. Working on a twelve foot long clay 'dillo was gonna be endless.

I had hoped that happy hour each day would revive me and my crew, but unfortunately for Daddy-O, Weatherford was situated in a dry county, meaning neither the 7-Elevens nor any grocery stores were allowed to sell beer. So on my way to the foundry each morning, I would stop at the same 7-Eleven in Fort Worth and buy a case of beer and a couple of doughnuts. After a while, the clerks started looking at me funny.

With the help of a couple of local "detail experts" we finally finished the clay original. After they pulled the mold, the Bucking Armadillo was cast by Metz and Joe and a bunch of their family assistants. It took eighty sections all welded together.

The unveiling party at Pasadena Town Square was held in a dry county, so we had to go back and forth to a party room on the other side of the shopping mall complex to get a drink. We made several trips. Lionel had his baby blue lasso, and by about the sixth trip, this girl walks up to him and asks, "You can't really use that rope, can you?"

"Why, sure I can!" Lionel said.

So she bent over, grabbed her ankles and said, "Well, rope this."

I have a great photo, with the loop laying right over her ass.

Who would bronze a little white lie? The corporate dudes, that's who.

On the plaque they cast is a mythical story about *Daisy Belle,* which is the sculpture's name. It makes reference to one of the last of the famous exotic breeds of giant armadillos that were on the endangered list for a number of years and now have become extinct. But in the early days of rough and rowdy Texas, some of the rodeos utilized bucking armadillos in some of their events. This statue is dedicated to the memory of one of the most famous, Daisy Belle.

# Chapter Fifteen

# The Bonnie & Clyde Mardi Gras Mobile

N 1982, the Center for Contemporary Art in New Or-
leans sent out a letter to
thirty different artists asking
them to come up with a bizarre and funky vehicle. They gave each
of us $1,000 either to embellish an existing auto, or go out and buy
something. We were responsible for getting the vehicle to New Or-
lans in time for Mardi Gras.

Each year at Mardi Gras a whole bunch of big and little parades
lead up to Fat Tuesday. Each one is sponsored by a particular
"krewe." The krewe that was sponsoring our parade of weird vehicles
was called the Krewe of Clones.

Driving down the road in Dallas one day, I passed a gas station with a "For Sale" sign on a tasteful, dark-gray delivery van. It was part of a fleet of trucks owned by a high-class North Dallas laundry establishment. It looked like a gray, boxy, UPS truck, but was smaller. I paid $700 for it. It ran great and was totally empty inside. It was the coolest.

At the time I had been keeping up with a story about a guy in Garland, an outlying city in North Dallas, who had a rifle range and rented machine guns. He was always in court claiming it was perfectly legal to rent machine guns for people to shoot on his range. Since he was outside Dallas's jurisdiction, he was able to keep doing it. Having shot up cars with the "Waco Boys" for the PBS *Jackelope*, I decided I would use the remaining $300 of the my grant to have the truck shot up. I called the owner of the range.

"I know it sounds crazy, but I've got this vehicle that's going to be in a parade for Mardi Gras. If I brought it out there, could I hire you to shoot up my van?"

He was ecstatic.

"Come on out!"

The reason the cars shot up by the Waco Boys looked so good was that the car was white and the bullet holes showed up better than they would on a darker color. Don't get me wrong, the Waco Boys would shoot anything. I needed a color that would be fun, yet light enough for the bullet holes to show up.

On the way to one of my favorite Mexican food joints I spotted a sign that read TRUCK PAINTING. Not only did this establishment paint trucks, they painted a lot of school buses, so the painter had hundreds and hundreds of gallons of school-bus-yellow paint. That color would be cheapest. That's all I needed to hear. I told them not to bother masking anything off, including the bumpers; nothing but the windows and tires. Just paint the sonofabitch. A school-bus-yellow van with bullet holes would look pretty funny. Dark on light. Perfect.

Once I got that bugger painted I drove it out to the machine gun range. I was getting low on funds, so I asked exactly what it would cost me. He told me it would be ten dollars for labor—the act of machine-gunning the van—and $100 for bullets.

We agreed up front on a few things: He couldn't shoot the gas tank, the motor, or any of the windows or tires. I still had to drive the thing to New Orleans. The rest of the truck was fair game. He blasted the van. Afterward you could tell it was done by a machine gun: That type of gun climbs diagonally to the left, and it gave me lots of beautiful diagonal holes. When he finished, there were still blank spots that looked awkward. The owner put his machine gun down, went into his office, and came back with a beautiful chrome-plated long-barreled Colt. It was the biggest damn pistol I'd ever seen in my life.

I'd point to an area I wanted shot up and he'd tastefully plug that area.

"Give me about five right here."

Boom. Boom. Boom. Boom. Boom.

"How about three over there?"

Bam. Bam. Bam.

After he was done the van looked beautiful. It never occurred to me before driving it back into town that I was fixin' to run into some kind of trouble. Think about it: Dallas is one of most tight-assed policed cities there is. If the average Dallas police officer saw a school-bus-yellow truck driving down the road riddled with bullet holes, they'd figure I just robbed a bank. I was stopped several times. The officer would ask, "What's the deal?"

I resorted to carrying the letter from the Contemporary Center for the Arts in New Orleans saying that I was an artist and had been sent a thousand dollars to create this vehicle, blah, blah, blah.

The Center also invited the Texas Kid to participate. He had already decorated his funky pickup truck, and also had an old-time black Cadillac limo with weird stuff all over it. He planned to take both cars to New Orleans. An entourage of five cousins and nephews planned to help him drive. Then there was me, driving my bullet-holed laundry van. A few girlfriends and a back-up car joined me, and we caravaned our way to New Orleans. What a happy caravan it was: a shot-up yellow van, an eccentric outsider art pickup truck, and a dark, decorated limo. We were sure we'd be stopped at least once an hour, but we got lucky and were stopped only once in Louisiana. The cops were nice as could be, and we came into New Orleans grinning like jackasses eating prickly pears.

The Center had arranged a room each for the Texas Kid and me, but they didn't have rooms for the six other girlfriends and pets we had brought along. Lionel Bevan flew in wearing a bigger-than-life cowboy hat and boots, a long yellow duster Marlboro man coat—

the whole works. I checked the Texas Kid in, wished him luck, and bolted. The rest of the krewe scrambled and found rooms. After a night of French Quarter partying, we were ready for the Art Car Parade.

In Mardi Gras parades, almost every float throws stuff to the crowds, usually cheap plastic beads, which they call "gimmies." This comes from people along the parade route constantly shouting, "Gimme, mister, gimme!" Everybody told me I had to toss something but I didn't want to throw beads, doubloons, or chocolate candy; I wanted to do something creative. Since we were driving a van full of bullet holes, I thought, why not throw something related to guns? I drove to the dime store and bought hundreds and hundreds of little ugly green plastic army men with rifles, bazookas, and grenades. I also bought six-shooter water guns with long barrels. I planned to throw the army men to the crowd as we drove down the parade route, and then hose them a little with the water guns. I also had a stuffed calf with me that had been used as a roping and branding display. It was positioned so that it was laying on its side with one leg in the air and its head all twisted around. Without the ropes and brands, it looked bizarre—real Texas. I tied it to the front of the van. It looked like we had just hit it on the highway.

All the artists and their vehicles met up at the art center. My friend from the Paris Biennale days, Tina Girouard, was in it too. As the parade route snaked its way through town, our van wasn't all that well received. Our entry, while great as art, didn't especially fit into the Mardi Gras spirit. In fact, we were probably the first and only Mardi Gras parade unit in the history of New Orleans that was roundly booed. Maybe nekked girls on the roof wearing criss-cross gun belts woulda helped.

After a wild night on the town, and with Lent setting in, the Texas Kid and his relatives and I decided to split in different directions. My companion and I decided to drive the van on to Houston. [Fifi] had to sit on a makeshift bar stool we rigged up since there was only the driver's seat. After hours on that bar stool in a bouncy van going fifty-five, we decided we had enough driving the van. In Houston I tried to talk my friend and former student, Andy Feehan, into taking the van on indefinite loan. He could carry band stuff in it, and I knew that if I drove it around Dallas, I would end up in jail. Houston, of course, hardly cared.

I named the Mardi Gras van the Bonnie & Clyde Mobile. Anyone who has ever seen the movie can understand why. Bonnie and Clyde loved to have their pictures taken with guns, and lots of my gun-toting friends had that same mentality—the Bonnie & Clyde Syndrome. The Bonnie & Clyde Mobile did its deal in Houston. It transported rock and rollers, moved junk, grossed out a few stuffy gallery functions, and eventually slowed down.

In 1984 I was asked to set up a small survey of my work at the Cultural Activities Center in Temple, Texas. It was a small show in a small town, but it showed balls that somebody wanted to present an overview of my art. In addition to weenies and photo canvases, I planned to exhibit a giant inflatable pontoon outside next to the Bonnie & Clyde Mobile.

George Prater, the curator at the center in Temple, was a former student of mine in Waco. He was hot to bring the Bonnie & Clyde Mobile to Temple, and he had a pickup truck we could hitch it to, so we didn't have to drive it. The two of us met at Andy Feehan's house to tow the van to Temple.

We hooked it up and pulled out of Andy's. Down the road a ways, I noticed a maxed-out front yard complete with weird concrete animal statues, cactus configurations, religious grottoes, and exotic flower arrangements. It was my kind of stuff. I had my camera so I asked George to stop. It never occurred to me that we might attract attention—you know, a pickup truck pulling a big yellow vehicle full of bullet holes. In Houston, which is one strange city, it probably didn't look weird at all. I jumped out to take a few quick pictures of the front yard phenomenon.

From the backyard came a yell in a thick Hispanic accent, "Hey, motherfucker! Get the fuck outta here!"

I figured, shit, eccentrics are eccentrics.

I jumped back in the truck. Let's hit it, George! As we haul it, I notice the guy running from the backyard to the driveway and getting in his car as if he's going to chase us. "Why is he chasing us?" I begin to wonder.

Ten minutes later we were on the freeway, hauling ass out of Houston and cruising easy, when we see the same Chicano dude driving alongside in an old Plymouth granny car. He was irate.

"Pull this thing over! Gimme the fuckin' photographs!"

George had always been patient. It turns out that when he was in the service, he specialized in negotiating and psychology. Now he was asking me, kinda shaky like, "Wade, what's the deal here?"

I shrugged. I had no earthly idea.

Meanwhile the irate driver was screaming and blasting his horn. "You took pictures of my house! You can't take pictures of my fuckin' house!"

We were going fifty-five, as fast as we could go with the Bonnie & Clyde Mobile hooked up behind us. We just wanted to leave Houston. We were scared shitless.

Finally the guy disappeared from our rearview mirror. Sigh of relief. Thank God he's gone. We're out of here.

Five or ten minutes later, I looked in the rearview mirror again.

It was like one of those horrible movies.

He's fucking back.

I looked at George. This was a serious deal. I had some pretty cool shots on my roll of thirty-six, but if I had to give up the film to get rid of this horror show, I would. He waved us over, so I decided we should pull over to the side of the road, and I'd give him my roll of film. I'll lose some cool pictures I snapped in Houston, but shit, it's better than dying, right? After George pulled over to the side of the road, I got out of the car and walked toward the old Plymouth. Suddenly he yells,

"Don't come any closer! Step back."

There I was, reaching, stretching toward his open window, so I could give him the roll of film without stepping any closer and he's screaming at me.

"Okay man, okay."

I got back into the pickup truck and sighed to George,

Let's get outta here!

We drove off. I always knew the Bonnie & Clyde Mobile could bring trouble; that's why I didn't want it in Dallas. It's the iconography of bullet holes and bad shit.

Further on down the road, I check the mirror one more time.

Crazed motherfucker was back again, still shouting about the photographs.

At that point, I'd had enough, so I put it to George this way. "We're on the outskirts of Houston and we're running out of 7-Elevens, which is the best place to ask for help and make an emergency phone call. Find the next exit that looks like it might remotely be 7-Eleven-ish, pull off quick, and I'll race in and call the cops."

We pulled off the freeway into a 7-Eleven.

Here's a couple of grown men in a pickup truck, towing a van shot full of bullet holes, pulling into a 7-Eleven. One guy jumps out of the truck and runs into the store and claims that some guy is following them down the highway. I pleaded with the cashier who finally called the cops, who, literally, pulled up in about thirty seconds. The flipped out dude had parked across the intersection just off the road, watching us. While all this was going on, George—who was taller and older than me and had been in Korea, Vietnam, or somewhere—got out of his truck and walked over to the car.

A whole bunch of Houston cops were now at the 7-Eleven parking lot. The first thing they wanted was my driver's license. I handed it over and noticed that they started running a check on *me!* Suddenly I was the bad guy! Sure, I was talking a mile a minute and my story about this guy following us must have seemed pretty weird.

George was walking back now and came over to reassure the police that everything was under control. George's army training had paid off. He found out that this guy's mother had been involved in some kind of lawsuit with an insurance company over a fall and was trying to score a huge sum of money for a back injury. We were photographing the yard and the cement chickens, but they thought we were working for the insurance company, hoping to find evidence that her back was in good enough shape for gardening.

As the cops were leaving, George was walking back over to the guy's car, mumbling something about giving the guy some gas money to get back. George gave him the art center business card and we all left. It seems the guy offered to send me the rest of my pictures once he'd processed the film and kept the photographs of his garden. Oddly enough, a few weeks later Andy found the photos on his porch. There were no negatives, just some silly pictures of Andy and his tattooed pig on their front porch.

The Bonnie & Clyde Mobile eventually ended up in my studio backyard in Dallas, where it lived for a few years. At one point the inside was mysteriously furnished and decorated with car seats and graffiti, and served as a home for winos, some homeless people, and assorted weirdos from the It'll Do Lounge next door.

Eventually my good friend from Fort Worth, Johnny Langdon, took a liking to it. At the time he was about to marry his high school sweetheart so I promised it to him as a wedding gift, provided he could get the thing to Fort Worth. Sure enough, he did; he called Lionel and Bulldog to move it, and the Bonnie & Clyde Mobile now lives happily in a beautiful open field where it's sometimes used to store hay for the horses.

Its a long distance between the hay and the grass.

# Chapter Sixteen

# Eight-Foot Frogs Allegedly
# Dancing the Tango

*ewsweek* covered another
one of my controversies with
a rhetorical headline that has
haunted me for much of my
career: ARE THEY SIGNS OR ART?

"Daddy-O and his dancing frogs," read the 1983 article. "Yet another battle between the true Texas sensibility and the cult of good
taste." *Newsweek* put me on the side of "the true Texas sensibility"
while my enemies, the Dallas city sign commission, was dubbed "the
cult of good taste."

"Only in Dallas," *Newsweek* continued, "the town that once
banned pinko artists like Picasso, would any bunch of rubes in three-

piece suits fail to see the frogs as art. Daddy-O got more than 25,000 bucks for his frogs, which must mean they're art. Would a sign painter get 25 grand? . . . Daddy-O himself is philosophical. 'I expected a little trouble, but I hope Dallas isn't too small a pond for my frogs.' "

Texas is more than just a sanctuary for cowboys, six-shooters, tall tales, chili, and bravado. True Texas sensibility, I feel, also stands for varmints and critters—like my famous eight-foot frog sculptures.

It all started when Dallas/Fort Worth club owner/restaurateur Shannon Wynne opened a place called the 8.0 in the early '80s in Dallas. He asked me if I would be willing to bring over a large dragonfly sculpture for the grand opening. It was stored in my 5110 studio, Daddy-O's Patios in Dallas.

The dragonfly's appearance at the 8.0's media reception sparked Wynne to offer me an even more ambitious commission. In 1983, he decided to open a large, cavernous dance nightclub on Greenville Avenue, Dallas's nightclub row, inside a former bank building with huge vaulted ceilings. The location had also served as an abortion clinic for a number of years. Wynne leased the building and attracted a group of investors. The nightclub, dubbed Tango, was to have a stage and dance floor, an upstairs video area, several cool bars, and a high-tech ambiance. There would be big-name, live entertainment.

There was another reason Wynne and I hooked up for this new project. According to an article by Texas music writer Chet Flippo, Wynne had been in New York City looking for inspiration to help launch this new club when he visited the Lone Star Café and saw my infamous Iguana perched on the roof. When he came back to Dallas, he tracked me down to talk about doing something for the roof of Tango.

Wynne and I had known each other for a long time. He had been doing some bicentennial projects while I was slaving away on my *Map of the United States*. He and I had also tried, unsuccessfully, to launch a zany art deal called the Limited Edition Replica of Oswald's Screen Door. We wanted to put together some bronze replicas of Lee Harvey Oswald's actual screen door with its bucking bronco design on the front. Together we sent out a prospectus for investors so we could buy the real door, have fifty or so fabricated, and make some bucks. By the time we were able to get past the documentary TV crew at Oswald's, the door was gone.

Shannon was a clever fellow whose dad was very well known for having worked for Walt Disney when the Disney Studios first opened, and later for becoming a celebrated entrepreneur when he returned to Texas and opened Six Flags Over Texas, an amusement park chain between Dallas and Fort Worth. Ironically, Shannon's brother, Angus, was the music director who booked bands for all of the fraternities during my college days at UT. In fact, Angus Wynne was the one who booked the Hot Nuts at our Kappa Sig parties.

Shannon hired me to create something that would knock the socks off Dallas café society. He wanted something with the same impact the Iguana made at the Lone Star in New York.

By then I had amassed an extensive collection of stuffed frogs, armadillos, and various other Mexican curiosities. Monk was still bringing me stuffed frogs from Puerto Vallerta. In fact, at one point, all of my frogs were displayed in the Dallas Museum children's wing as part of a line, color, and texture exhibition.

One girl frog was decked out in a bikini; some were playing dominos and drinking beer; some wore sunglasses. But most of them looked like they were part of some Latin band routine, playing trumpet, saxophone, bongos, or bass fiddle.

Monk's stepson Alex also had a collection of stuffed dancing frogs, too. One of the little critters had his leg kicked out and his arms outstretched, as if he were doing some ballroom stuff. I'd seen them playing musical instruments, but I had never seen them dancing. The minute I saw them, I knew they would figure into the whole project. I built a model of the building, borrowed the frogs, and stuck them on top. I never returned them to Alex because they had bugs in them and eventually deteriorated. They get eaten from the inside out. A lot of these souvenirs from Mexico were stuffed with sawdust, and microscopic mites would get inside there and live. Each morning it looked like the frogs shit sawdust.

Monk finally figured out a way to solve the mite problem. Every time he came back from Mexico with a critter, he'd immediately put it inside his freezer, which would kill all of them.

That was it then. I pictured a combo of frogs playing up on the roof of a joint called Tango. It made total sense to me. I tested my plan on Monk and he loved it, so I presented Shannon with the idea. One way or another it evolved to include six frogs. Shannon liked the symbolism. In the spirit of Six Flags Over Texas, it would be Six Frogs Over Greenville.

The possibilities seemed endless. How about a guy and a girl frog dancing, and the other four playing instruments as the combo, like the ones you saw at a bar in the '50s when you took your date out for highballs and cocktails? We all agreed it was a great idea, so we drew up a contract and said, "Let's go!"

It turned out that one of the club's investors had a warehouse with twenty-foot ceilings almost exactly across the street from Tango. It became the Frog Factory. I could work on the project there without having to pay rent. The Frog Factory became *the* cool place to drop by. Shannon, Monk, or the club investors would constantly visit and bring their friends—much like when they'd come to Daddy-O's Patios on 5110 Lemmon Avenue.

Ronnie and Derek, a couple of the Texas Kid's relatives, became my assistants. They were inseparable. They reminded me of those two black calypso characters in *Night of the Iguana*: they were never apart. One was thin and handsome and the other was short and pudgy, and they worked together, side by side, wherever the work was.

They usually started the day at the Frog Factory with fried chicken and a malt liquor with a boom box playing in the corner. Ronnie and Derek's main job was framing out the Frogs. I taught them how to weld and bend metal frames. A blues musician named Dennis also helped out on welding. Dozens of people would come through day and night to check up on our progress. We'd work late into the night, and limousines would pull up and out would jump these slick Dallas yuppies with their skinny, leggy dates.

We held up giant cardboard frog cut-outs on the roof to see if they showed up well enough from the street, and then I made photographs to help figure out the scale. After making preliminary sketches, we welded up the Frogs, just like the Iguana and Boots. I had my internal framing system down pretty good by then. Urethane foam would ensure that bumpy, amphibious texture. One frog would play sax, another would play trumpet. A female in a bikini with big eyelashes (whom we nicknamed Miss Maracas) would hold a pair of maracas, and the fourth would strum a guitar. Plus there were the two dancers. Of the six frogs, two of them were female, not too bad as far as politically correct ratios go.

From the very beginning, I didn't want these critters to be static— just standing there. If at all possible, I wanted them to be motorized. If we played it right, based on our budget, there would be just enough money left over to get some eccentric wizard to come up with a system to motorize them. Somebody suggested I talk to a member of the Motorized Bar Stool Club.

It was typical of Dallas to have an organization like that, so I put the word out. One day the doors of the Frog Factory opened and in came a dude on a bar stool that had a little motor attached underneath. Little levers on the seat steered him right and left. He was a charter member of the Motorized Bar Stool Club.

"Watch this," the guy said as he did his motorized routine around the warehouse.

We hired him on the spot. I had built each frog on a square-base framework, so they wouldn't fall over, and I told him I wanted the frog band to move from left to right and the dancers to spin around like a turntable. He went to work on this concept.

Time for foam! Foamers were usually funky-looking characters who quite often didn't even wear protective masks. Every time I've supervised these jobs, whether it's been the Iguana, the Boots, or the Frogs, the urethane foam dispenses a spray that I suspect is somewhat toxic for the first few moments. Once it hits the surface and expands, it hardens and dries. It's the initial mist that you must be careful of. In fact, you can hardly scrape it off your safety goggles. Urethane foam sticks to stuff really well. When I did the Boots in D.C. the crew had to go up and down the street to make sure there were no cars parked within a city block of where we were spraying. The stuff could go up in the air, swirl around, and land on all the parked cars and stick to their windshields and paint jobs. The police are now using portable foam guns to shoot globs of urethane onto criminals or rioters.

We lined up all six frog frames for the foam men. They shot the whole half dozen in one day, and, God, they looked good. We took a couple of dozen snapshots afterward with the crew of foamers posing proudly in front of the unfinished critters.

Next it was time to get out the old pruning saw and rasps and carve some details in and around the eyes, the nose, the fingers. You tighten up some details, although not much, around the body. This is where doing all those ice carvings in college came in handy.

Frogwise, we were coming right down to the lick-log. Our deadline was approaching fast. Shannon was under a lot of pressure to make sure everything finished simultaneously. The last thing he needed was an artistic snag on my part. When it comes down to synchronizing construction on art projects, timing has always been something that's cost me a lot of sleep. Another difference between an artist creating in a creative vacuum and a Daddy-O building public art.

Meanwhile the mechanical guy had the motorized process pretty well figured out. He rigged up odd motors with weird springs and rods that almost resembled an oil well contraption, enabling the sculptures to lean to the left, to the right, or back and forth.

The Frog combo's musical instruments were fabricated separately. The trumpet was made out of some galvanized air-conditioning metal. The saxophone was cut out of plywood, a painted silhouette. The maracas looked real but were carved from urethane foam. We painted the dancer's hands as if she were wearing white gloves. We were getting there.

Each year, the St. Patrick's Day Parade in Dallas always took place on Greenville Avenue. It was a serious deal for the city, serious as cancer, so Shannon decided to sneak-preview three of the Frogs in the parade that year, with each one wearing newsboy caps and riding in a pickup truck. They easily won the grand prize.

We had one preliminary coat of paint on these rascals when we hoisted them with a crane onto the roof of Tango. Imagine the vast square footage of each Frog, with its chest billowed out to resemble that stuffed, puffed-out look. Each paint job, not to mention all six, was a massive undertaking. The only way we could secure these things—you couldn't bolt down through the roof—was with long pieces of steel angled up so that they were hooked together. Then we draped lots of sandbags over the steel and the framework to keep them from tipping over.

No matter which direction you were coming down Greenville Avenue, the Frogs looked impressive. People had a great view from both Tango's angles. I was up on the roof adjusting and painting this obsessive creation. The arms of the Frog dancers were extended out, and at one point someone, maybe it was Shrop, yelled. "Daddy-O! Look out!"

Had I not ducked, the motorized frog arms literally would have pushed me right off the roof, down two and a half stories, and I would have looked like a blister from a new pair of boots down there on Greenville Avenue.

On the day of the opening, my girlfriend Lisa and I were up on the roof, doing typically last-minute detail painting, trying to get the spots just right. Count Basie was booked to open the club. It was a big private tuxedo-and-limousine affair and instead of basking in glory down on the street, here I was, feverishly slaving up on the roof. It was very windy and I was using spray-paint. Lisa would hold up a piece of cardboard to block the gusts of wind so I could aim and spray or paint a circle. Paint was swirling everywhere.

The opening was incredible, and I was introduced to the cheering crowds. People waited in long lines. There were twinkle lights, Tijuana Brass music piped into the trees, and searchlights flashed up on the moving Frogs. They were an immediate hit.

Tango was in hot water with the city of Dallas from the git go. On both sides of Greenville Avenue, right behind all of the nightclubs and restaurants, were residential neighborhoods. I don't believe there was ever any real problem with the neighbors against the Frogs; it had more to do with the sound, the traffic, and the parking late at night.

The city of Dallas was contacted about each problem, so they sent inspectors in, and the nightclub had to respond. It only took one phone call to stir up the fire. They inspected the club and ascertained that, besides the sound and traffic, the Frogs could possibly be illegal. Was there a permit for the Frogs? Did they exceed standards of height? Our contention was that the Frogs were art, not signs. They weren't bound by the same rules.

What ultimately set the city off was that a brand new committee had been appointed to study Dallas's sign ordinance problem. We had stirred up this new gung-ho subcommittee, and we were its first case! Dallas is very clean and patriarchal—unlike Houston, where there is little zoning and anything goes. This current situation was getting stickier.

One of the problems was the fact that the Frogs were motorized.

Did they attract the attention of the motorists or the passersby, therefore touting the goods or services offered inside? The city laws seemed ambiguous and open to debate regarding art versus advertisement. If, in fact, the two dancing Frogs are doing the tango and the name of the club is Tango, isn't that indeed a direct advertisement to come dance and pay a cover charge?

I had to appear in front of the city hall investigative hearing, which was an unbelievable circus. Every reporter and TV station was there; the hall was packed. Shannon brought in a museum curator who actually didn't really want to be associated with the Frogs because they were not what one would call intellectual—as in fine, minimalist art hanging on a museum wall, but since I had art degrees, eleven years of teaching, and a track record of exhibits and installations, how could they say that I wasn't making art?

The curator stood up and said that Mr. Wade was a recognized artist and, therefore, if I said it was art, then, by golly, it was. It was an old argument that had been used many times: Its quality can be argued, but if a recognized artist proclaims something, whatever it is, as art, then that's it—it's non empirical. One of the questions they asked me when I testified was, "Mr. Wade, aren't those dancing frogs in fact doing the tango?"

My answer was, to be honest, I really didn't know how frogs danced, much less tangoed.

The debate polarized the pro-Frogs camp and the anti-Frogs contingent. The anti-Frogs were the sign ordinance people and others who felt that if such frivolous behavior was allowed, then who knows, there might be some guy who would actually get up on the roof of a Safeway Store and fabricate a giant gorilla holding two heads of lettuce.

The brouhaha with the city council splashed across the television airwaves and the front pages of the newspapers. The Japanese news wires picked it up, reacting to an article in *Newsweek* sporting a four-color picture of the Frogs laid out along the top of the story. By blowing this whole incident out of proportion, the city of Dallas embarrassed itself.

The city finally decided they would allow the Frogs to stay if they passed some kind of engineer's inspection. What happened in New York and what ultimately occurred in Dallas was an engineer inspected the frogs in relation to the rooftop and how the structures were supported. Since the building housing Tango used to be a bank, and the rooftop was constructed to prevent criminals from drilling holes and dropping down inside, it was probably one of the most fortified buildings in Dallas. So much for any structural problems.

We agreed to make any suggested fortification or repairs to anything they might have found during their inspections. The council was finally satisfied that the Frogs were art and not doing the tango. It was decreed they could stay. People then started visiting the roof to have their pictures taken with the Frogs. Almost directly across the street from the club was Little Gus's, one of my favorite breakfast joints in all of Dallas. Every time I'd come off the road, I would race over there and grab a table by the window so I could eat and gaze up at my creations.

I usually work right up to deadline on a project or a painting, and the next day it's gone and I might never see it again. In my haste to finish, I generally don't have time to relax and savor a piece. Sure, I worked on it, but sometimes I was too close and involved to appreciate it. With the Frogs, I had the chance to sit at the window and just stare across the street. As with all of my public projects, I had lots of fringe collaborators, such as crane operators, city councils, and newspaper reporters. Stuff takes on a life of its own.

Wouldn't you know it, after all the work, hearings, and publicity, the nightclub started going downhill. The Frogs, meanwhile, were still on the roof doing their motorized routine. Tango came to an end, closing less than a year after it opened. The plywood guitar was jerked out of a Frog's arm and used to board up the rooftop door. Everything was ordered to be auctioned to pay a mountain of bills, including the Frogs. This seems to happen to me quite often. The Iguana was auctioned off when the Lone Star decided to close down its Fifth Avenue location and reopen up on 52nd Street. Like barstools and silverware, the Frogs were auctioned off to pay the bills.

# Chapter Seventeen

# I Don't Want to Change You . . . But Just

# Don't Get Any Worse

**VERY** year for our anniversary, Lisa gives me the same card. It reads, "I Don't Want to Change You . . . But Just Don't Get Any Worse."

I met Lisa in 1982 at a big art weekend in Santa Fe that she was covering for an art magazine. Artists and dealers came in from out of town to attend the concerts and parties. She was renting a house in Galisteo from a doctor who was traveling around the world, and she was having a dalliance with a musician who happened to be playing that night. They'd met that year in Boulder and there he was in Santa Fe.

I was in town to do some bidness with Amarillo Dave, who had just published a set of lithographs of one of my Waco Boys pieces. We had attended a concert and were headed to a late after-party at his house, when . . . there stood Lisa. I only had to take two steps to meet her. At first I thought she was the sister of somebody I knew. I tried my best at conversation.

She bit my head off. "I don't have a sister! Who the hell are you?" I introduced myself. "Bob Wade."

"Oh!" she said in a huff. "I've heard about you. You're a crazy fuckin' artist from Dallas. Get your hands off me! Don't touch me!"

For some reason, I took out twenty bucks and tried to give it to her.

"I don't want your money!" she said to me. "Just leave me alone."

Catching herself, she apologized and told me that she had just had a fight with her boyfriend. I was sympathetic and hopeful, and we talked through the rest of the party. After everyone left, we ended up staying a bit longer, as I was hoping to get a ride to my hotel in her Porsche. Luckily I got the ride and a bit more. I couldn't even remember her name. I had to called a buddy of mine, Palmore, to find out what to call her besides "Oh, baby."

The next time we met was at the DeVargas Hotel in Santa Fe, where the St. Francis is now. There was a fight in the alley behind the hotel, so I had to throw beer bottles down from my room to break up the fracas. I showed her the color Xeroxes of my Bonnie & Clyde Mobile, which I had just completed, and she acted like she dug it. Later that night I was back in Texas, gone from Santa Fe as fast as I'd arrived.

A couple of days later I phoned her and invited her to Big D. She was attracted to my childlike nature, and said she'd think about it. She eventually called me back and said she'd go only if I could guarantee air-conditioning. She'd heard the nights were a bit warm in Dallas. I must admit, that's the first time I'd ever courted a girl with air-conditioning.

I met her at Love Field airport with a gardenia. As we were walking through the airport, an old Denton friend of mine wearing a big cowboy hat came running by, a lot like O.J. Simpson in the Hertz car rental commercials.

"Hey, Daddy-O!" he said. "How ya doin'?"

"Good to see ya, man," I waved back to him. Three federal mar-

*Bicentennial Map of the U.S.A.*, 1975–76, Farmers Branch, Texas. 300 feet wide.
(Photo: Stu Kraft)

*Texas Mobile Home Museum,* 1977, at the Paris Biennale. 1947 Spartan Trailer
coach.

Daddy-O and *3 Frogs*, 1992, at Chuy's in Dallas. 8 feet tall,
urethane foam and steel. (Photo: Elizabeth Grivas)

En route to Cal State,
Los Angeles, for
TEX/LAX show, 1976.
Wade and friends
transport stuffed horse
"Funeral Wagon" and
Texas art.

*The Boots*, 1979 to the present, installed in front of North Star Mall, San Antonio. 40 feet high by 30 feet long, each; urethane foam and steel.

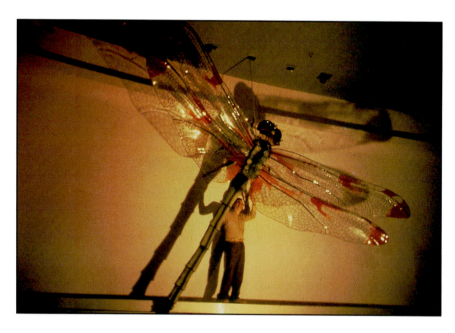

*Dragonfly Texanus*, 1980, appearing in New York City en route to the Lone Star Cafe. 12 feet by 16 feet, plastic and steel.

*Bonnie and Clyde Mobile*, 1982, en route to Art Car section of the New Orleans Mardi Gras parade. Laundry van painted and machine gunned. (Collection of Mr. and Mrs. John Langdon)

Daddy-O wears Julian Schnabel's coat and shows off *Daisy Belle*, 1982, a bronze, 12-foot, buckin' 'dillo for Pasadena Town Square, Pasadena, Texas. (Photo: Ron Phillips)

*13 Cowgirls*, 1979. 4 feet by 10 feet, oil on photo linen. (Courtesy of Mr. and Mrs. Lee Bass, El Coyote Ranch Collection)

*El Salsero*, 1987, make-over of 1950s fiberglass soda jerk for La Salsa, Pacific Coast Highway, Malibu, California. Urethane foam and serapes.

*Bad Guy Gets Drop on Good Guy*, 1950, a Daddy-O childhood drawing. Crayola on paper.

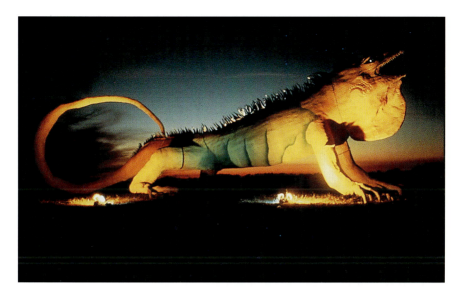

*Giant Iguana*, 1978, posing at Art Park, Lewiston, New York, prior to its trip to Manhattan. 40 feet long, urethane foam and steel.

*Giant Iguana* arrives at the Lone Star Cafe, New York City, October 1978.

*Smokesax*, 1993, commissioned by Billy Blues, Houston. 70 feet high; upside-down Volkswagen, car parts, beer kegs, surf-board, steel pipe, and plastic.

*Map of Texas*, 1973, University of St. Thomas, Houston. 40 feet by 40 feet; stuffed animals, rocks, hay, sand, and beer signs. (Photo: Robert Smith)

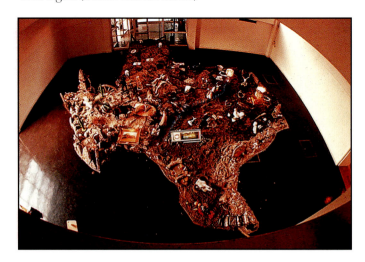

shals followed in hot pursuit seconds later, chasing the guy through the airport terminal. An impressive start, I thought to myself.

Back then it was still sorta legal in Texas to drink from an open container in a car; I carried my fruit jar with a screw-on lid full of vodka and orange juice. Lisa was twenty-six. I was thirty-nine. She told me she had never dated a forty-year-old. I told her I hadn't exactly made it to forty yet. We drove around Dallas in my big station wagon and I took her to a place called the Hot Klub, a punk hangout with bleachers. I found the place in the weekend guide, a "young place" I thought she might like, also a place where nobody, especially a girlfriend or two, would run into me.

Afterward we went back to visit my studio, but I had arranged for "great air-conditioning" in a hillside motel in Oak Cliff that had the postcard view of downtown Dallas. Lisa had no idea what Dallas was like. I was obviously hiding her because I still had a carload of girlfriends around town.

We did bump into "Fergie," my old Iguana-Concorde buddy who forced us into his open air Jeep for a thrill tour of our hangouts. Poor Lisa was forced to meet all these nutsola fools who still hung out at Tom Garrison's P. The round table at the P soon filled up with my old happy hour crowd; Monk, Dirty Little Shrop, Frank X Tolbert, Dickie Bob, and lots of darlins. Jay Ungerman and Buffalo George were usually in there, too, enjoying the antics.

The P is where Daddy Jack and the 7 Screamin' Niggers would crank out fabulous soul and blues tunes while customers had fistfights and threw chairs through the windows. Lisa liked it. Still does.

When we started dating regularly, I would pick Lisa up at Love Field after her $35 flight and take her to my studio, where there was always some party going on. My studio on 5110 Lemmon was a bit much, and she wondered how anyone could live and work in such chaos. I sensed that Lisa was the organizational type, and found out she had been an archeologist out west at the University of New Mexico in Albuquerque. But more than that, her very presence calmed me down and focused me, so I asked her to help me change the sheets on the bed where, unfortunately, she found earrings, and bras, and lipsticks lying around. Whose gold sandal was that over by the front door? One of my friends' dog clawed the wall by my side of the bed, I explained.

During the early stages of our relationship, Lisa and I alternated a lot between Texas and New Mexico. I came back to Albuquerque a lot in 1982 because I was working on a cowgirl print at Arber and Sons. I would borrow Arber's pickup truck and visit Lisa. Before you'd got to Santa Fe, there was a road that cut across to get to Galisteo. I'd drive that route looking at the panoramic Santa Fe vista, and pass through four or five different weather conditions singing, "Rollin', rollin', rollin'. Keep them lithos rollin', Rawhide."

From the day we met in 1982 until now, the longest Lisa and I have ever gone without talking to each other is two days. We've never broken up. Wherever I traveled, I'd ring her up. I'd call from places like Brazil or send weird, funny telegrams. I used to send her flowers until she noticed I was charging them to her florist.

On one trip to Santa Fe, I brought a black-and-white barbed-wire photo piece on photo fabric. I rolled it out to show this visiting art collector and he thought it was great. He told me if I could finish color-tinting it before he left to go back to New York, he would buy it for $300. I was broke at the time and jumped right on it. I went to the local hardware store and bought wood for the stretcher. I stretched the canvas, got hold of some photo oil paints. I borrowed Lisa's Subaru wagon, and rounded up Julia, my Apache female assistant, who was also in town. My assistant and I worked on it together in the parking lot of Bert's Burger Bowl, where we opened up the back of the Subaru, folded out the tailgate, and while waiting for our green chile cheeseburger, we hand-tinted that barbed-wire photo canvas. It became my first art done in Santa Fe. I raced it back to the collector and collected my $300.

I began spending more time in Santa Fe than Dallas. It had no bugs and no humidity! I would come up and stay for a week at a time and do paintings on Lisa's front porch. I enjoyed the idyllic scenery away from the Dallas hustle-bustle. I had been hand-tinting cowgirl lineups with watercolors on photo paper. I knew Elaine Horwitch from years earlier when I was making annual passes through town to visit artist friends.

One day Lisa and I walked into the Horwitch gallery. I had a rolled-up finished cowgirl piece and I showed it to Elaine. She grabbed it out of my hand, ran across the gallery to a group of loud Texans, and told a rich rancher lady she must have it. The rancher lady bought it on the spot. Guess I had just joined the Horwitch gallery.

When I first met Lisa, I used to keep my photo canvases on the studio floor, rolled and rotting. One of the first things she did was find a climate-controlled storage area and take all my fragile pieces there. She stood them up and began wrapping, labeling, and organizing. I was still a madman. I'd give away original slides. People would come over to the studio late at night and I would *give* them paintings. I would turn up at a party and one of my pieces would "mysteriously" be hangin' on a total stranger's wall. Lisa had museum experience and if she was going to stay at my studio, she wanted to start somewhere. I was organized when I was teaching, but after my divorce it was up to my girlfriends to organize me and my art. It's tough for a woman to play so many roles in an artist's life—manager, curator, and girlfriend.

At 5110 Lemmon Avenue I kept an old black couch I found at a Salvation Army drop-off spot. Because of my credit history—or lack of one—none of the utilities was in my name. I was forever running around town with money orders to pay the gas, phone, and electricity using the different names of friends the utilities were under.

Monk paid $14,000 for 5110 Lemmon Avenue and let me live there with the agreement I would move on when someone offered him $100,000. That became Daddy-O's Patios #1. At four o'clock in the afternoon, a crowd was either going to the Stoneleigh P or friends would drive by Daddy-O's Patios, which was between a car wash and liquor store. The rule was if there were more than seven cars parked out front, there was a party going on.

People on the outside assumed that 5110 was a deserted unpainted furniture shop. The car wash next door had a little outdoor speaker that pumped out happy Muzak all day and night. On weekends, people would pull up at all hours to wash their cars. The floodlights stayed on, and people would slap the floor mats against the side of my studio. The kitchen and living space was at the back end of the studio, by the car wash, so we'd constantly hear the *whhaapp* of car mats being slapped against the side of the studio. People would turn up their radios while they were drying and vacuuming just to avoid listening to that speaker that was pumping out the Muzak. I spent years listening to that happy-sounding Muzak until one night I finally had enough. I grabbed a gun, went outside, and shot out the goddamned speaker. Finally, it was quiet. Lisa always wondered, Why hadn't I done that years earlier?

The bed was on top of the bathtub, and for our first Valentine's Day together, I built Lisa a shower. It was a lot of work just to take a bath. She was tired of having to flip the bed up and put the hose into the bathtub to try to wash her hair. The tub's drainpipe was a radiator hose.

I planned a big party to show off the shower. Everybody treated it like another one of my art projects. We put four sliding glass panels together to form a large shower next to the kitchen stove and across from the bed. When it was completed, it was huge, like the isolation booth for the *$64,000 Question,* with absolutely no privacy.

The burner on the old stove was our heat. There were so many gaping holes in the building we never had to worry about asphyxiation. Then the pipes would freeze. For the first year, there were rooms Lisa never went into for fear of what she might find.

Lisa ended up staying in Dallas a lot longer than she planned, driving me around, taking care of me after I had broken my leg out in front of the Texas Kid's house.

It all started when I stopped by the Texas Kid's house to work on a grant application that had to be mailed out that night. An old girlfriend of mine appeared out in front of the Kid's house as I was getting ready to go drop off the letter. She wanted to try to patch up the relationship, so I reluctantly agreed to ride with her to the post office. Things didn't work out, and on the way back to the Texas Kid's house we had another big argument. I was furious and perhaps a little inebriated. She pulled up and parked in front of the Kid's pickup truck which had big chrome reinforcement bars on the front grille.

When I got out of her car, I noticed a neat stack of her stuff in the backseat. In my fury, like some childish, low-rent hillbilly, I grabbed all the stuff and threw it into the gutter.

She ran around to pick up her precious items as I stood in front of the Kid's truck, hyperventilating with anger. As she was bent over I gazed at her rear end not amorously but with the intention of kicking it from Dallas to Waxahachie. I aimed and somehow missed. I spun around and like a bronc rider banging against a corral fence, smashed my leg against that grille of the Kid's pickup.

After a few weeks of my pissing and moaning, Lisa finally took me to the emergency room at Presbyterian Hospital. I found out my leg was broken and was already healing. I didn't have a cast put on my leg. While my leg mended, I carried a beautiful folk art wooden cane carved into a snake that a friend gave me. It looked so real people in crowded airports would move off to the side when they saw me coming.

Since Lisa wasn't the girlfriend who came around right after my marriage or after anything long term, none of my former girlfriends seemed to have animosity toward her. She fit in surprisingly well with my crazy friends and nothing seemed to faze her. Many say Lisa saved my life by later getting me the hell out of Dallas. Dallas was wild for me in those days. It was hard to get anything done. If any of my friends had a date that night, they would always stop by 5110 first for a solid round of drinks. Once after a hard night working on the Frogs, for instance, I came home and went straight to bed, plenty tired.

Honk, honk. Bang, bang on the door.

I slipped on my robe to find two girls from Fort Worth in a limo parked out front.

"Hey, Daddy-O! Come get in the limo, let's go get some French food," yells [Baby-O].

The other one opened up her fur coat and there's nothing on under it. They were shameless (so was I) and I was Mr. Fun. Temptation usually overrode wisdom. When people came over late, I would seldom admit I was sleeping. I'd get up, and the bar was open. Daddy-O was the only thing some of my friends knew about art. They weren't the usual people who would go to galleries or museum openings or collected art, but if I had an opening, they'd all be there. At the very least, I brought in a whole different crowd and element to Texas art.

My openings were always chaotic and crazy. Compared to openings in major cities, the ones in Texas are always much louder and more boisterous. People would fly in on their private jets from all over Texas. I'd always had the attitude that art openings should be fun, and music should be playing. Occasionally a snob would yell, "I don't come to a gallery opening to hear music, I come to look at the art!"

Just getting the crowd to leave was sometimes pretty tough. When flashing the lights failed to get the drunks out the door, I would stage a head-'em-out cattle drive routine. Three or four guys would roam the room making cattle sounds with another four or five guys yelling "Yee-haa! Yahh! Get on out!" and cracking make-believe whips.

Monk sold the 5110 Lemmon property, so it was time to drive around Dallas and look at other possibilities for a new building. Monk and a few others decided to invest in a building.

Real estate hunting with Monk was a trip. Lisa was thoroughly amused. We'd drive around to look and, like dogs, pee everywhere. At every building site, like a couple of water-witchers, we'd pee in the backyard and discuss it.

"What do you think about this one, Daddy-O?"

The plan was that we'd purchase another building in Dallas, re-model it, and at the same time work on projects I had in the works. Still, all through our engagement Lisa and I would alternate between living in Dallas and Santa Fe.

We bought a red brick building on Elm Street adjacent to a for-mer redneck beer joint called the It'll Do Lounge. It was a Hispanic rock 'n' roll hangout that was very loud on the weekends. You'd hear the squeal of tires and loud arguments in the parking lot at closing time over who was going to take whom home.

My old friend Jim Napierala from Art Park had experience re-modeling New York lofts, so he agreed to fly in and help redo the interior of this big old empty building on Elm. My Rasta friend Clement was in the backyard welding the Indian head project while two characters from Georgia burned up four Skil saws doing the woodwork on it. South American guys from next door taped and bedded.

The Elm Street building was great, but the neighborhood was a little hardcore. That was probably one of the reasons I eventually ended up in Santa Fe. One night just after Lisa and I went to bed, we heard gunshots, and I heard something ricochet. Luckily the bed was lower than the actual windowsill. The next morning Lisa found a bullet that had come through the window and bounced around the room. Once, somebody came knocking on the door in the wee hours and for twenty bucks we were the proud owners of a previously-owned color television. I could get a lot of work done even though we had our share of visitors just like at 5110. Duane Thomas of the Dallas Cowboys came by, as did Monk's crowd. After finishing the remodel and Indian head sculpture, I started a project for one of Buddy Holly's original Crickets, Tommy Allsup.

Tommy got backing to do a country-western joint called Tommy's Heads Up Saloon in 1988. Richard Chase was the wheeler-dealer head guy. The logo was a side-view outline cartoon of Tommy's profile on a round coin. They named it the Heads Up Saloon because Allsup was the one who flipped the coin to determine who would stay behind and who would ride in the plane to Buddy Holly's next gig in Wisconsin. As it turned out, Allsup and Waylon Jennings lost the toss and took the bus, and Buddy Holly, Ritchie Valens, and the Big Bopper died that night in that horrible plane crash. The club was to be a grandiose place; it was part of a plan to develop the Deep Ellum area.

I designed the facade: a twelve-foot stucco cowboy hat and boot with a thirty-foot steel piano keyboard coming out of the boot. Everything was backlit with blue neon. They also wanted me to create huge longhorns to hang over the stage. It was a last-minute gig, so I had to hustle up my crew and crank out a pair of twenty-five-foot steel and plaster monsters, complete with red Naugahyde center.

I dragged Lisa down to Austin for the one hundredth anniversary of the chapter of the Kappa Sigs. I said to Lisa, "If you survive this weekend, we'll talk about getting married." There were also two other Texas tests she needed to pass—Willie Nelson's Fourth of July picnic at Carl's Corner, and the Terlingua chili cook-off.

Somehow we got a little off tour and ended up in Acapulco with artist friend Carl Johansen. I got drunk on Coco Locos and when I woke up, I was engaged. Lisa said I could change my mind, but I said, "Hell no, let's go get a Mexican interim ring!"

When we got back to Dallas, a summer's worth of mail lay inside the front door. Inside one of the letters was an NEA check for $15,000 for a sculpture fellowship. There is a God, I thought.

I had had enough of the craziness of Dallas and enough of living in grungy lofts. The Horwitch Gallery in Santa Fe was selling a lot of my art and I didn't have a gallery in Dallas. Still, Texas was the place to fire up welding torches to do work on the big sculptures. Our eight-month engagement was up. I sublet the Elm Street building, packed up the '57 Chevy, and towed it full of stuff to Santa Fe. Daddy-O and Lisa, looking like Ma and Pa Kettle in "Big Blue" full of stuff, towing "Little Blue" full of stuff.

Our wedding was a poolside blowout on Canyon Road in Santa

Fe. The Chief Justice of the Supreme Court of New Mexico married us—after we walked out to the "Love Boat" theme. It was a great bash of Texans, New Mexicans, Californians, and New Yorkers. Later we made two lists: Those who got laid and those who did not get laid.

With the birth of Rachel in 1989, I became a family man again. Lisa remembers the first time she saw me with my oldest daughter Christine; here was this wild crazy guy asking his nine-year-old daughter if she had brushed her teeth. She must have seen another side of me I had forgotten existed. I could have been a better father and I have regrets about not being around Christine more. After dropping her off at the airport after she visits, I'd come home with sunglasses on. Lisa knew I'd been crying. Now Christine is a Tri-Delt college girl. I hope some sick Kappa Sig doesn't gross her out.

# Chapter Eighteen

# The Sex Pistols and the Del Rio Six-Shooter

**HE** Sportatorium was a wrestling ring in Dallas, a huge Quonset hut that attracted the low-rent, white-trash crowd. When they had their fill of overweight guys throwing each other around, they'd go down the street to an authentic Dallas landmark, the Longhorn Ballroom, for a little two-step and a few brews.

The Longhorn Ballroom on Industrial Boulevard was an urban version of roadside art. It was surrounded by peculiar junk shops and tired liquor stores. A twenty-foot cement longhorn steer on a five-foot-high pedestal with cactus sprouting out stood proudly in the front. Around the back was a big fiberglass figure of a cowboy.

Lots of prominent country stars like Dottie West and George Jones played at the Longhorn. The waitresses were the early prototypes for the Dallas Cowboys cheerleaders. They wore these cute little outfits with revealing little vests and white boots. The Longhorn also had a giant Plexiglas map of Texas that showed all the cities and which country star was born where. But nothing compared to the night the Sex Pistols played there in January 1978. Monk and I figured that it was gonna be a big mistake for the Pistols to appear at the Longhorn Ballroom. Maybe it was an accidental booking, but who knew? Maybe whoever booked the acts at the Longhorn Ballroom mistook them for some sort of female country group who wore low-cut outfits and short skirts. There was a Chris Colt and Her Fabulous 45s, but she was a stripper who used to play the Dallas strip circuit.

Back in the early '60s, the Dallas strip joints were run by guys like Jack Ruby. There were lots of cheesy posters of strippers like Candy Barr, with big knockers, dressed in a short cowgirl skirt, a little cowboy hat, and a white leather holster. She'd hike one leg up on a chair and point her big, shiny, chrome six-shooter at the camera from under her leg.

The good ol' boys all over Dallas were fixin' to show up in droves for these Sex Pistols, hoping to see some group of cute cowgirls with six-shooters and skimpy costumes again. Instead, out came this punk band. Monk and I went to the show because we wanted to see what would happen once the cowboys found out the Sex Pistols were British punks. There weren't many punks in Dallas at the time, so the audience was split between skinny little rat punks and big tough beer-bellied cowboys. Big bouncers were usually around in case the cowpokes got pissed off and charged the stage, only I didn't see any extra security that night.

When the Sex Pistols came out on stage, the crowd started going nuts and people stood on chairs to get a better view of the action. Then somebody put chairs up on top of the tables and longnecks started smashing to the floor.

Monk and I were stuck up against the back wall. We didn't want to miss anything, so we piled a table on top of another table, then stuck our chairs on top of that. We balanced our way through the show like two circus performers.

The crowd started booing after the first few songs. Somebody reached out and popped Sid Vicious in the mouth, and he defiantly blew teeth, spit, and blood back out into the crowd. Johnny Rotten sneered at the audience, then Sid forgot his bass guitar parts. There was a skirmish here, a drunken scuffle there. It was chaos; it was excellent.

Back to Bonnie & Clyde. In 1982 after I completed the Bonnie & Clyde mobile, I was invited to do a guest lecture in Fort Worth at TCU's art department. I decided it might be clever for Lisa and me to drive over in it so the students could see it live. What could be a better way to showcase this example of art and outrage?

I was scheduled to give the lecture in Fort Worth in the student union building. In front of the building was a sprawling circular drive where the students hung around during lunch.

As I drove onto the TCU campus, I spoke with the campus police and mapped out my plan. I was to arrive late, after all of the students were inside and seated in the lecture room, and park the Bonnie & Clyde Mobile up on the curb at an angle as if a high-speed chase had just occurred. It was to look as if the cops were on our tail and we had jumped the curb, dashed out, and run off like bank robbers. We had the campus police block us so we couldn't back out and drive away.

I gave a professorial lecture—made the students laugh a little bit and showed them some slides and videotapes of past projects, then Lisa and I strolled out of the lecture room. I shook hands and answered a few remaining questions as the students followed me out the exit. I then signaled the campus police to turn on their flashing lights.

There was the Bonnie & Clyde Mobile making its debut on campus, looking totally depraved, with the cops sitting there. It was a great laugh and we had them going for a long time. It was what I labelled as criminal art.

Lisa and I climbed back into the Bonnie & Clyde Mobile after that and hauled out. We stopped off to eat and visit some friends, and we decided not to drive the bullet-holed van to Dallas. It was dark and I wasn't quite sure how the headlights were working. We pulled into the nearest Holiday Inn, and retired to an inexpensive room. We planned to get up bright and early the next morning.

All we had was my briefcase, a Nikon camera, videotapes, and some jumper cables. Since we couldn't lock the doors, I wrapped the cables around my shoulders and Lisa grabbed the Nikon. It must have looked very suspicious—a dirty old man with jumper cables and a young girl with a Nikon climbing out of a bullet-ridden van.

The look on the night clerk's face as we checked in reminded me of some of my contorted sideshow photos.

We had to drive the damn thing back to Dallas the next day, and ordinarily you could clip along at 55 mph. Sixty was pushing it. As we cruised along the turnpike heading back to Dallas; traffic slowed to an unfortunate bumper to bumper situation. The Bonnie & Clyde Mobile started to overheat. Under curious scrutiny from the other cars, we barely limped into Dallas, looking like crazed white trash.

I was invited by the Del Rio Council of the Arts in 1981 to deliver a lecture and perhaps construct a spontaneous project down in Del Rio, a town on the way to hardly anyplace. I had been in a Mexican jail near there during my college fraternity days, so I was somewhat reluctant to go back.

I was asked to deliver the lecture at the Old Fire Station Art Center. I gave my slide show, did the meet and greet afterward, and arranged to pick up my small honorarium. The fellow who arranged the lecture was familiar with my reputation and asked if there was any way I could get some of his students together and create something out of the blue.

I asked, "What kind of budget do we have to work with?"

"We don't have anything," they answered.

I wondered if they really expected me to hang out in Del Rio for a while and raise money for a spontaneous project. They said that if I would create something, they would boost my honorarium. I accepted the challenge because it seemed like a chance for Daddy-O to leave his mark in Del Rio, plus maybe go back to Mexico again.

I didn't have much to work with. We were on a city block that had only two buildings. The Old Fire Station Art Center was on one extreme corner of the block, and alongside the other corner was another little building that housed the local gun shop where everybody bought their firearms.

It was in that place where, every morning, police would congregate to chitchat, drink coffee, and buy ammunition. I never found out why they were using so much ammo every day, but it seemed like they were there every morning to buy more bullets.

I walked into the gun shop early the next morning after the lecture, and the first thing that impressed me as I looked around the store was a beautiful chrome-plated Colt .45 pistol with an extra-long barrel. It looked to me like a collector's item, and while I don't collect guns, I sure admired its aesthetic design. Garry, the owner of the store, was real friendly, and I decided maybe I could construct a giant version of this Colt .45 six-shooter. Coincidentally, outside the front door where all the cops hung out was a little concrete slab with threaded rods coming up out of it. Something had previously been bolted onto this little five-foot-square spot. Since the bolted foundation was already intact, all we had to do was hustle a few materials and we'd be ready to do something special.

Later that same day, I met with the gun shop owner and sketched a couple of drawings. I explained to him that we would use students to do the work and with a little bit of money he and I could own this giant pistol together. If it ever sold we would split the money. He thought it was a good idea, so we wrote out an agreement and he fronted some cash.

It took us a couple of days to round up the labor and materials. We installed steel framework that fed its way up from the handle all the way up to the barrel. We cut up a fifty-five-gallon drum to resemble the bullet chamber. The barrel was made from shiny tubular duct work we got at an air-conditioning supply store. We put wire mesh over the steel framework of the handle and got a couple of stucco guys to come out and plaster this beautiful, smooth, pearl-looking handle. The twenty-foot-long piece pointed upward at a thirty-degree diagonal. The side that faced the street was completely finished with refined details right down to the trigger. When the law enforcement guys saw our giant six-shooter, they loved it. However, one of them approached us.

"There's only one problem," the officer said. "It's pointing over at the courthouse."

I had used up all the money and it was time for Daddy-O to leave. I made a quick run down to Villa Cuña for old time's sake. The next morning, I did a quick radio interview and split, leaving the six-shooter just as I had finished it. The courthouse was still safe.

A photograph of my Del Rio six-shooter ran in *Time* magazine in 1995 with an article about the Brady Bill. In the picture, the large-bellied sheriff of Val Verde County is standing in front of the giant sculpture. A few weeks later, *Texas Monthly* magazine also ran a photo of it. Neither had my name.

❀  ❀  ❀

My theory is if you're a good ol' boy on any level and you've lived in Texas and you ain't been "downtown," as they say, there's got to be something wrong.

I once borrowed a giant crew cab pickup truck from my buddy Lionel Bevan in Fort Worth. For some reason I had to go through downtown Dallas. Another car cut in front of me and I had to swerve to miss him. When I did that, the policeman on the corner directing traffic motioned me to pull over. He ascertained that I was either drunk or robbed a bank or there was something mighty suspicious going on. That's how Dallas police think; if you behave even a little bit off center, they immediately grab you. I gave the officer my driver's license and they ran a check on me.

I had unpaid tickets.

The old downtown jail was across the street from where I got stopped.

"Mr. Wade," the officer said calmly, "I'm not going to make a big deal out of this, so just leave the keys in the vehicle right there, sir, and quietly follow me across the street. We'll just walk in this door over here."

It was daytime and I was being a nice guy. I hadn't even had a beer and now I was going to jail.

It was the same old story. I checked in and they left me inside a large holding cell with a miscellaneous group of characters while they decided where to put me next. Wasn't too unlike the jails in Mexico, come to think of it.

Like most artists, I depend on the phone to wheel and deal. At the Dallas jail, you could make collect calls. First I called my attorney and then I stepped back while the others made theirs. As I helped the other prisoners reach their bail bondsmen, it occurred to me that I could be making some third-party calls while I waited for my attorney to come down and get me out.

I decided that since I was stuck there I should do some business. I started dialing up some numbers and wheeled and dealed on some upcoming art projects, charging the calls to a third party. The other prisoners were puzzled.

"What's this guy doing? He's talking about sculptures, deadlines, and materials."

Actually, I lined up two solo shows and one piece of ass.

❊   ❊   ❊

*Ghostriders in the Sky* was a quickie project. A team and I did it in two days in 1980. A fellow art professor who was teaching at the Florida School of the Arts in Palatka, Florida, not too far from Daytona, asked me to come out and do a little two-day workshop: show slides, lecture, and execute a project. Unlike the Del Rio Six-Shooter project, the college had a little money to fly me in. The plan was for me to meet with the students, show slides in the afternoon, then get together with the students and plot a twenty-four-hour art experience. We discussed the parameters and the possibilities of a spontaneous, indigenous art project. The idea was to start and complete the project in one day, which meant we absolutely had to be done by 5:00 P.M. the next day.

The clock was ticking. I focused on the aura of Daytona, which hosts all kinds of great motor races. One of the main events is a big international motorcycle race. There are lots of trees in the area, and there are logging mills, so I figured we could probably get a wooden telephone pole for free. I suggested we mount a couple of motorcycles on a telephone pole. We planned to meet the following morning at eight o'clock, split into a couple of groups, and by ten o'clock report back with what both groups had hustled. The idea was to do the sculpture on campus right in front of the art building near its circular drive. We had an open area of grass to work on, with a full view from all of the college buildings, but most of the faculty members, especially those in the art department, were skeptical about us accomplishing all this in one day.

First we needed to go get a pole and get it to the campus. Then we had to figure out a way to have a hole dug. The other trick was to score two motorcycles that were so shot that they would be of no use to anyone. I was teaching the students the whole Daddy-O art experience—set the goal, figure out the easiest strategy, silver-tongue your way through the project, and then deal with the authorities, in this case the college administration.

We got two motorcycles without motors. Then we scored a pole. With two pieces of plywood in the shape of motors, we faked a little paint and brushwork and put them where the motors used to be. At a distance they looked genuine. Next we rigged them in such a way that one motorcycle looked like it was going up one side of the pole while the other looked like it was coming down other side of the pole. We bolted and strapped the cycles so there was no way they could fall off. A couple of the students thought it would be fun to create tire tracks by dipping the tires in paint and rolling them up and down the pole.

We hustled up a gasoline power digger, and dug down six feet to make sure the structure would stay up. It was getting late. It was four o'clock and the sculpture piece was nearly complete, but our goal was to finish at five. There was nary a faculty member to be seen. They'd poke their heads out occasionally through the day just to see what was going on, but they were basically hiding out in their offices.

The only thing between us and the deadline was that the pole was too long and too heavy to just push and lift into the six-foot hole. There was no money for a crane. With an hour to go, we had to dig a gradual trench that led to the hole and hook up three guide ropes. We felt that with the help of a wrecker we could lift the pole up. One of the students knew a tow truck driver. She ran off and, ten minutes later, she returned with both the truck and the driver. The wrecker was skeptical about lifting the pole. I suggested that by maneuvering the guide ropes in a certain way he could pull the long rope forward, and with the other two lines, we could keep the pole from flopping left to right by pulling the ropes taut on each side.

The pole was six feet off the ground at an angle down in the hole. Four students on one side held a rope, another four students on the other side held a rope. The wrecker slowly drove off in his tow truck at the signal. The sculpture was swaying back and forth. By twenty minutes to five most of the faculty were leaving the building. They did not want to be part of this fiasco.

With five minutes to spare, after struggling with the ropes and the wrecker, the sculpture slid into the hole perfectly. The wrecker drove away as we filled the dirt in and took the ropes off the top— at exactly five o'clock. In twenty-four hours, those students learned a whole lot about making art.

The deal was done and we celebrated that night with four or five cases of beer, a quart or two of tequila, and orange juice. The next morning, before leaving Florida, I came back to photograph the finished project on the way to the airport. As I jumped out, Johnny Cash's "Ghostriders in the Sky" was playing on the radio. I took my slides and photos and left, still humming that song.

Johnny Cash, Waylon, Willie, and the outlaws, were kinda making me homesick for a chicken-fried steak at a Texas truck stop.

*Chapter Nineteen*

## The Saga of Carl's Corner

**ADY** Bird Johnson chose Interstate 35—a stretch of highway that runs through Dallas, past Oak Cliff, and on to Waco and points further south like Austin and San Antonio—to be the recipient of her grand, Texas-style beautification plan. Thanks to the powerful wife of LBJ, the highways and byways of I-35 are festooned every spring with miles and miles of wildflowers and bluebonnets.

Along the road out of Dallas, on the left-hand side is the outstanding city of Waxahachie. One of my favorite Texas good ol' boy sayings is "Bend over, baby, I'll drive you to Waxahachie." Waxahachie was the home of the Supercollider fiasco, one of the biggest government technology spending boondoggles in history. Waxahachie was supposed to become a boom town. The little corridor of land outside the nearby town of Hillsboro also seemed destined to be worth a fortune. Down the road from Hillsboro, toward Waco and Austin, is a little town called Abbott, where Willie Nelson was born.

My buddy Monk had always been active in real estate. He'd acquire big chunks of property, on his own or with partners, and resell them for fun and profit. In 1980, he ended up with a piece of land near Hillsboro, which is a little over an hour outside of Dallas and thirty minutes north of Waco. Instead of designing a fancy sign to advertise the land for sale, Monk drove down to the lumberyard and bought a four-foot-square piece of plywood. He took out his brush and a bucket of paint.

LAND 4 SALE, CALL MONK with a phone number.

I remember looking at the property with Monk, Pam, and Lisa. It was called Two Ponds, but in reality there was only one pond. Lisa knew better than to ask.

A gentleman named Carl Cornelius called Monk about the property and they worked out a deal. Carl is one of the prime characters in all of Texas, one of the most outstanding examples of the Texas good ol' boy ethic that I've ever known.

I first met Carl when Monk drove me down to see the property. Monk explained that Carl had just put up a used-car lot on the land and in lieu of a partial payment wanted to give him one of his funky old vehicles. We drove outside of Dallas to a typical Texas roadside used car lot with maybe a half dozen vehicles for sale. Off to the side was a temporary wooden shack with electricity and a phone and that was about it. Inside sat Carl. He had three fingers missing on one hand. He was sitting there, leaning back in his chair. He had the best Texas accent in the world. He also had a big nose, a big hat, and cowboy boots, and, boy, he could ramble on forever. While we were there, I spotted a great-looking four-door 1957 Chevy.

Every time I went to Dallas to visit Monk we'd take a ride out to Hillsboro and find that Carl had done a little expansion. He actually wanted to build a gigantic truck stop with showers, a restaurant, a tavern, a convenience store, and plenty of pumps for diesel and gasoline. As time went on he poured a giant concrete parking lot and continued adding more buildings to existing buildings, letting it all sprawl out.

The building codes in that county must have been rather relaxed. Carl knew everybody in Hillsboro. Soon he struck a deal with Fina, one of the big Texas gasoline firms, and Carl's truck stop started looking pretty legitimate. Carl's old friend Willie Nelson hung out at the truck stop, playing dominos with him whenever he was near his old hometown of Abbott. Carl's restaurant served chicken-fried steaks the size of Rhode Island with mountainous blobs of snow-white mashed potatoes smothered in homemade gravy.

Carl's truck stop service did have one little extra nice touch. Truck drivers who wanted to park in his lot overnight and sleep in their cabs could leave a wake-up call. Cute little waitresses handled the calls as follows: One of the ladies in a tight little white outfit would go out with a squeegee on a long stick and a little bucket of water. She would knock on the truck door. When the truck driver opened his door she would hand him a cup of hot coffee and then go around and squeegee off the windshield. It was a hell of a good deal.

Carl had created his own little empire. Eventually he figured he needed some kind of monument that was visible from down the highway—something that would tell the average traveler that they were fixin' to come upon something fantastic: Carl's Corner Truck Stop.

Carl asked me to come down and figure out what we could erect along Interstate 35. Since it was illegal to just slap up a new billboard, what he really needed was some kind of giant sculpture to grab the attention of motorists zooming out of Dallas on their way to Waco and Austin.

How about a 150-foot long, eighteen-wheeler cattle truck? I thought.

I had used telephone poles a lot over the years for outdoor projects, and loved putting stuff on top of them, so we hired a friend of Carl's to erect a bunch of telephone poles off the freeway on the way to Carl's Corner.

Next I acquired thirty or forty galvanized cattle gates. These gates had a similar geometric pattern to cattle truck sides, which have diamond-shaped holes so the cattle can breathe. If I clustered a bunch of them together and mounted them to the poles in a long rectangular configuration, the cattle gates would create the illusion of a giant cattle trailer.

The scale of this roadside attraction was immense—150 feet long by 30 feet high. By using cattle gates, the wind could blow through the open holes, thus eliminating any problems of wind drag, which could blow the entire structure over.

As Carl's guys mounted the cattle gates, I drove down to Lake Whitney, another little town twenty minutes from the truck stop, and hooked up with a local welder/fabricator named Orlis who lived in a house trailer with cats and goats roaming around his property. Lake Whitney is a typical Texas resort town with cabins and boats. There's a lot of bait and, as a consequence, a lot of fishing.

Orlis fired up his welding torches and created a giant, flat steel cutout of the cab—the tractor, as they call it—complete with fake lights, bumpers, and smokestacks: the whole works. I then salvaged some massive Caterpillar tires for wheels, since you could get worn-out ones for almost nothing.

Finally, I welded some gigantic steel cutout letters across the trailer. Because of state and local ordinances we couldn't legally post something like "Carl's 1/2 Mile Ahead" or "Carl's Next Exit," so to keep within the legal boundaries of art on the highway, the giant eighteen-wheeler merely said "Carl's."

In exchange for erecting the giant eighteen-wheeler, I was paid some cash, the four-door '57 Chevy I'd been eyeing on Carl's lot, and this fabulous carved wooden cowboy couch with gigantic cowhide cushions. I still drive the '57 Chevy from time to time. In fact, I cruised around in it regularly in preparation for writing this book.

Even though it was fifteen minutes outside of Hillsboro, Carl's place was still out in the middle of nowhere. As the truck stop thrived, some of the transients working for him decided they wanted to live on the property, so Carl acquired some travel trailers and mobile homes and put them on the other side of the highway. He rented them out to the cook, the hired hands, and his maintenance staff.

Carl's truck stop was originally situated in a "dry" part of the state. Texas law stated that if Carl had enough people living in this little trailer community, he could incorporate as a city. Then they could vote the town "wet" and legally sell liquor. It wasn't too long before the numbers worked out, and Carl had the minimum amount needed to create his little city. As soon as the town was formed, Carl and his employees officially voted the new town "wet." It was announced in the papers across the state: CARL'S CORNER, NEWEST TOWN IN TEXAS. Carl then opened a bar inside his truck stop, right next to where the truckers ordered their chicken-fried steaks. My buddy Mike Young noticed the lollipops on the counter in all different flavors. Raspberry, blueberry, boysenberry, and his favorite flavor, Marion Berry. Only in Texas.

When Carl's Corner became a city, people flew in on helicopters for the official grand opening. Sunset Carson, an old Western movie star making a comeback, was there to shake hands. They had bands playing; it was an enormous event. Carl phoned me shortly after the celebration. "You know, Daddy-O, I've got this bar here, and now we've got some strippers, too."

He named his bar Le Barn.

I drove down to Carl's Corner and, sure enough, there was a great lookin' bar with a little stage on the side. Carl had bought all kinds of stuff from a defunct rib restaurant chain called Victoria Station, which had decorated each of their locations with real railroad club cars. Le Barn became the victim of an eclectic decor. Here were Victoria Station railway booths mixed in with some other stuff Carl had purchased from an old Mexican restaurant that had gone bust. I always loved Carl's brand of scavenger ticky-tack.

Once I stopped in Carl's truck stop to check out the strippers, but the place was empty—no bartender and not a single person sitting at the bar. The stage, with its pole that dancers shimmy up and down, was bare. I walked into the adjoining restaurant where there were about a dozen truck drivers sitting at the tables wolfing down chicken-fried steaks and slurping coffee. I saw Carl, gave him a shrug, and called out, "Hey, Carl, what's the deal? Where's the bartender? Where are all the strippers you were telling me about?"

"Well, I'm going to be the bartender in just a second," Carl said. He spun his head around and spotted a waitress—dressed in her white outfit and name tag—who had just delivered some chicken-fried steaks to another hungry group of truckers.

"[Marie]! Get in there!" Carl yelled.

Carl followed me back into the bar and I hopped on a bar stool and watched him do his bartender ritual. He poured me a beer and cranked up the jukebox. Pretty soon, from some little secret passageway that led to a little curtain, Marie came out in a skimpy little baby doll outfit. She was a little chunky, but she did do a fairly decent bump and grind to the jukebox music. She proceeded to take what little she had on off.

I felt awkward. I knew this whole little scenario wasn't really going anywhere, but I wanted to be nice to Carl.

"That's pretty good," I said to Carl at the bar as I looked at my watch. "Hey, man, it's been great. I better be goin'."

Carl answered back, "Hell, that's nothing, Daddy-O. You oughta see her when she stands on her head and gargles peanut butter."

During the mid-'80s when my Dallas "Tango" Frogs were being auctioned off, Carl attended the bidding and ended up going home with six Frogs for the reasonable price of a few thousand dollars. They had been on Tango's roof for only about a year so they weren't in too bad a shape.

Carl sent up an eighteen-wheeler flatbed to fetch the Frogs. I planned to be in town briefly before the Frogs left Dallas, since it was decided to have a "good-bye Frogs going-away party" at a rock 'n' roll nightclub, fast and cool, run by one of Shannon Wynne's buddies. Everybody was there, and Nancy Smith, the social columnist, wrote it up. The Frogs, loaded onto Carl's funky flatbed, were parked outside the club. They were roped off and lit up by klieg lights. The deejay cranked up the blues and a hip member of the city council stood up and officially said good-bye to the Frogs.

I waved good-bye to my amphibious urethane buddies. Even though I no longer owned the Frogs, I figured they would be put to good use. They were hauled to Carl's truck stop where three of them were mounted onto the roof of one of Carl's gas pumping stations. The other three were displayed off to the side. They were immediate crowd pleasers.

In 1986, I was invited to submit something for a touring exhibition of six sculptors scheduled to start in Austin. The idea was to feature large outdoor sculptures by well-known Texas artists that could be loaded onto flatbeds and trucked around for two years, whistle-stopping small communities like Amarillo and Marfa. Annette Carlozzi was curating the exhibition from the Laguna Gloria Museum in Austin.

I didn't have any large sculptures available, but I thought I could get the truck stop to loan me three of the Frogs. Carl had three on his gas pump rooftop, so he agreed to loan the show the other three. He figured it was good publicity for him and his truck stop.

It was time to call my man Clement of St. Croix. Clement was a great welder and rigger who helped me with the Indian head and Tommy's Heads Up Saloon stuff. Clement and I drove down to Carl's Corner to secure the three loaner Frogs onto a thick wooden platform for traveling, rigged so a crane could grab onto the curved steel rods and lift the unit on and off a truck for two years.

Carl said he'd let us stay in an Airstream trailer nobody was renting at the time. I packed up my tools, and picked up Clement. Luckily, the three loaners were the ones out back and consisted of the two dancers and the trumpet player.

We had a little trouble getting electrical power out back so we tapped directly into a nearby power pole. The Frogs' original mountings weren't meant to be seen up close, so we built a flat wooden facade around the bottom and beefed up their boots. We arranged them fairly close to each other and bolted them tight so nothing would shake loose. We touched up their makeup and kissed them good-bye.

During the course of the tour, I got calls asking how to repair the Frogs' fingers. I finally realized that wiseasses along the way were bending the fingers to create that well-known insult.

By the time the Frogs returned from their tour, Carl had built a gigantic swimming pool out back of the truck stop. You could walk out the back door of the bar and be poolside. Monk and I went to visit, and found Carl was trying to fill up this huge concrete hole in the ground with a garden hose. Monk looked down at the bottom of the pool.

"Carl! Where's the drain?"

Carl looked down, dumbfounded. "God damn! I forgot the drain."

Mobile homes, divided in half like motel units, surrounded the pool. You could crash there for twenty bucks a night. Carl decided to put the three returning Frogs out by these mobile home motel units. Eventually the mobile homes were removed, leaving the Frogs sitting by themselves, still mounted on their platform out by Carl's drainless pool.

I received yet another Frog request, this time from Joe Hobbs in Oklahoma City, regarding a Festival of the Arts celebration. Here we go again, I thought: They want Frogs to put on a rooftop. I hated to bother Carl, but the city's arts council had enough of a budget to ship them. Since the other three were on the Texas tour, Carl generously let me borrow the three critters he had on the roof of the gas pump island. We wanted to be fair to these three—plus, I had an idea which needed these particular Frogs.

Just sending the Frogs up "as is" seemed incomplete. I heard a funny saying years ago about Texans: "A Texan is a Mexican on his way to Oklahoma."

People hear it, look at you funny, and kinda laugh. They don't really get it. I decided each Frog would hold a flag—Texas, Mexico, and Oklahoma. We removed their instruments and fixed up their hands and sent the Frogs up to the Festival of the Arts for their second fifteen minutes of fame. We ordered the poles and flags, and Hobbs kindly completed the joke for us.

When they returned, they were put back up on the roof of Carl's pumping station. All six Frogs were eventually reunited, and they became something of a landmark. Besides his regular trucker clientele, parents driving from Dallas to Austin to visit their kids at college or vice versa, as well as families with station wagons full of whining kids, would all pull off the road to see the Frogs.

Then in 1989, when I was living in Santa Fe, a photographer friend from Dallas called. "Daddy-O. This is J. Allen Hansley. Carl's truck stop is on fire! The flames are fifty feet high! The entire place is in flames! It's on the television right now. I'll send you some photos later."

I flashed back to a time when Carl had called me on the phone, out of the blue. He had handed the phone over to his friend. It was Willie Nelson. "What do you say, Daddy-O? What the hell are these Frogs about? What are they for?"

I put my wife, Lisa, on the phone with Willie to explain the Frogs.

The next morning someone overnighted me a copy of the newspaper coverage of the fire. J. Allen had gotten there fairly quick and videotaped the tail end of it. Helicopters circled as the press documented the blaze.

I later flew down to Carl's to inspect it with my own eyes. I walked through a charbroiled, burned-out wasteland. The truck stop had literally burned down to the concrete slab foundation. Le Barn was gone; the restaurant with the chicken-fried steaks was gone. Fire had razed everything, except for the fuel pumps. It was a miracle there weren't any gasoline explosions. On one of the rooftops stood the three Frogs, a bit charred but otherwise safe.

Everything had perished except some steel beams, the metal gas tanks, the three Frogs on the roof, and, believe it or not, the other three Frogs, which were out by the pool off in a corner away from the main building. At the other set of diesel pumps where the semis filled up, Carl had an actual truck mounted up on the rooftop. A driving school had paid to put it up. It survived the fire, too. From the highway all you could see were dilapidated, burned-out buildings, the metal gas tanks, and three Frogs.

The *Houston Chronicle* spiced up its coverage of the incident without realizing that the color photo of some tourists in front of the surviving Frogs was actually a prank. While appearing to be gesturing like the Frogs with their arms and legs, these rascals were spelling out the letters F-U-C-K.

It was bad enough to have everything burn to the ground. What could be worse?

Carl had no insurance.

Everybody asked, "Carl, why didn't you have any insurance?"

"Too expensive," he answered. "I wouldn't have been able to pay the monthly nut for a policy on a place like this, with gasoline and all this rickety stuff."

Meanwhile, Monk was being paid back little by little from Carl's enterprises. Holy shit! Now it was gone and there was no insurance settlement. After they gathered their wits, Monk and Carl came up with a couple of ideas. One was to hold a benefit in Dallas with the free services of Willie Nelson. A gig was scheduled at the Longhorn Ballroom to bail out poor Carl.

Every country star in the world has played the Longhorn Ballroom one time or another, including Bob Wills, who played this honky-tonkin', two-steppin' joint regularly. Anybody who was anybody and had ever been to Carl's Corner showed up for the fund-raiser. Carl, Monk, and I had ringside seats, ten feet from the stage. I designed the official T-shirt for the event: Frogs and flames with a picture of Carl emblazoned on the front.

Then came another idea.

Mike Young owns a popular restaurant chain down in Austin called Chuy's. Mike is a clever guy, and after being successful in Austin, he opened up more and more places throughout Texas.

One day Mike phoned and asked me if by chance Carl would be interested in parting with the Frogs. I told him that even though Carl was badly in need of money, he had grown attached to them; they had become part of his life. Under these new circumstances, though, I said Carl might be willing to part with three of them. Mike asked me to call and see if he was interested in selling.

Between Monk, Mike, Carl, and me, we struck a deal for three of the Frogs, which gave Carl some much-needed capital.

We made arrangements for Young to turn the Frogs' trip to Austin into some kind of P.R. event. Another "bye-bye." We decided to meet at the truck stop, which Carl was already rebuilding. Mike brought up a flatbed trailer big enough to hold the three Frogs, and he rented a limousine to tow it.

The newspapers and television showed up to cover the crane lifting the Frogs off, one by one, and put them on the trailer. We timed it so as the sun was going down we drove off into the Texas sunset.

I rode in the limo with Mike and as we approached the outskirts of Austin, the local hip radio station broadcast our entry into the city.

We dropped the Frogs off at Chuy's, and the next morning I was interviewed at length by a newspaper reporter. Two days later, the paper printed a big photograph of the Frogs and a long article outlining the latest addition to Mike Young's thriving empire.

Young's ultimate idea was to take the Frogs to Houston, so I agreed to hang around Austin for a couple of days to meet with the guy who was going to refurbish them. Carl hadn't done much touching up and the sun was starting to eat up the urethane foam.

Before these three "road warriors" went south, they wore their new paint jobs north to Dallas and resided in front of the Dallas Chuy's. Then it was back to Austin for a Christmas parade, where my daughter Rachel rode on the trailer with the Frogs done up as elves. A long article, "Saga of the Frogs," and photo appeared in the New York City newsletter, *The Homesick Texan*.

Chuy's made arrangements to have the newly remodeled Frog sculptures towed to Houston just in time for Foto Fest '92. The critters were jazzed up with glitter and new spots were painted all over their varmint bodies. The girl Frog wore an elaborate bikini costume and long eyelashes. With my ten-foot-by-twenty-foot Pancho Villa photo mural on Chuy's roof, and the Frogs in the parking lot, a giant party broke out. In an appearance organized by socialite/fund-raiser Carolyn Farb, former governor Mark White, and Houston quarterback Warren Moon helped unveil the huge Pancho mural.

The Frogs remained in the parking lot for a few weeks, and then moved into the new Chuy's where they are to this day. The other three Frogs are still on the roof of Carl's rebuilt truck stop. They survived a treacherous fire, a two-year trek around Texas, plus trips to Oklahoma, Austin, Dallas, and Houston. Art critics love to ask, will they survive the test of time? Fuck the test of time. Not only were the Frogs disaster-proof, my art had gone through fires, tornadoes, court battles, drunken cowboys, squatters, chainsaws, gypsies, theft, tourists, and me.

# Chapter Twenty

## El Salsero, the Malibu Man

T a party in Los Angeles up on Mulholland Drive in 1987, a guy came up to me and introduced himself to me as "Howdy." He said, "Howdy." He understood I was an artist and told me that he had just leased an old 1950s-style Frosty Freeze along the Pacific Coast Highway in Malibu. His company wanted to turn it into a place that sold Mexican food made with natural ingredients. He told me about an old fiberglass soda jerk wearing a little cap and holding a giant hamburger that had been standing there for over twenty-five years. Howdy said it wasn't appropriate for his Mexican place, La Salsa, and asked if there was any way that I could transform the soda jerk into something that would work for his new restaurant. I said I'd think it over.

Before leaving L.A. I drove past that figure of the soda jerk and took some photographs. I studied the photos back in Santa Fe, made a few notes, and then sent Howdy a few preliminary drawings with a rough estimate on what it might cost. Howdy flew me back out to meet his partner, Lou Adler, the record producer. I had never done a makeover on an existing piece. Since I wanted to make a clean transformation, I showed them some of my previous projects and we negotiated price.

The plan was to transform what I nicknamed the Malibu Man (dubbed El Salsero by the owners) from a soda jerk into an hombre dressed in a sombrero with a serape draped over one shoulder. Instead of holding a hamburger, he'd be serving a tray of tortilla chips, salsa, and chili peppers, and waving a *cuchera*, a knife used in Mexican cooking.

The Soda Jerk was an unofficial landmark of the Malibu area. When we started our work on the site, concerned people would pull over and ask "You're not taking this down, are you?" or "You're not taking this Jerk off, are you?"

I found out that the Soda Jerk had a somewhat notorious past. There were some apartment buildings behind the restaurant overlooking the beach. One day a fellow from the apartments approached me.

"I've got something I think might interest you," he said. "During the time the hamburger joint was closed, some Pepperdine students pulled an interesting little gag on the Soda Jerk man. Here are the Polaroids."

The photos reminded me of my college days at UT. The students had created a urethane and rubber dick about six feet long and rigged it, using wires, to make it look like the Malibu man had an enormous boner. According to the guy who lived near there, it stayed on for a few days, and caused a commotion. It was even reported in the newspaper. The Soda Jerk had also been cast in some kind of B movie. Upon closer inspection, one saw that the movie company had done a bit of a makeup job on his face, darkening under the eyes, blushing the cheeks more prominently, and jazzing up his hair.

I soon realized I had seen this fiberglass fellow before in various regalia, holding tires, doughnuts, and mufflers. You could order different heads or do him up as a cowboy. The bodies came from one mold, and it appeared from the label I found inside that these guys had been made in Riverside, California, some thirty years ago.

Lisa and I stayed a block and a half away on the PCH in an old oceanside motel called the Tonga Lei. It was getting ready to be torn down. Because we were working up the street and because the bulldozer wasn't due to arrive for another six weeks, we stayed two weeks, even though it was closed to any new guests. Right next door was the old Beachcomber, which had already been gutted. The Tonga Lei was an infamous motel where Hollywood types from decades past would meet for nooners and extramarital affairs. We were the last couple to stay in room number four, overlooking the Pacific ocean. It had a beautiful, romantic view.

Once I was sure we were going to be working with fiberglass, I set out to find a nearby surfer type who specialized in working with it. My friend Jim Ganzer, a well-known sculptor from the early Venice days, designed surfer outfits in Malibu, known as Jimmy Z. He suggested a hardworking surfboard craftsman named Scottie, who became my main man on the work site. A contractor named Jens was set to refurbish the rest of the building. He had all the equipment and cranes I needed. As far as help went, I was ultra-covered. My next move was to order up enough scaffolding to surround the Malibu Man. I found enough from the guy who had supplied scaffolding for one of the space shuttles and the Statue of Liberty restoration.

Our first job was to climb up and get rid of the hamburger the soda jerk was holding. I decided to slice around the top and bottom bun, right where it and the meat came together. Just then, Howdy drove up with Lou. They loved what was being lowered down and made jokes about who was going to own the ring of meat. I said it looked like the biggest asshole in Malibu. They said they knew bigger ones. When we lowered the top part of the hamburger bun and flipped it over, hollow side up, I flashed.

The brim of the sombrero!

Looking back up at the lower half of the hollow hamburger the Malibu Man was still holding, I flashed again. A shallow Mexican terra cotta tray! I filled in the hollow bun with a form-fitted piece of plywood to hold the giant foodstuffs.

Standing atop the scaffolding, beer in hand, I gazed out at the post-card view of the Pacific with its ships and sailboats. Babes and surfers drove by in their convertibles and honked their horns. There was a cool breeze coming in as the fast PCH traffic whizzed by.

The next task was to remove the hat. I pulled it off and found a nicely coiffed hairdo that nobody had seen in thirty years, wavy and neatly parted. To put on our sombrero, and reinforce it inside the fiberglass structure, I still needed to cut off the top of the Soda Jerk's head. Since the sombrero was going to sit just above the eyebrows and ears, its angle could hide the missing part of the Malibu Man's head. As Scottie handed down the top of the head, I flashed again.

The bowl for the chips!

The Soda Jerk's head had the perfect texture; it looked like a decorative Mexican bowl. We filled the upside down converted head with tortilla chips made out of sliced urethane foam (coloring it with guacamole and yellow-corn hues), and bolted it down on the Malibu Man's plywood tray. Since the restaurant was also planning to feature Mexican light beer, I decided to add a longneck bottle of beer on the tray. I fabricated the bottle, complete with label, out of carved urethane foam. I also constructed a giant *cuchera* and a green chili pepper over four feet long, full of erotic curves with a bright red stem. I still needed to finish a giant serape and sombrero. I worked out of a small utility shed, and the friends and rock 'n' rollers began stopping by. Of course everybody looked great and had good deep tans. My art dealer from Beverly Hills, Janie Beggs, was always bringing clients by. I had done shows with Janie in Aspen, and her crowd always seemed to "get it."

Another thing I had to do was to change the ethnicity of the Malibu Man. Soda Jerk was the whitest guy you ever saw. California had changed. In order to change him into a suave Mexican waiter, I needed to figure out what color to paint his skin. I stopped by the paint shop, borrowed their big ring of cardboard color sample swatches, and drove down to the Old Town Mexican marketplace. My goal was to find a merchant whose skin tone I liked and, if he wasn't offended, I'd hold the swatches up to him and match the color. In exchange, I'd buy all the serapes we needed from him. I found an understanding guy right away, got the right color, bought the serapes, and went back to work.

I fiberglassed the combined serapes onto some wire mesh and

draped them over the Malibu Man's shoulder. I repainted the Ma
ibu Man's skin and bolted on a long handlebar mustache. His ha
was then reinvented since the original style was a straight-arro
post–World War II haircut—high around the back and clean arour
the ears. El Salsero got neat long sideburns, his hair got longer
the back (El Paso style), and I reworked his eyelids. Originally So
Jerk's eyes were wide open and he looked a little like he had ju
been goosed. I didn't want to be accused of creating a sleepy Me
ican image, but I did in fact lower the eyelids enough to make hi
look a little more casual.

All that was left was the sombrero, and that was tricky.

I cut a hole into the top part of the detached hamburger bun th
I had elaborately converted into the sombrero, lifted it up, ai
rigged it perfectly on top of the Malibu Man's head. The hat stay
on with steel reinforcements going down into the body. After I fa
ricated a top out of fiberglass for the sombrero, I bolted it on, lac
fancy rope around the brim, and gave it a beautiful paint job.

One finishing touch was to change Soda Jerk's big black wo
boots into huaraches, Mexican sandals with the tire-tread soles (
the bottom. Scottie picked up some used tires to bolt cut pieces
tread up under the bottom of the shoes. Since the restaurant w
going to have a drive-thru window, the cars were going to drive rig
underneath the man. When they looked up, they would see th
huaraches' tire-tread soles.

The Malibu Man turned into one of my smoothest projects an
was completed on time without a hitch. A really weird thing ha
pened when I met a guy named Chappy, who was not only an a
sociate partner of the business, but—as the young son of anothe
restaurateur—had been the original model for the Big Boy!

I heard rumors that some politicos might not dig the update
roadside art, but I spoke with Howdy recently and he said El Salser
was holding up great. Like my dancing Frogs sculpture, the Malib
Man proved, again, to be a real survivor, having fought off the recen
rash of earthquakes, mud slides, hurricane-style gales, fire, floods
and storms that continue to plague the Malibu area. Now that I'
stuck a lizard on the roof in New York and put up a Mexican waite
on the Pacific Coast Highway, it was two coasts down and one t
go—the Third Coast.

# Chapter Twenty-one

# Smokesax: The Giant Saxophone versus the

# City of Houston

**NE** of the biggest seaports in America is found in Houston. This port supplies the city with a constant flow of ethnic groups, giving Houston a lot of Third World folks you'd never find in landlocked Dallas. Dating back to the final battle of San Jacinto, lots of people equate the beginning of an independent Texas spirit with Houston's multicultural population. Hence, the city was reluctant to tread on anybody's personal rights or freedom. Houston also had a much more diverse economy compared to Dallas, which was mostly insurance and banking. Houston still has all kinds of economic bases, which made it one of the first cities to stage a comeback after the big recession of the '80s.

It used to be that you could never accuse Houston of being as ultra-tidy and anal-retentive as Dallas. Zoning was never a priority; the city of Houston encouraged people to open up stores and work the free enterprise system. Big money contributed to the large buildings. Houston's freeways were always much bigger and Houston's cars drove faster than Dallas. Then things changed.

There was once a time when a notorious giant saxophone terrorized the city of Houston. It all started innocently enough as a project for Billy Blues, a nightclub eatery cum food corporation rooted in the supreme Texas ideal: a great, successful, barbecue bar 'n' grill that sold a little sauce on the side.

Billy Blues was a fictional character created by two grade-school buddies, Bill Gallagher and his partner John Coleman. The way I figure it, they must have hung out one night and talked about great barbecue places, and the sauces that saturate such establishments. Since it wasn't such an off the wall idea, they decided they'd try it, too. Coleman already owned a chain of small drive-in grocery stores all over greater Houston and was a whiz when it came to anything that involved marketing, supplying, and shelving. Gallagher and Coleman figured they'd fiddle with this entrepreneurial project, and together they created an alter ego, Billy Blues. Every time they weren't sure how to proceed, they'd look at each other and ask the proverbial question, "What would Billy do?"

Gallagher was a wild man from way back. I'd known him through some business deals he had been involved in with some of my old college buddies. He was a Kappa Sig a few years before me, and had been nicknamed "Super Chicken" after a cartoon character. He and another group of characters were partially responsible for what you might call the *Animal House*-style fraternity behavior at UT— as in how gross can you get and have a good time while partying for as many years as you're in school? A question I asked myself frequently during my own superior college career.

Super Chicken married a wonderful woman named Penny who I knew at UT. During my solo show at Carrington/Gallagher Gallery (which Penny owned), Kim, a writer from the *Dallas Morning News* once asked Super Chicken what made Kappa Sigs act so crazy. Without even stopping to think, Gallagher cited his answer: the GI Bill.

Gallagher and Coleman's first restaurant-nightclub opened in San Antonio, and catered mainly to carnivores who enjoyed listening to blues talent ranging from B.B. King to the Fabulous Thunderbirds. Gallagher fancied himself a blues expert, and had a head full of obscure dates and names.

Gallagher's first call came in the late spring of '92. They wanted a big, elaborate, razzle-dazzle sculpture out in front of their new joint in Houston. Super Chicken was rattling ideas off so fast I thought he was half crazy, but Penny, who was one of my smartest gallery reps, was asking the right questions. They wanted to come out to our house in Santa Fe and show me the blueprints of the restaurant so I could get a sense of the building scale. They wanted me to make something that would attract a lot of attention—they wanted something in the spirit of the Iguana and the Boots. Their kids came along, so we had quite the gathering of fools at the Wade house in Santa Fe. Super Chicken—with Penny and their daughters in tow—trundled up our long driveway with a beer cooler.

Gallagher always moved fast and kind of jerky, like he was excited about something. After we exchanged our hellos and secret fraternity handshake, Gallagher tripped on his way to the swimming pool and the beer cooler crashed to the ground, sending all the beer and ice rolling out onto the concrete.

Gallagher didn't even stop to pick up the beer. Instead, he cannonballed into the pool. He never even looked back. That's when I realized I'd better be ready for anything. Super Chicken wasn't messing around. He had things planned out.

After swimming for a couple of hours we retired to the Daddy-O studio to look at all the funny stuff on the walls, including some old fluorescent orange and dark blue silk-screened R&B posters that I'd collected over the years. Gallagher and Penny pulled out their blueprints. They had the whole deal down: the logo, the architectural drawings, the floor plan, brochures, figures, and numbers. It was well thought out—impressive, I must admit—all put together and ready to go. Super Chicken was ready to roll. We set up a loose deadline to begin around Christmas. But for what? All we knew was it had to be big.

Gallagher's architect friend Ted Heesch was on this project, and was a veteran of fun and unusual Houston gigs. It was decided that Bill, Heesch and I would coordinate our efforts so that the building and sculpture would work well together.

Everything in Houston is done on a grand scale. Strange manifestations crop up in Houston, or as Kinky would say, "Down there in Hootin'!" Bill had a firm notion of what we didn't need, and that was any more guitar motifs.

I got an idea in the shower. Daddy-O was in a daze, daydreaming and idea fishing, when something suddenly came to me. I'd bought a couple of music magazines devoted entirely to jazz and blues and spent the previous evening drinking beer, leafing through 'em, and looking for clues. What came to me in that steamy shower was a saxophone with all the bizarre pads that open and close, long pipes and intricate tubing, the funny reed and the mouthpiece at the very top. It was so complex a design that unless you were a repairman, you couldn't even draw one perfectly, which lent to the sculpture's abstract potential. This in turn left lots of room for interpretation and design, which left a lot of room for Daddy-O. Plus it made sense for Billy Blues. You hear a lot of sax solos in blues music and the instrument lends itself to *assemblage,* a technique of assembling and attaching lots of stuff or found objects. I recalled the stories about Picasso taking a wagon to the dump in search of throwaways, tools, and other objects. He was one of the first to spot art in broken toy cars, adding ears to one and calling it *Baboon* because it ended up looking like a monkey head. A sixteenth-century artist named Giuseppe Arcimboldo painted all kinds of fruits and vegetables assembled into the shape of a grotesque face. The idea of taking different things and putting them together to create yet another image could give me just enough historical rope to hang myself.

Based on the floor plan Super Chicken had provided, the sculpture needed to be vertical because the club was long and horizontal. I did a scaled paste-up drawing just to see how big this thing would have to be in order to have real impact. While studying my daughter Rachel's toy saxophone, I realized that the bottom curve was gonna be the hardest part. Then somehow it occurred to me that the curve of a saxophone closely resembled the overall shape of a Volkswagen bug, and I thought, what if I obtained an old Volkswagen, turned it upside down, and started with that?

One of my automotive art influences was a sculptor named Ed Kienholz. His work attracted my attention while I was in graduate school in Berkeley. He constructed a famous piece at the Los Angeles County Museum in 1966 called *Back Seat Dodge*, which was comprised of a chopped old car. The car door was open, and in the back a stylized couple was going at it, banging away. It wasn't realistic, but neither was it any more surreal and creepy than a lot of Kienholz's other works. When I finally drove down to see it, the museum board had gotten so much flak that they closed the car door. That experience was very symbolic, and it put the fight in me when it came to making a stand in favor of controversial public art.

My original agreement with Gallagher and Coleman called for "the artist to create a giant saxophone outdoor sculpture (a memorial to rhythm and blues) on the site of Billy Blues in Houston, Texas." According to Super Chicken, Houston was known as a headquarters for the recording of contemporary blues primarily because of Don Robey, who lived there during the '50s. Houston became a mecca because it had a network of hip recording studios. That's partially why Gallagher was so adamant about building this monument.

The agreement—dated January 28, 1993—defined the structure as "built of objects both purchased and found in the assemblage tradition, such as hubcaps, car bumpers, pipes, miscellaneous steel, cultural icons, fun and strange things to create the shape of a saxophone." The contract also defined the support crew: Daddy-O, R.A., Big Bill, and Lick Lick—all working for Super Chicken. The contract mentioned "budget for purchase of objects, paints, materials, and rentals," but it didn't say how much. A hell of a deal, I thought, plus I maintained control of the copyright associated with the sculpture. The original title was *Memorial to R&B* or *Sax Memorial*. Ultimately the Billy Blues folks shortened it to *Smokesax*.

After sketching more preliminary drawings, Super Chicken and Coleman gave me the up-front money, after which I created a more elaborate set of final drawings. I must say, the Billy Blues people were the best patrons I ever worked with. There wasn't even mention of a budget. There were no parameters. It was the only time in my life I didn't feel constrained by size or budget.

I hired my buddy R.A. (semi-engineer, wrangler, all-around good ol' boy who always keeps an engineer's Bible in his truck) to do some initial investigation of the site. R.A. has worn an oversized

Stetson, the biggest cowboy hat ever made, day and night for years. He's bow-legged as hell, a genuine cowboy. Since he's from Houston, and had worked in the oil fields with oil field manufacturing and pipe, I thought he'd be the best guy to get things started. I told him to look around the junkyards for a Volkswagen.

R.A. knew a woman who rented an apartment not far from where Billy Blues was being built. She had a son who had abandoned his Volkswagen, which had been towed a bunch of times by the Houston police. We bought it for a hundred bucks and towed it to the Billy Blues site. After R.A. measured the Volkswagen's length and width, I borrowed Rachel's gold plastic toy saxophone again, which had enough detail and proportion that I could literally outline in order to get the outer shape. Based on the Volkswagen's measurements and the shape of the toy, I figured out how tall the sculpture had to be. I decided early on that the saxophone needed to be high enough off the ground to keep people from messing with it, but that they should be able to unlock the Volkswagen for photo opportunities. As with the Iguana, the idea was that people should be able to enter into the upside-down Volkswagen, get laid, climb a ladder inside the saxophone, and stick their head outside the bell. I pictured people like B. B. King or groups like Z. Z. Top standing inside the bell, waving. Since most of the saxophone would be made of huge lengths of steel oil-field pipe, and counting the suggested twelve feet off the ground, the top could reach a total of some seventy feet in the air!

That made me happy for a couple of reasons. The Boots I designed were forty feet high, not counting the four-foot platform. This also meant we could outgun Big Tex! Big Tex is the fifty-foot cowboy who greets everybody as you enter the Texas State Fair. My personal goal had always been to construct a piece of public art taller than Big Tex. If you're going to bother to make it, always build it a little bit bigger. (The San Jacinto monument is taller, on purpose, than the Washington monument.) Or as Dirty Little Shrop would say, "Honey, it's not very long, but it's as big around as a beer can."

I was faxing and FedExing a storm of ideas to San Antonio when I got the final go-ahead from Super Chicken. That meant coming up with all the preplanning, the exact measurements, and staying in touch with R.A. so he could work out further details with the engineers. How deep of a hole would we need to dig to mount it?

How much concrete would we need? If anything was going to be put into the ground, it had to be able to withstand hurricane wind forces.

R.A. purchased forty-foot bits of pipe and had holes drilled in the ground. He had already received all of the proper clearances to avoid cutting through any telephone or power lines belonging to the city of Houston. This triggered an army of inspectors. Someone asked if we had the necessary permits we needed in order to erect a sign. We alerted the city that we were putting up a sculpture and not a sign. Still, someone downtown felt that we still fell under the department of signs for the city of Houston—a city which, ironically, was famous for its lack of zoning laws. Here was a town where you could have a barbershop next door to a mansion next to a Korean grocery store next to a museum. Houston was a shot-loose boom town kind of place in the spirit of the movie *Giant*. While Gallagher and Coleman might ask, "What would Billy do?" I asked myself, "What would Jett Rink do?"

Houston had entered a new era in the '90s: a new regime of city committees and departments dedicated to "improving the city." Anybody who put up a sign now had to conform to very strict rules. They even had laws on how high a flagpole could be. We began to get nervous. From the very beginning, I was asked to submit my credentials to the planning commission so they could evaluate me. They were aware of the Lone Star's scrapes with the law concerning the Iguana in New York and Tango's Frogs in Dallas. We were soon targeted by the mayor's task force who challenged us on the basis that the saxophone was not art but rather a sign. If we went forward, they said, citations would be issued. Super Chicken maintained that he commissioned me to build a monument to the blues, entitled *Smokesax*. That was my role, and I was to proceed no matter what. All my art heavies were behind me. Marilyn Oshman, Bill Hill, Carolyn Farb, and Lynn Goode all kept their "Fabulous!" mantra going.

The city's arguments were similar to the ones officials used in New York and Dallas: Anything that causes motorists and people to look, that "causes attention to itself and represents either a product or a service that is being sold inside or on the premises," must be a sign. Yet would a signmaker be given an unlimited budget to create a sculpture? My main argument would eventually make headlines nationwide: "I don't make signs. I make art."

Most of the fight waged with the city occurred while we were still in construction. Super Chicken was betting on my track record in New York and Dallas. That might have been why I was hired in the first place. If we were going to create a controversy, at least we would go in with a winning record. We ended up with publicity you couldn't buy.

All the while, more pipe was being delivered to the site. I had detailed drawings and a clear concept in my head of how I wanted this thing to go. On February 1, 1993, an art fabricator named Big Bill jumped on a plane with me from Santa Fe to Houston. Big Bill had built dragsters and flown air force jets. He also possessed the mechanical and engineering skills I lusted after. We were joined by a third guy, someone who went back even farther, one Keith Turman, who had been dubbed "Lick Lick" by Monk White. Lick Lick oversaw a warehouse I shared with Monk in Dallas. He had lots of experience in automotive and industrial spray-gun painting. These guys, along with R.A., became my beer-drinking, good ol' boy crew. On February 2, 1993, we all began working. All we had was a sturdy base pipe cemented into the ground. The rest of the work was to be done horizontally on the ground—or so we'd hoped. Parked nearby was this pitiful little Volkswagen plopped down next to the pipe, with flat tires. Meanwhile, lots of contractors were hustling and bustling and building the restaurant. We all had a common deadline.

The day we arrived, R.A. had already been there a couple of months. We had a quick meeting and after that it was lunchtime. One thing the contractors all knew was the nearby strip joint, a very classy place frequented by businessmen, that served a great lunch. Strip joints and Daddy-O go way back.

I had my own etiquette: Act like a gentleman even though you're there to see T&A. Don't get loud and drunk and don't gyrate. A lot of arm motion will alert the bouncers. No grabbing, no lurching, no lunging. Leering is okay, although it's not gentlemanly. I've seen bouncers really take guys out. I've seen guys break beer bottles over other guys' heads. Since a lot of people in these joints are of questionable character, you have to be careful.

Our estimated time in Houston was pretty ambitious: seven to ten days of work. By the time we got going, we were working pretty fast. When people asked me how long it took to make this thing, I said three and a half weeks, but Big Bill corrected me. It took two and a half weeks. We had support beyond the strip joints. The Hills brought beer, Cock Dog cashed checks, the Tolberts drove us around, and Robert Cozens arranged for the local PBS station to pay us a number of visits. The "backstage" area was the usual drawing board, beer cooler, car seat scene with my rented car's radio cranked up all the way—every day.

One of the first things we had to do was gut the Volkswagen, which included taking out the engine and the seats, thus converting it to a shell on wheels. After seeing some of the faxed drawings, some of the contractors were dubious that we could crank out a sixty-foot saxophone in ten days. There we were, torches fired up, gutting a Volkswagen, rubber catching on fire, transmission parts and fluids splashing onto the newly-paved concrete parking lot, creating squalor right on the spot—junkyard dogs destroying the construction site's natural order. We planned to do most of the building horizontally, but we had no such luck. We painted horizontally, but most of our work went on in midair, courtesy of Johnny, our crane expert, whose company, ironically, was named Houston Sign. I'd hate to see that crane bill.

The Volkswagen looked like shit, and the more we added, the more ridiculous the structure looked. Gallagher and Coleman would drop in, gaze at my unconventional drawings, and exchange worried glances. Most of the guys on the site suspected we were lunatics, not artists. But at least we were entertaining, and had great-looking women stopping by all the time.

Most of the work was done from the ground up, using a variety of strange ingredients. We constructed the bottom of the saxophone bell from circular galvanized cattle troughs. Some ranchers use them as miniature swimming pools. I knew that hubcaps could serve as a lot of the circular keys, and as luck would have it, there was a used-hubcap store six blocks away. I took a bunch of invitations to the Billy Blues grand opening party and traded for all the hubcaps I needed. Clear-coated shiny galvanized electrical tubing served as the rods going up and down the saxophone. When I ordered room service at my hotel, I noticed the stainless-steel room service tray covers and immediately thought, More saxophone keys! We used pieces of a twelve-foot aluminum canoe for flaps. After having lunch at a place called the Beach Club, which used surfboards for snack tables, a surfboard became our reed. The mouthpiece was fashioned from beer kegs. Volkswagen trunks and hoods created more keys. It was going.

The big half of the bell was handmade, and it represented the final component. At first we were looking for something like those giant horns you see on the deck of luxury liners. The diameters turned out to be too small, so we created a linear inner skeleton framework using steel rods that were lightweight but strong enough to withstand the wind. After surveying our options, we collectively decided we would wrap the bell skeleton with six-inch-diameter plastic electrical flex pipe. Halfway through, we exhausted every running foot of flexible PVC in all of Houston. We found more flex pipe in Huntsville, Texas, but we were still short about one hundred feet. As we were starting to get desperate and depressed, a visiting contractor heard about our dilemma and remembered he had a couple of wooden spools of the same flex pipe in his warehouse, which he just gave to us.

Painting the saxophone was an enormous task. Lick Lick came up with a beautiful dark blue, not because of the name of the club, but because one night I watched Branford Marsalis play a blue tenor saxophone on the *Tonight Show*. I'd never seen an instrument so beautiful. The shiny stuff would show up great with blue. How would you chrome-plate a seventy-foot sax anyway?

To celebrate the opening, the Billy Blues people had printed up fancy invitations to the opening parties, three nights in a row featuring the Fabulous Thunderbirds. Opening night was for all the people who had worked on the restaurant. The series of parties blew the city out of the water with all the noise—so much so that Billy Blues was required to provide extra soundproofing. That opened a whole new problem: sound ordinances. And what about those pesky inspectors?

Jacqueline Pontello of *Southwest Art* magazine posed the question in July 1993:

> When is art not art? Well, if inspectors from the city of Houston, Texas are to be believed, it's when art draws attention to a commercial establishment, in this case, Billy Blues Barbecue Bar & Grill. The inspectors decided that Bob 'Daddy-O' Wade's sixty-three foot *Smokesax* at Billy Blues' entrance fell in the category of sign, not art. As a

sign, the sculpture fashioned from a Volkswagen bug, a surfboard, beer kegs and other found objects was too tall for display under the city code, and so must come down.

Deja vu? This *Smokesax* fracas was eerily reminiscent of the 1983 controversy in Dallas when Wade's *Six Frogs Over Tango* was banned from its perch atop a nightclub. Only this time, the politicians were keeping an eye on public opinion. Petition drives to save *Smokesax* garnered much newspaper ink until Houston's city council which heard the case on appeal decided not to decide, voting [instead] to defer to the Municipal Art Commission.

Quicker than a scalded cat, the Municipal Art Commission ruled that, of course *Smokesax* was art, and so it can stay.

I still think of *Smokesax* as my second most permanent erection. Still, I was maxed, taxed, and faxed out. It was time to leave barbeque and humidity for more altitude and green chili. Time to piss on the fire and call in the dogs, as Kinky would say.

*Chapter Twenty-two*

# My Heroes Have Always Been Waco Boys

# and Cowgirls

 was flipping through my col-
lection of vintage black-and-
white photo postcards one
day, and I noticed that the
old photographers always enjoyed having people line up in a row.
Even in old Hollywood Westerns, directors loved to line up the
lawmen, the outlaws, or the frontier townspeople and pan the camera across their rustic, dustridden faces.

I met a modern version of these Wild West characters whom I
affectionately dubbed the Waco Boys, and they became subjects for
a couple of my best works. One especially telling photo, taken in the
late 1960s in Uvalde, Texas, depicted the Waco Boys and a couple

of their women on some kind of rattlesnake hunt. It was one of the most provocative photos I had ever seen. Four guys, three of them wearing modest cowboy hats, are standing in the back row holding machine guns, shotguns, rifles with bayonets, and one long dead rattlesnake. Their expressions range from somber to menacing to smiling. Two glowingly attractive women with short hair—one blonde, the other brunette—are kneeling down in front, equally rambunctious with rifles and bayonets. The dark-haired woman has an ammo belt draped across her chest.

The Waco Boys loved having their pictures taken. The Waco photo store had an easel in the front window with a variety of enlargements stacked together. The boys would often drive by the shop with their friends and family to make sure their particular favorite was prominently displayed. The original photo was taken by Harry Hornby, the editor of the *Uvalde Leader News* in July 1969, on the very same day man first walked on the moon.

I loved the enlargement so much they eventually gave it to me, thinking I would do something sensational that would make them even more visible and larger than life. People have a craving for photographic documentation. Throughout history lawmen posed with guns drawn at the end of a successful manhunt. Bonnie & Clyde, as they shot their way around Texas and Oklahoma, often had their pictures taken by strangers and anonymous newspapermen.

I eventually used the Waco Boys' picture in a couple of pieces, one of them an eight-by-ten foot photo emulsion canvas simply titled *Waco*. It started out as a black-and-white canvas, push-pinned through the grommets flat to the wall, that was first shown at the Tyler Museum in January of 1973 at an Oak Cliff Four group show. Later that year, it was exhibited at the Whitney Museum in New York and included in other traveling exhibitions around the world, with stops in Chicago and São Paulo, Brazil.

After I shipped the *Waco* canvas to the Whitney Annual, I heard the opening promised to be a zoo, so I flew up to take a quick glimpse of my big canvas. As I strolled the museum with Robert Doty, the curator, I came around the corner where my piece was hanging, but when I looked at it, I noticed it wasn't flat against the wall; it draped a little bit with a kind of a wave in the canvas.

I said, "Oh my gosh, we need to get one of the guys up here to flatten it out."

"Oh, no," said Doty. "We did this on purpose."

"Why?"

"To give it the New York theatrical effect."

That was an artistic awakening. I used to think that everything in Texas was bigger, but New York is exaggerated and bigger in terms of theatrics and lighting, be it the Broadway stage or the Whitney Museum. Because there was a bit of a ripple on the canvas, it wouldn't look so flat, and resembled a decal roughly glued to the wall. They wanted it to look like it was hung on the wall spontaneously rather than coming off as a flat, pasted-on presentation.

In 1975 I made my own Waco Boys photograph as part of the *Jackelope* documentary. I lined them up in the same order as the earlier 1969 work. Since I lost track of one of the four men, I donned a shotgun, cowboy hat, and a pair of sunglasses, and stepped into the picture in his place. Prior to James King's taking the photo, we machine-gunned an abandoned white, stripped-down automobile for the *Jackelope* film crew in the hot sun. Later we blew up the car with explosives and again stood in front of the pulverized heap, looking proud of ourselves. Real "Texas boys."

By 1977 I happened upon another interesting photo in an antique store in El Paso. It was a 1922 lineup of rodeo cowgirls, which struck me immediately as a special picture. I had dabbled with a lot of Southwestern themes in my early photographic projects, and many became as well known as my sculptures.

Since the late '80s there seems to have been a renaissance of the cowgirl phenomenon, something I've been interested in since my buckaroo childhood. Many Westerns featured cowgirls alongside their cowboy counterparts. Roy Rogers and Dale Evans are only one example. The cowgirl was neglected for a while, only to inch back into popularity. Barbara Stanwyck played a tough ranch-owning cowgirl on the long-running television series *The Big Valley*, and rodeo cowgirls in particular have become a recurring popular image these days. They're a theme I still utilize in many of my photographic canvases.

It all started when I was asked to come up with something for a

1979 charity auction that was to be held in the giant ballroom of the Adolphus, a famous hotel in downtown Dallas. I decided to enlarge that cowgirls photo I found a few years earlier. It was about four feet wide on photo linen. I hand-colored the hell out of it and donated it to the auction for all the café society socialites and the crazy-wilds to bid on. Monk White was in the audience, of course, and when my piece came up for auction, the crowd went nuts over it. They loudly applauded it and started bidding the thing at five thousand bucks. Up until that time, I had never sold a canvas for that much. It sold for $14,000.

As a result, a famous rodeo cowboy named Larry Mahan approached me to do a cowgirl commission for his wife Robin. That's when my interest in cowgirls accelerated. Occasionally other great cowgirl photos would come my way.

In 1986 I was asked to apply for inclusion in a touring exhibition sponsored by the Western States Arts Federation, WESTAF, headquartered in Santa Fe. The group exhibit was scheduled to start at the Brooklyn Museum of Art and travel around the United States for a couple of years. Charlotta Kotik, the curator of the Brooklyn Museum, visited my studio in Dallas and soon after sent me a letter of acceptance. It was decided that I would create a ten-foot version of the thirteen cowgirls, and another ten-foot-long double photo canvas of the Texas Boys. The title "Texas Boys" came from Erica Billiter, who was curating a show for the Kunsthaus in Zurich in '77 titled "Photography and Painting in Dialogue." She asked me to participate, and requested I send her some "Texas Boys." Then she giggled.

They were of course my Waco boys.

I joined two photos side by side of the Texas Boys in front of the car, before and after the explosion. On the "before" side, there's me and the three other Texas Boys, and on the "after" side, two of the Texas Boys are absent. Hence the title of the photo piece, *Four Minus Two Equals Waco*. A professional crate-maker built a special container to handle the two years of travel. I even attended three of the openings. Hundreds of boisterous people attended the one in Brooklyn, and I felt I had struck a great artistic chord for Texas. Charlotta said, "I was going to hang the two canvases one over the other, but I didn't know who should be on top, the boys or the girls."

Before the tour, the WESTAF people asked me if I would be interested in doing a postcard or a T-shirt—a memento of the exhibition that would go on sale in the bookstores and gift shops at each museum. Taos artist Bill Gersh had his work on shirts done by a company called Art Wear, who wanted to do my images too. They had state-of-the-art screen processes for high quality photo reproductions. I met with Peter at Art Wear and Cheryl at WESTAF about putting the Cowgirls on the T-shirt. Because of the extra-long lineup of cowgirls, we could only fit seven of the thirteen across the front. The shirt toured with the exhibition and I started to receive letters, forwarded to me by WESTAF, from relatives or people who had known some of the cowgirls. Sometimes it was plain old fan mail, sometimes I felt I was onto something special. The cowgirls were a positive, historical icon of American womanhood.

The cowgirl-shirt developed its own momentum. WESTAF submitted my design to a national museum products design conference competition and it won an award. At the end of the tour I was told the cowgirl shirt was an overwhelming crowd pleaser. Art Wear presented me with a contract and asked if I would be interested in continuing the production. During the WESTAF tour, I had donated the royalties. I started seeing the shirts everywhere: Aspen, New York, Los Angeles, Anchorage, Hawaii, and Santa Fe. Giant social events would purchase a couple hundred to give out as contributor gifts. Twenty valet parkers at a Fort Worth social function would be outfitted in cowgirl shirts. I began marketing a denim jacket with the cowgirl image sewn on the back, padded to look 3-D, that sold in Japan and at Harrod's in London.

A place in Santa Fe called me about reproducing my cowgirl canvases on postcards. I figured you don't have to be a deceased artist to have your paintings on a card, and besides, they became good calling cards to give to people who visited the studio. Each month I'd receive dozens of letters as a result of the postcards. Magazines began reproducing my photo canvases in articles. Publishers used them on book covers, and they also graced the artwork of a CD. People all over the world loved the cowgirls.

The cowgirls' heyday came during the '20s, when performers like Lucille Mulhall specialized in rope tricks and bucking broncos. Mulhall started in Wild West shows and made a career out of the rodeo. Daughters of early ranching families in Texas, Oklahoma, and Wyoming could ride, rope, and herd cattle just like their brothers and became as skilled as their dads. They became tough women. Mulhall exhibited some great qualities, and Will Rogers (who was also from Oklahoma) spotted her and became one of her biggest fans. She went off to Madison Square Garden in New York with Will Rogers and with other big troupes as early as 1905. It's hard to say who was the first rodeo cowgirl, but Mulhall was the first to be recognized in these big events. In fact, Rogers would write about her in his newspaper column, in which he referred to her as "the world's original cowgirl."

"Cowboy" and "cowgirl" were fairly new terms at the turn of the century. Before "cowboys" took on today's connotations, they used to be referred to as "cowmen." In fact, some experts believe the term "cowgirl" should not be used unless a woman does, in fact, work primarily with horses. She doesn't necessarily have to herd, brand, and rope cattle.

It was mostly women who wore flamboyant Wild West outfits made of satin, fur, large swatches of color, and huge bow ribbons they wore on the back of their heads. Trick riding was a big deal back then. They'd perform bizarre flips or hang upside-down underneath the horse at a full gallop.

Of course, all the photographs I've ever seen were black-and-white because color photography as we know it today didn't really come along, in terms of snapshots, until the mid '40s. When color postcards were developed, they were mechanically printed on the offset system, much like a magazine. The photographers of that grand precolor era ran around with large view cameras and shot great big beautiful black-and-white pictures, which were then turned into photo postcards and sold to the contestants and the fans the following day. Thousands of these photo postcards were printed on actual photographic paper, and on the back side there was a place to put the stamp and lines for the address—hence they're called "real photo postcards."

As I hand-paint the canvases, I have to imagine the colors. I prefer the term "enhance" over "colorize" when it comes to painting my photographic canvases. Colorizing is a process that came along with Ted Turner. Computer effects companies would alter original black-and-white films into full color. Quite often these movies were designed to be shot in black-and-white rather than color, whereas with the old photo stills I work with, black-and-white was all they had. Plus, computer coloring doesn't seem to have the Daddy-O touch.

Enlarging a black-and-white to the scale of twelve feet unfolds lots of details and objects you would have never seen before, making a stunning impact. It's like the difference between watching football on a tiny Watchman as opposed to a giant wide screen.

Enlarging cowgirl postcards transports me back in time seventy or eighty years. The past becomes current and alive. Unless you're a collector, a historian, or a curator, many of these photos are sights unseen. By very softly applying color to these old photos (so as not to overpower the original photographic quality) you subtly enhance the details already there, literally breathing new life into a photo that was taken in the '20s or '30s.

I was putting finishing touches on a group of cowgirls one particular night. Cowgirl performers, after all, did coif up before a big show. In essence, I was applying the makeup: a little bit of blue above the eyes, a little blush in the cheeks, and a little show biz exaggeration on their red lips. I was concentrating heavily on facial features, and while they weren't physically moving, their faces became a little bit animated and gained a little extra expression.

It was one of those surreal, late-night TV kind of nights. The canvas kind of shivered around a couple of the cowgirls. I swear to God one of them said, "Thanks for bringing us to life one more time."

I felt like I had time-traveled to 1922. They were frozen in time and I was releasing them from the dark and dingy, black-and-white, teeny-weeny documentation that confined them.

At the end of the WESTAF show in 1986, I loaned out the accompanying double painting, *Four Minus Two Equals Waco* to Southwest Texas State University in San Marcos in conjunction with a Southwest writers' collection containing archives from early writers such as J. Frank Dobie all the way up to Larry McMurtry. The grand opening featured many Texas celebrities. Jerry Jeff Walker played; then-governor Ann Richards was there, whom I had met casually once or twice before. I shook hands with Governor Richards and left the party soon after. Later on, as I attended a gathering at the university president's house, I was taken aside and told that the governor was looking for me. She had found out that the Texas Boys canvas was on loan, and she was trying to wrangle the painting out of the university and into her office in Austin.

Truly! The governor of Texas wanted to hang Texas Boys over her desk! I arranged for the painting to be moved to Austin. If there was a tough Texas woman around who would appreciate *Four Minus Two Equals Waco,* surely it was Ann Richards, a neat lady who hunts, shoots, and, ironically, comes from Waco. When I went to see the painting in its new environment, I presented Ann Richards with the cowgirl denim jacket.

The next year, the actual guys from Waco who are in the *Four Minus Two* painting were attending an official ceremony in the governor's office. Upon seeing the painting for the first time and not believing it, the "Texas Boy" introduced himself. "Hello, Governor, I'm Parnell McNamara," to which the governor replied, "I know who you are, Parnell. I live with you every day!"

My work often turns up on television, and even in movies. The Iguana has been featured in movies and television shows. My Pancho Villa T-shirt appeared in the movie *Reversal of Fortune.* The film *White Men Can't Jump* with Woody Harrelson made for another movie appearance. From a small six-inch postcard in a junk shop to a close up on the big screen, the cowgirls appeared again.

"Thanks for bringing us back to life one more time."

While I've done a lot of cowgirl pieces for museums and galleries, I've also done commissions and portraits for people who have found their own "little buckaroo" photos or pictures of family members decked out in early western wear.

I like commissions.

I got a fax from Shannon Wynne in 1992 about a project he wanted me to do, some kind of a big mouth bass for a restaurant he was opening in Dallas called The Big One. The basic concept was that it would have seafood decor, but not necessarily seafood fare. It would be a hamburger place, but in a tongue-in-cheek way, dressed up like a crazy seafood joint. Besides having a fishy interior, he wanted to have "a big mouth" on the roof.

Shannon sent pictures of the building and I did a small-scale mock-up. I made arrangements to do the piece at the same time I was scheduled to go off to the Kansas City Art Institute. I was to serve once again as artist in residence for Dale Eldred for a couple of weeks. I thought it would help the students if we worked on Shannon's fish head sculpture.

While I was putting together the steel framing, one of the students who was helping out approached me about some of his motorized kinetic sculptures. Although it was not part of the original idea, I suggested he help me rig the head so that it would be motorized.

Instead of urethane foam, I sprayed the head with fiberglass to give it that shiny fish look. I hired a student to truck the finished piece into Dallas, where I lined up my crew to do the paint job and the final detail work. The sculpture ended up on The Big One's roof, even though the restaurant was short-lived. It was bought out by my buddy Mike Young and became another Chuy's. As part of his buy out, Mike ended up owning the big fish and eventually moved it down to an Austin lakeside restaurant he developed called the Hula Hut. Between homes, it lived for a short while at the Dallas Museum in the big circular fountain of the modern wing.

"Big Mouth" is real happy now in the water by the Hula Hut docks. The whole thing is hooked up to a device that requires two quarters. When scantily-clad UT coeds put in their quarters, the head moves, eyes light up, and smoke billows out of the mouth. Hook 'em horns!

I also did a lineup commission when my friend Glenn Frey called up during the first leg of the Eagles' *Hell Freezes Over* world tour. Glenn loves quality art and asked if I would consider doing some artwork for a T-shirt. I went up to Denver to see the Eagles perform, and brought back selected black-and-white photographs of the band. I blew one up about five or six feet wide and airbrushed a bright, strong orange/red fiery background behind the group to signify hell freezing over. I brought the guys to life with other Daddy-O tricks. The painting was reproduced on a T-shirt and sold during the tour.

Roy Rogers once said, "Show business in your blood is about the most incurable disease, they say."

*Chapter Twenty-three*

# Smoke Rings: My Three Visits

# with Roy Rogers

**R**oy Rogers's mother was Mattie Womack. My maternal grandmother was Virginia Lee Womack. They were sisters. That makes Roy my second cousin.

1943 was a big year for Roy and me. Roy got the cover of *Life* magazine and I got born.

Roy came to Austin in 1943 when I was two months old. My family was living there at the time, and Roy was in town for a big rodeo in nearby San Antonio, so he stopped by to visit his cousins, my Aunt Mary and my mother Pattie. Roy liked the way my mom had taped my ears back to my head for training. As part of the P.R. for the rodeo, Roy rode Trigger into the lobby of the Gunter Hotel, where my father ended up working years later. Trigger was set up in a high-class stall, complete with bales of hay in the lobby.

How could I have known in 1949—when I was six years old—that cowboys would influence my life in such a big way? Since we had no TV, I went to the Saturday morning movies. I knew Roy Rogers was a huge star. I was lucky that he was in my life.

When he was headlining rodeos in Texas towns like Beaumont or Galveston, Roy would often stay at the hotels my father managed. Roy would drop by the manager's suite and Little Pard would sit on his knee. At the time Roy was a big cigarette smoker. He could blow dozens of smoke rings from twenty feet away—maybe it was that yodelin' stuff that helped get the rings to float so well.

Leonard Slye—Roy's real name—and his father Andy Slye came from Cincinnati—not Texas or Nashville. He was born during a time in America where everyone struggled to do the best they could do. I still have original eight-by-ten photographs of his visits that Roy's publicists sent to my parents. My favorite picture is of Roy, my parents, and me behind the chutes at a rodeo in Beaumont, Texas. It is a fabulously posed shot, perhaps a little bit odd by today's standards because my hand is on Roy Rogers's belt buckle. I distinctly remember the photographer wanting me to do something with my hands, so he placed one of them on Roy's buckle.

Having Roy Rogers as my second cousin always made me special and a touch better than the next guy. While other kids' great-grandfathers may have drilled for oil in the 1890s, my Roy Rogers lineage allowed me to equal them. Sure, your family may have $200 million dollars, and I may be broke, but at least I'm Roy Rogers's second cousin.

I didn't see Roy again until I was a teenager visiting Los Angeles. It was well before he moved to Apple Valley. He was in Southern California at his huge family compound and I remember lots of dogs. Roy was a hunter and owned dozens of hunting dogs. During the visit, someone who worked for Roy asked me, "Do you want to go see Roy's closet?"

It was an interesting concept.

I walked into Roy's closet and saw a hundred thousand boots, shirts, and cowboy hats. His "closet" was as big as a football field.

Endless. The biggest western wear store in Texas wasn't as big as Roy's closet, and the closet was much cooler. Of course, everything was monogrammed "Roy."

The singing cowboy is coming back larger than life. Roy—the second singing cowboy after Gene Autry—was the forerunner of contemporary mainstream singing cowboy-types like Clint Black, who even shares Roy's slanted eyes. There are dozens of concert-hall versions of the singing cowboy. Roy, I think, had a big hand in starting it all.

The original superstar, Roy Rogers at one time had over five hundred licensing agreements—lunch boxes, yo-yos, T-shirts, you name it. In those days, it helped to be associated with Roy Rogers. He was, and still is, the ultimate all-American nice guy. In addition to catching the bad guys every Saturday morning, Roy and Dale helped countless kids and have done enormous work for charities. Plus, he can yodel.

Every year my parents got the Christmas card: "Merry Christmas from Roy and Dale."

It was always a heckuva big deal in our house. In fact, after my Dad passed away, I called Roy's secretary to have the address transferred, to keep the cards in the family. I get two thrills each and every Christmas: a card from Prince Albert of Monaco, who owns pieces of my art, and one from Roy Rogers and Dale Evans.

In return, I always sent Roy stuff in the mail: gallery announcements, postcards of my work, and clippings of my achievements.

When my youngest daughter Rachel sent Roy a Valentine she got back an autographed eight-by-ten of Roy rearing up on Trigger. It said, "To Rachel," from "Roy Rogers and Trigger." Forty years earlier, I got an almost identical eight-by-ten. Mine said, "To Robert," from "Roy Rogers and Trigger."

The third time I met Roy, I took my wife Lisa with me. We were on our way back home after building the Malibu Man and went through Victorville. At the time there were two adventures Lisa had never experienced. One was Las Vegas, and the other was meeting Roy Rogers. Since we were going in the direction of Las Vegas, I figured I'd help fulfill her two dreams at once. We called ahead to Roy's compound and sent a follow-up card telling him how much we'd love to stop by and see him. The concept of someone opening up their own museum was a kicker to an artist like me.

We were slated to see Roy at noon. Sure enough, he was there, so we went right upstairs through the ground-floor museum, a rambling, fabulous, easygoing, funky place. Roy's museum features Nellybelle the Jeep and lots of stuff from the movies and TV shows. Trigger was rearing up like in our photos. He was stuffed—just like Funeral Wagon—and his famous dog Bullet was there too, stuffed in the growling position. Roy claims that when he dies, he wants Dale to have him stuffed and put up on Trigger. I was thinkin' that maybe I could join the totem pole when I die and be put up on Roy.

Roy's private office was upstairs, the kind you'd expect an oil tycoon would have: huge desk, guns and photos on the wall, gigantic leather couch. Roy looked great and exactly the same. He brought out photos of the family; we took pictures. It was a great visit.

During our visit, Roy announced, "I want to sing you a little song."

Before the song, he introduced us to his hound dog. It was then that it finally occurred to me that Roy Rogers had actually prepared for our arrival. There I was, a pitiful little cousin to this living legend. Needless to say, I was extremely moved.

He sang us a song titled—appropriately enough—"The Lights of Old Santa Fe." Lisa and I sat enthralled on the big black leather couch as Roy, sitting on a stool, sang to us, his dog next to him. At one point during the song, his dog howled on cue.

On our way out, at the top of the stairs, I asked Roy, "How's your health?"

He wasn't feeling that bad, he said. He had a pacemaker recently installed inside his all-American body.

"Do you want to see it?"

He unsnapped the pearly buttons of his shirt, took Lisa's hand and put it where the scar was. Lisa felt the beating of the American heart of my youth.

A few years before our visit, my oldest daughter Christine stopped off at the Roy Rogers Museum to see Roy, too. The cousins hugged and kissed.

"I think you know my father, Bob 'Daddy-O' Wade."

And that's when Roy said, "Yes, he's the guy that sends me all that weird stuff."

I've always found the rest of the world to be just like Roy. If you think people see your art the way you do, you're absolutely crazy. It sounds simple, but art is truly in the eye of the beholder, and the eye of its creator. I've learned—usually the hard way—that the definition of art is bandied around not only inside museums, universities, intellectually sterilized journals, and educational safehouses, but inside city council chambers, barrooms, city streets, shopping malls, honkytonks, and beer joints. All my life I've relied on the myths of the Old West and my El Paso roots to guide my slightly twisted vision of painting and sculpture. Roy Rogers grounded those memories with a family-based, gut-level sense of reality.

Yeah, Roy. I'm the guy who sends you all that weird stuff. And there's more in the mail where that came from.

# Afterword: Kinky Gets the Last Word

**TEXAS** culture, in which Bob "Daddy-O" Wade is certainly a leading, not to say Olympian, figure, has long been regarded by some pointy-headed intellectuals as an oxymoron. This jaundiced, jaded view flies in the face of truth, beauty, and everything—well, at least some of the things—we hold dear in America. Like the freedom to create weird shit and make it bigger and better than anybody else. This, after all, was basically the approach that God had in mind when He worked for six days and created the earth and all that is in it. There are, of course, those of us who feel that He might've taken just a little more time.

All that notwithstanding, Bob Wade almost *had* to be a Texan. Not for him to spend a lifetime perfecting masterpieces in miniature. Not for him to reside in coffeehouses on the Left Bank of Paris or New York or L.A., embroidering and vampirizing the thinking of the day. Daddy-O needed a little more spiritual elbow room. For it is out of that aching expanse of emptiness that is sometimes called Texas that that rarity of rarities, a truly creative and original idea, is now and again born.

Though Bob Wade's work takes many forms, gracing everything from postcards to shopping malls to art museums, the creation of his that I'm the most familiar with is the Giant Iguana that once seemed to live and breathe on the rooftop of the old Lone Star Café in New York. Andy Warhol, John Belushi, John Matusak—all of whom have subsequently stepped on a rainbow—and multitudes of others from all walks of life have experienced a personal communion with this mystical child of Daddy-O's in the midst of the madness of the city. Part of Wade's genius, of course, was making that monster look like many of us felt at that particular time in our lives, which was usually moderately amphibious as well.

It's never easy for an artist to create. It's even harder for the artist to tell you how, in fact, he did it. This often funny, often outrageous, always insightful book is Bob Wade's latest and most definitive attempt to explain why he creates strange and wonderful things. But just as the Iguana has finally found a home in the country, the innovative talent of Bob Wade has certainly found a home too, in the eyes, hearts, and sensibilities of the legions of Americans who love his art, even if he deliberately makes it sometimes a little difficult to collect.

Oscar Wilde once observed: "No great artist ever sees things as they really are. If he did he would cease to be an artist." There's very little danger, of course, of Daddy-O's ever seeing things the way they really are and that's a blessing for us all.

—Kinky Friedman, April 11, 1995

Kinky Friedman is the author of eight mystery novels, including *God Bless John Wayne* (Simon & Schuster).